The Cost of Emotions in the Workplace

Bottom Line Value of Emotional Continuity Management

by

Vali Hawkins Mitchell, Ph.D., LMHC

Kristen Noakes-Fry, Editor

ISBN #978-1-931332-58-3 (Perfect Bound)
ISBN #978-1-931332-68-2 (eBook)
ISBN 978-1-931332-65-1 (Hard Cover)

Rothstein Associates Inc., Publisher
Brookfield, Connecticut USA
www.rothstein.com

ISBN 978-1-931332-58-3

Library of Congress Control Number (LCCN) 2012952669

Disclaimer

PUBLISHER:

Philip Jan Rothstein, FBCI

Rothstein Associates Inc.

The Rothstein Catalog on Disaster Recovery

4 Arapaho Rd.

Brookfield, Connecticut 06804-3104 USA

203.740.7444 • 203.740.7401 fax

info@rothstein.com

www.rothstein.com

Keep informed of the latest business continuity news.

Sign up for Business Survival™ Weblog: Business Continuity for Key Decision-Makers from Rothstein Associates at www.rothstein.com/blog

DEDICATION

Dave, this one's for you
for sharing this E-Ticket Life with me.

ACKNOWLEDGMENTS

I would like to offer deep and whimsical gratitude to Philip Jan Rothstein, my publisher, for believing in my work. Thank you for not giving up, even when it would have made sense to do so a hundred times over.

Thanks to Kristen Noakes-Fry, my editor, for sprinklings of wisdom and support through her editing magic and becoming a new friend in the process.

Very special thank you to Lyndon Bird and Martin Greenwood for your thoughtful comments and support of Emotional Continuity.

So grateful to my husband Dave, for his brave "first draft" editing, business wisdom, twisted humor, and daily heroic contributions to our life so I can continue my "walk-about-work."

And thank you to all the people who have shared your amazing and heart-rending stories with me over the years.

Foreword

At the Business Continuity Institute, we have always defined our mission in terms of "promoting the art and science of Business Continuity Management (BCM)," and I have often been challenged about what we precisely mean by that phrase. The "science" part is easy – techniques and methods for ensuring operational continuity will suffice. However, the "art" side has been altogether more difficult to explain, but, now that we have this new book by Dr. Vali Hawkins Mitchell, I suspect that the "art" of BCM will no longer be hard to explain. I can now point questioners to *The Cost of Emotions in the Workplace: The Bottom-Line Value of Emotional Continuity Management*, confident that they will understand precisely what we mean.

I wonder how many BCM professionals have ever considered an "emotional tornado" or an "emotional terrorist" as a major risk to their organization? Do they know how to read the warning signs that human emotions could spin out of control to cause a catastrophe? Well, they should, and after reading what Dr. Vali says in this book, they certainly will in the future. Traditionally, in the world of BCM we talk about risks and threats to our organizations, such as computer failures, natural disasters, supply chain disruption, or a pandemic. This book examines the risk and threats that people can pose to a business, such as brand and reputational damage, litigation, employee turnover, and even criminal behavior.

Although people are always considered in BCM plans, they are often treated as a recoverable resource – numbers to be counted and skills to be replaced. However, actual human behavior in BCM is rarely thought about in the planning, response, or recovery phases, and where it is mentioned it is usually at the bottom of the priority list. Maybe after reading this book, and learning more about the fiscal risk and hidden costs of emotions, organizations will be persuaded to look more closely at this commonly overlooked subject and begin to see the benefit of emotional continuity management.

Many organizations take a "macho" approach to management, and for those companies, the subject matter of this book might be regarded as irrelevant to "the bottom line" or "getting the job done" in an emergency. This book effectively debunks that point of view, systematically producing evidence and arguing a compelling case. Dr. Vali connects human emotions directly to cost and increased risk, which should definitely take human emotions much higher up the board agenda.

"Emotional continuity" is not a soft subject; rather, it is about emotional readiness and paying attention to the way businesses and humans interact. In this book, the chapter on Emotional Continuity Management for Disasters is particularly fascinating for BCM professionals, as it talks about how to plan for the emotional consequences of disasters. Clearly, direct comparisons can be drawn between good practice in traditional BCM and good practice in Emotional Business Continuity Management. Thus, emotional continuity management is definitely high on the list of new topics for BCM practitioners to master. You will find Dr. Vali's book to be both an excellent read and a great catalyst for generating new ideas about how these concepts could be incorporated into your mission statement. If you are open-minded about BCM, I suggest you read this book now and start applying its principles – well before the next major incident impacts your organization.

Business Continuity
Institute

Lyndon Bird

Lyndon Bird, FBCI,
Technical Director
The Business Continuity Institute
Caversham, United Kingdom
May, 2012
www.thebci.org

The purpose of the Business Continuity Institute is to promote the art and science of business continuity management worldwide.

The BCI was established in 1994 to enable individual members to obtain guidance and support from fellow business continuity practitioners. The BCI currently has over 7000 members in 100+ countries active in an estimated 2,750 organizations in private, public and third sectors.

Foreword

A computer will do only what it is programmed to do. The thoughts, emotions, and actions of people are far more complex, have far more variability, and are far less predictable. As an undergraduate, I majored in Business but my curiosity and desire to better understand the human condition led me to complete a degree in Psychology, as well. While I ultimately completed an MBA in Management Information Systems, I never lost my interest in Psychology and the human condition. Thus, as an IT leader, I can contrast the behavior of computers and the behaviors of people.

In *The Cost of Emotions in the Workplace: The Bottom-Line Value of Emotional Continuity Management*, Dr. Vali Hawkins Mitchell provides the concepts, theories, and real life examples that put much of the behavior I've seen as a corporate leader into context. Her book compels us to accept that people have emotions and to consider that those emotions – when out of control and unmanaged – have real, measurable impacts on an organization. While most people will accept these propositions in theory, very few companies currently provide training for their managers in what Dr. Mitchell calls *emotional continuity management*.

Like myself, many readers of this book will inevitably bring to mind many real life examples corresponding to situations and characters Dr. Mitchell describes here. For example, in one company, I recall a manager who was smart and talented and whose team was well respected. From the outside, it looked like a well-functioning team and he appeared to be dedicated, hardworking, and demanding. What people didn't know was that when he was alone with his staff, he would ridicule and berate people in front of their peers. He was a perfect fit for what Dr. Mitchell describes as a "workplace bully" or even an "emotional terrorist." Eventually, a member of his group brought his behavior to the attention of HR. Looking back at that situation, I can only speculate how months of that treatment impacted the morale and productivity of his group. After reading Dr. Mitchell's book, I wonder if only he, his people, and his superiors had been trained in *emotional continuity management*, would his behavior have been identified and addressed sooner and more effectively – for his group and for the corporation?

Unfortunately, the behavior I just described is not limited to lower levels of management. I remember a Senior VP at one company, who was known for using well-attended conference calls to loudly and aggressively attack individuals – not only members of his own group but members of other groups. His behavior was completely destructive, but it was tolerated by the highest decision-makers due to this VP's level, his power, and his significant contributions to the company. Still, one can only imagine the direct and indirect costs, both in terms of productivity and the bottom line.

Dr. Mitchell explains the need to understand human emotions in the workplace, helping the reader to understand the difference between normal emotions and reactions and destructive behaviors, providing a context for identifying warning signs of problematic behaviors and situations. She approaches the subject not from a purely theoretical view but through a wealth of real life examples of organizations that ignored situations until they became toxic to the bottom line of the business.

We all understand that emotions are going to happen; after all, that is what makes us human. However, these valuable, real life examples help us to understand how and when situations go beyond the normal emotions that quickly pass, and start becoming endemic or out of control.

The Cost of Emotions in the Workplace: The Bottom-Line Value of Emotional Continuity Management will cause you to think about a subject that many in the world of business choose to ignore until they run smack into it. Dr. Mitchell makes a strong argument that everyone in an organization needs the tools and training to manage emotions, and that *emotional continuity management* will be effective only when there is buy-in from the most senior management.

As an experienced IT executive, I have led teams ranging from a few people to several hundred, managing and motivating them effectively, delivering tough, aggressive projects on time and on budget. Great teams with great people, time after time, came together to achieve success. Because I have managed user support organizations that deal with people who are often in highly agitated states, I can see clearly the value of providing training on emotions in the workplace. Like many executives, I have dealt with people and their emotions in the workplace without any formal training or conceptual context for identifying and dealing with strong and sometimes destructive emotions. Because of these experiences, I am writing this foreword to acknowledge Dr. Mitchell's good work and to recognize the beneficial value that training in emotional continuity management would invariably have for everyone at all levels in an organization.

Martin Greenwood
Former Executive Director, Verizon Communications
Executive in Distributed Technology
      & End User Computing
Montebello, New York
November, 2012

Table of Contents

Chapter 7: Emotional Continuity Management for Disasters 231

Preface

When I was gifted with the opportunity to provide mental health services in New York City immediately following the World Trade Center attacks, I walked in the presence of the energetics of anguish in exact proximity with miracles. It was phenomenal. The full range of emotions present created a "Quantum Field of Sacred Ground Zero." It felt familiar, like the openings that happen when babies are born or someone passes away, a place where something so authentic is happening that there is no missing it unless you are made of stone. A place where everything has meaning. Our work has meaning. I have had the opportunity to go to meaningful worksites that are, in my opinion, similar to Ground Zero, places where things are happening that influence the entire world. No matter where I go, I find that some employees know the meaning of their work, others just show up for the paycheck, and still others just come to cause chaos. But all of them bring their human experience with them. All their energies create the essence of their environment.

Nearly anyone who has been employed for any length of time in the real world has seen or been touched by the emotional experience of a co-worker, from a small breeze to a catastrophic tornado event. The costs to the organization range from simple to profoundly complex. Middle-level threats to well-being eat away at stamina, productivity, company loyalty, absenteeism, health care costs, mental health care costs, EAP costs, and managerial conflict-resolution time, and they just make work a toxic environment.

The event that inspired emotional continuity management:

A few years ago, a large corporation hired me to help counsel some disruptive and violent employees. Two rowdy employees had become physically violent over some work-related decision — and no one saw it coming. It was like an emotional tornado had wiped out this company and all that was left was the remnants of the former organization. Walking the halls, I saw, felt, and heard the disruptive effect created by these workers on over 600 people. It was like experiencing the rubble of any other disaster. There was no physical wreckage, but the full range of emotions was exactly like that of any natural disaster where I had served as a counselor. Nothing was hidden. Everything was exposed and raw as if a common energy had stripped away the veneer of civilized behaviors.

No one felt safe. No one felt protected. No infrastructure kept people safe in the presence of these out-of-control employees. People took sides, hid, ran, quit, overworked, underworked, ate too much, drank more, complained more, went silent, changed jobs, exited, and so forth. They reacted as if all their systems had been tossed into the air and were never going to land again. From that experience, I became sensitized to the differences between small gusts of emotions that have no power and the catastrophic force of emotional tornadoes and their impact on business.

I realized that if only this company had recognized the risk and had been prepared with corporate policies and procedures, they could have defused this situation before the human and financial costs were ever incurred. I began my research here and, as a result, I ultimately developed a corporate initiative you can put in place called *emotional continuity management*. In these pages, I provide plans and methodology you can act upon right now to avoid costs to your company in decreased productivity, injured goodwill, employee turnover, plummeting morale, and severed business relationships.

Why do the policies and practices currently in place at most companies constitute high risk behavior?

The old paradigms of separating humans from humanity during work hours is antiquated thinking and has had limited upgrades in the last few decades. While computers must be upgraded regularly, human emotional management hasn't had an upgrade. Ignoring emotions is not only antiquated, it is high risk behavior.

Historically, the work of managing emotions has been left to internal Human Resources personnel and internal or external Employee Assistance Providers. There has been a mythology that emotions are someone else's domain. Most current policies and procedures are inadequate because of 1) ignorance, and 2) resistance.

Ignorance is easily managed by offering new and efficient information that is now available by studying the concepts of emotional continuity management. Resistance is not as easy to manage due to the complex dynamics of humans who do not perceive danger even when it is in their domain. As they say, "Resistance is futile." The world is changing rapidly, and either your company can be current or it will lag behind. It isn't rocket science! It is tough to keep up and stay competitive. It is even more difficult to stay compassionate. But it is doable.

How you can use this book to start reducing risks?

- The critical first step is to understand the concept that emotions: 1) are going to happen, 2) range from small to large, 3) can influence systems (companies are systems), 4) have measurable costs associated with them, 5) can get out of control, 6) can be managed in a compassionate manner that supports people and the bottom line, 7) don't go away just because they are suppressed, ignored, or disvalued (in fact, they will distort and become even more lethal), and 8) can be turned into positive energies that support growth and development, loyalty, and buy-in.

- The second step is to achieve a realistic buy-in from those at the top of the system – meaning the CEO, the owner, the leadership – and briefly teach them the key tools. When such awareness is in place, emotions rising in the system can be reflected back into the system in a healthy format with tools that increase loyalty and strength-building aspects of the company. Managers at all levels feel supported from the top down and can manage the ebb and flow of the changes of wind velocity, knowing that if a "tornado" breaks out, supports are already in place, and if it is just a temporary emotional "dust-devil-breeze" that it isn't necessary to go ballistic!

- The third step is to teach everyone, everyone, from the bottom up, all the tools to manage emotions. No one can be left out of the trainings. No one. The primary key to emotional continuity management is that everyone is on the same team using the exact same tools, creating comradeship as well as intelligent procedures and policies. Anyone who isn't on board with the desire and ethic to work in an emotionally healthy environment can be identified easily as a risk to success. Such employees can then be remediated, repurposed, or removed. Usually, once they see that the environment no longer serves their need for chaos, they will choose to either get on board to keep their job, or move on because no one is willing to spin into an emotional frenzy with them anymore.

The next step is up to you!

Where you, your co-workers, and your employees work is sacred ground because where you work matters to you. Emotional management should not be the sole protective domain of a few employees. If everyone is awake and aware of the concepts, there can be no hidden agendas. Of course, not every company chooses to be awake – just as there are the gamblers and risk-takers in "tornado alley" who ignore the warning sirens and people who build houses directly on top of earthquake faults. You get to decide how much risk your company can absorb. While waiting until a disaster happens is one approach to change, taking action now to reduce the risk will serve you, and it will serve the bottom-line of your company.

I keep researching, exploring, and discovering new tools that find productive and compassionate ways to mix the oil and water of finances and emotions.

Dr. Vali Hawkins Mitchell
Seattle, Washington USA
November, 2012

Introduction

Bottom-line Impact of Emotions in the Workplace

0.1 What Does it Mean, What Does it Matter?

"Former discharged employee kills boss, leaves 3 bystanders and a child dead."

"Love triangle in the workplace leads to multiple layoffs."

"Woman sues company over misunderstanding, company in financial ruin."

"Charges of sexual harassment leveled on CEO, he denies allegations."

"Domestic violence spills over into workplace, woman hospitalized, 2 other key employees injured."

"Executive director quits company amidst rumors of misappropriation of funds."

Whenever I read newspaper headlines like these, first my heart thinks of all the staggering emotional ripples, and then I start doing the math in my head. The headlines identify specific people and situations, suggesting that some process of emotions spinning out of control is happening – or has been happening for a long time – but now has moved from the covert to the overt. And the personal and financial costs – both short-range and long-range – are complex.

Why would you or anyone in business care about this?

- Humans work and humans have emotions.

- Human emotions can make or break your company financially.

- Poorly managed emotional events at work can range from daily annoyances to deadly.

- Emotions and business are like oil and water.

How much does one hour of your time cost your company? Multiply your salary times the hours you spend managing emotional spins. Can your company afford this? Ask your chief financial officer if it is cost-effective for you to ignore emotions. How much do you think the costs associated with increased security due to the increased issues of fear cost your company? How much fear can your company absorb?

Take a few moments and do your own math. Consider the last few weeks or months of your work time spent mitigating workplace emotions. Now, multiply it by your salary. Now, take the salary of your boss and multiply it times the hours you spend reporting on problems. Extrapolate it out for the year. Now, call local counselors at a mental health agency or a counselor in private practice. Ask them how much they are getting paid by the hour to do what you do every day.

0.2 The Cost of Emotions Spinning out of Control

Some of the bottom-line costs in business context:

- **Fiscal:** The real costs in dollars and cents are expenditures, losses, revenue streams.

- **Goodwill:** Will customers continue to use your business or move to your competitors?

- **Liability:** Will your business be eaten alive by nickel-and-dime or catastrophic litigations?

▶ **Global:** Will your company be part of the world community or isolated to the point of no contact and ultimate extinction? Isolation is not viable.

▶ **Other Costs:** Can you think of other costs in your specific industry?

> A group hug isn't going to manage the fiscal risks of emotions at the worksite.

0.2.1 Fiscal

When you think about the headlines above, you will identify some of the obvious and hidden costs associated with managing emotions at the workplace. Such costs include unaccounted health care dollars spent, counseling fees, lost vendors, clients who never pick your business because of the rude receptionist, pencils stolen, and paper towels used by the obsessive-compulsive hand washer in the cubicle down the hall. A group hug isn't going to manage the fiscal risks of emotions at the worksite. At the same time, putting emotions in a category that doesn't place real dollar risks on the small and large emotional spins of employees is shortsighted.

Risk equation: To determine the exact cost of emotions in the workplace, figure your hourly salary times hours spent dealing with an emotional event, plus salary multiplied by time spent with the problem, plus the number of people affected by the spin times their salary times their hours lost, plus the salary of your boss multiplied by the time spent by the boss (who is now listening to you), times the number of projected days/weeks until resolution, plus any additional ancillary costs such as FICA/taxes, services, customers lost, PR, training dollars, and health care. The result equals a number that reflects the literal financial cost of an emotional spin.

Do this: Do the math

Don't: Forget that every hour you spend managing emotions costs your company money.

Figure 1: Computing the financial costs of emotions in the workplace.

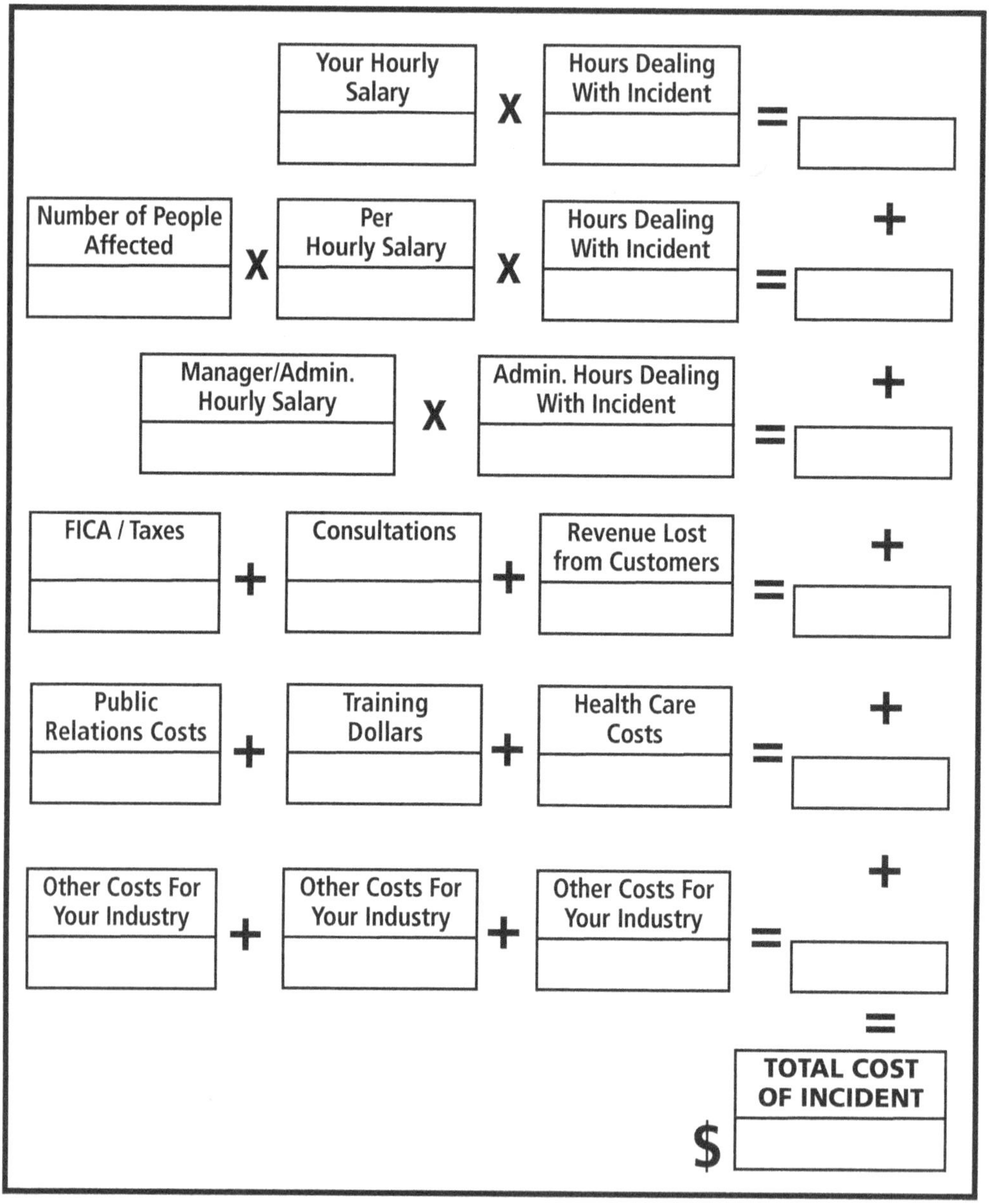

Your Hourly Salary	X	Hours Dealing With Incident	=	

Number of People Affected	X	Per Hourly Salary	X	Hours Dealing With Incident	+ =

Manager/Admin. Hourly Salary	X	Admin. Hours Dealing With Incident	+ =

FICA / Taxes	+	Consultations	+	Revenue Lost from Customers	+ =

Public Relations Costs	+	Training Dollars	+	Health Care Costs	+ =

Other Costs For Your Industry	+	Other Costs For Your Industry	+	Other Costs For Your Industry	+ =

=

TOTAL COST OF INCIDENT

$

The High (and Sometimes Overlooked) Cost of Employee Turnover

People leave. They resign from their jobs, request transfers, move to jobs with the competition, and sometimes just stop showing up – often with little or no explanation for their actions. Unfortunately – and unsurprisingly – a lot of employee turnover is the result of emotions spinning out of control in the workplace. The costs to a company in actual revenue are a consideration that is often underestimated – or not even addressed by companies – until a crisis occurs. Studies by the American Management Association and other organizations reveal that a pattern of resignations and transfers needs to be looked at carefully because such a pattern can add up to significant unrecoverable costs for the company. Here are some of the costs that are generally identified in U.S. business:

▶ Actual exit costs surrounding the person's departure, including lost productivity from a vacant position and loss of departmental productivity and delivery of key projects due to the disruption, costs of temporary staffing, HR personnel hours, severance pay, unemployment insurance, loss of skills, and loss of customers that a departing employee may take with him or her.

▶ Costs of replacing the employee, including advertising, recruiting costs, HR costs of handling and processing resumes and conducting interviews and performing background checks.

▶ Costs of onboarding a new employee, including HR costs of putting the person on the payroll, setting the person up with computer and passwords and other office-related costs, orientation, costs of persons doing training and providing training materials, lost productivity from supervisor and other employees who are training and mentoring the new hire and reviewing his or her work.

And that's not even considering the costs in company brand and reputation. Financially, the costs of employee turnover can vary according to industry, job level and experience of the employee. Generally, cost of turnover is calculated based on the annual salary of the employee, ranging from roughly 6 months' salary (for hourly workers) to 18 months' salary (for professional employees). A rough

> estimate of the cost of employee turnover can be computed as
> 150% of the yearly compensation of the departing professional
> employee, with a higher percentage for managers or salespeople,
> approaching 200-250% of salary. According to this formula, the
> departure of a professional employee earning $32,000 will cost your
> company a minimum of $48,000. Thus, multiple departures could
> add up to significant business loss – something to consider as you
> work with the concepts of emotional continuity in the workplace
> that we discuss in this book. – *Editors*

0.2.2 Goodwill

Think of the damage to the company's goodwill from these headlines! For most companies, goodwill determines longevity. Goodwill is mathematically factored by historical data, expectations of the industry, trends, and mythological predictions of future business. Predictions are fantasies. Certainly some fantasies match reality quite closely, but until a crystal ball is invented, or businesses hire psychics as consultants and their numbers are verified and repeatable, goodwill is a hope, not a sure thing. Many businesses attach a goodwill value to the selling price of their business. They have built up a reputation, and it is a valuable asset.

Clients and customers are attracted or repelled by goodwill concerns. Customer service is the subject of very expensive trainings and policy meetings for businesses that make an effort to keep people coming to their company for products or services. When people do not come, the bottom line is not maintained. And people don't come if they do not like you. This is one powerful domain of emotions at the workplace that can easily be translated into lost revenue. Large corporations spend billions on convincing the public that they are the "good guys." Loyalties shift rapidly, and one day the good guys are the bad guys and revenue dries up.

The loss of goodwill can span industries and revenue streams for decades. What does the word Columbine mean to you? What did it mean 10 years ago? The Titanic was pitched as the safest maritime product and service in the known world. The Titanic was sold as "unsinkable." Today the word Titanic is synonymous with loss and doomed failure. Some loss, like the Titanic, spans fiscal and goodwill costs for decades.

Do this: Consider goodwill as money on its way.

Don't: Think people aren't paying attention to the smallest ripple of attitude.

Do this: Assume that everything is completely visible to everyone on the planet at all times and someone is keeping score.

Don't: Ever forget that your next client is in the wings waiting to be either your client or someone else's client.

0.2.3 Liability

What are the risks of litigation from these headlines? Industries, businesses, employees, and managers are at extreme risk for litigation through civil, criminal, and personal liability suits. Emotional events at the workplace – from extreme events such as shootings and criminal incidents to small events such as an implied sexual innuendo or racist comment – routinely end up in court. The hourly fees and retainers of legal advisors add significant costs to companies. A day in court could ruin a small business.

Personal liability in a company is an emotional and fairly political topic.

Posturing and positioning during conflict can lead to verbal or physical threats and outright attacks. Threats of litigation are becoming more dangerous and powerful than real attacks. Legal saber-rattling from an adversary is intended to shift power so the other guy will back away first in compromise. Bullies love to scare anyone they can. Threats of litigation can be as terrifying as a real lawsuit.

Behavior that threatens litigation can create emotions that spin out of control and launch future spins through implications of future terror. When conflicts and power struggles exist, it means that someone will win and someone will lose. Some battles need to be fought for justice and ethical standards, and many conflicts originate with people who use litigation only for the right reasons. However, there are others, like bullies, who use litigation or threats of litigation for the wrong reasons, to start or maintain a spin or to gain position and power.

Do this: Call several local attorneys and ask their fees per hour.

Don't: Assume your company will cover your legal fees. Find out. If necessary, get your own lawyer and your own malpractice or liability insurance – and if it is that risky, perhaps a new job or a different career!

0.2.4 Other Costs

Then there are the costs that are personal, local, national, or global. I think about the employees and the managers and the spouses and the children and the counselors and the lawyers and the classroom teachers and the day-care providers and the grandparents – and the other business and personal outcomes that will be a natural consequence of these headlines. I know that the headline is the tip of the iceberg. I wonder if anyone is helping the survivors?

▶ Alcohol and other addiction behaviors will escalate in the home and the workplace.

▶ Domestic violence, child abuse, and other nasty side effects of fear and instability will wobble the local economy.

▶ Lawyers will be making plans to take their families to Tahiti after finishing the work that has been created for them.

▶ Doctors will prescribe more antidepressants, and more pharmaceutical products are sold.

▶ Children who are stressed because mom or dad is stressed will be more likely to be targeted as attention deficit disorder (ADD) when they act out their tension in the classroom.

▶ Some students will be put on medications because the teachers and the parents don't know how to manage emotionally spinning children or just don't have the financial resources to be as compassionate as they would like to be.

▶ The teachers won't have the support, and so their emotions will escalate into a spin. And perhaps no one will be there for them, either.

▶ The pharmaceutical industry may benefit, but pharmaceutical industry employees will be stressed, too.

> **One bully can bring a company and countless others to ruin like a bunch of cascading dominoes.**

0.3 Protecting Your Bottom Line

Many people believe that this "soft side of business" should be left to the HR professionals because it has nothing to do with the bottom line. In reality, it has everything to do with the bottom line. It is ironic that companies that would spend millions on software tools, customer surveys, and ergonomic furniture fail to spend needed dollars on emotional continuity management tools, too. Emotional continuity is about emotional readiness and paying attention to business and humans in the same location.

The bottom line here is that if you "turn on the lights" in your company, you could save a lot of time and money. One bully can bring a company and countless others to ruin like a bunch of cascading dominoes. Not a pretty sight. And you need to see the big picture to fix the problem here.

I hear stories. When I tell people I'm a traumatologist, or emotional continuity management consultant they say something like, "Huh? What's that…?" And then they say, "I've heard about emotional stuff at conferences – but how do you really do anything about people's feelings at work? What tools are there? How can you quantify emotions? How can you make policies about human feelings? Oh yeah, we've had people who created so much conflict and chaos that it was unbelievable. But can anything actually be done about it?"

Indeed, no one can mandate emotions nor can they predict and control the human mind, but work needn't be a madhouse. Countless user-friendly tools are available to better manage your own emotions and the emotions of others. Psychologists, mental health counselors, human resource professionals, management trainers, social workers, coaches, and people who attend 12-step meetings have better tools in place than most companies. Why? Emotional continuity management is not rocket science, nor the exclusive domain of some secret psychology club! Historically, businesses haven't had the time or inclination to put emotional continuity management tools in place. However, times have changed.

And the best emotional management tools are simple to use. This book introduces a few tools that have been well tested in real worksites with real people under real conditions. Just as everyone in a company needs to know how to use the fire extinguisher, everyone on your team needs to know how to use emotional readiness tools for whatever may happen. Continuity planning is about readiness. Mastery takes practice and rehearsal. You will be able to tell if your tools are working by how you feel and how people are responding.

0.3.1 How Emotional Continuity Planning Can Help

Recently, I ran into Dr. Fiona, the CEO of a medical clinic where I consulted a few years ago, who said she wanted to thank me. She and her partners had hired me to teach them how to deal with some emotional issues that were beginning to pick up traction. Doctors are not always trained in best business practices because they spend most of their time learning how to save lives. The staff was mostly women. The level of gossip and backbiting had apparently escalated past reasonable limits and, in fact, had led to serious hurt feelings, infighting, side-choosing, reprisals, and several resignations. Beyond what would have been normal attrition, they had recently gone through the expenses and transitions of hiring and training six different office managers in less than a year – only to have each leave suddenly with little or no explanation. After a review of the situation, I identified Zelda, a key player behind the scenes, as the one stirring up the mix quite well. A long-time employee, she was a highly trained professional who hoped to become a partner. She was one of the troublesome people whom I define in this book as an *emotional terrorist* (ET). Knowing that her position was critical to the function of the medical organization, Zelda thoroughly enjoyed her power and had a knack for making people angry while appearing superficially soft-spoken and pleasant. She thrived on chaos.

Even when they realized Zelda was the source of the problem, Dr. Fiona and the other partners, out of their need for her considerable, specialized skills, decided that it would be better for the overall deliverables of their company to absorb the loss of a few easily replaced managers than to lose Zelda – even though they admitted that she could be "difficult" at times. I encouraged the partners to consider what their fiscal and goodwill bottom line number was. In other words, how many people could they afford to lose as a result of Zelda's disruptive behavior? The partners came up with a clear number that they believed reflected the value of keeping this "talented" employee on board. Subsequently, two chaotic years passed before the tipping point. Finally, Harriet, a new office manager who had been doing a brilliant job of running the office surprised the partners with her resignation. Unlike previous departing managers, Harriet itemized in detail the treatment she had received from Zelda, saying that she was considering litigation. At this point, it was clear to the partners that the value of Zelda as a key employee did not justify the costs of retaining Zelda while facing the prospect of recruiting and training more staff, only to have her drive them away. It was then that Dr. Fiona and her partners took action. They invited Harriet to stay, and then they broke the news to Zelda that their plans did not ever include further promotions or a partnership for her. The ambitious Zelda "suddenly" decided to move on with her career. The doctors supported her in moving on to her next career opportunity, which was in the same community, but not a job that would impact the finances of their medical clinic directly.

In the end, this resolution apparently went well. Dr. Fiona said to me, "Thank you for understanding that we couldn't just fire her outright in this closed and tight local industry, that her technical skills are brilliant, and that it took us a long time to work through this without causing more long-term grief." However, once Zelda was gone, the partners reviewed the costs of employee turnover during the time Zelda was on the job undermining morale. Dr. Fiona concluded, "When we did the math at the end of this two-year period *after she was gone*, we discovered we had saved almost two million dollars by her exit, maintained goodwill, and feel really good about it. Your compassionate *emotional continuity plan* worked."

Questions for Further Thought and Discussion

1. Have you observed a situation in your community or workplace in which "spinning" emotions left damage in their wake?

2. Think about the medical clinic example given above, considering the claim that the company had saved $2 million in the two years after the disruptive employee left the company. Using the information in this chapter and your own experience, see how well you can do itemizing these costs. Do they add up to $2 million? Perhaps more?

3. Once again looking at the medical clinic example, would you have simply fired Zelda? How much do you think the company had been losing per year while she was still employed (think of the year that six office managers quit)? Or, by summarily getting rid of Zelda, would the partners perhaps have run the risk of other business losses?

4. What do you think might be some of the financial costs that could accompany a loss of goodwill? Think of examples of companies that – due to inappropriate or violent behavior on the part of employees – suffered financially for loss of goodwill (reputation, brand, etc.).

5. Imagine that a manager says to you, "We're not baby-sitters. Employees are adults and need to take care of their own emotions. Emotions are not something for line managers to concern themselves with – let HR take care of that weepy stuff." From what you have read so far, what would be your response?

Emotions and Spinning

1.1 Emotions Are a Part of Work

Questions: What emotions are appropriate at work and what emotions are counterproductive? What is okay and what isn't okay? How do you tell if someone is having normal emotions without getting an advanced degree in psychology? What if your co-worker, boss, supervisor, or manager is an emotional terrorist or bully? What if you are? Does your company have a policy and plan in place to manage emotions? How would you deal with an employee who is acting in a manner that is disrupting the entire organization?

Answers: *Reasonable variations of human emotions are expected at the workplace. People have feelings. Emotions that accumulate, collect force, expand in volume, and begin to spin are another matter entirely. Spinning emotions can become as unmanageable as a tornado, and in the workplace they can cause just as much damage in terms of human distress and economic disruption.*

All people have emotions. Emotions happen at home and at work. Different people have different sets of emotions. Some people let emotions roll off their backs like water off a duck. Other people swallow emotions and hold them in until they become toxic waste that needs a disposal site. Some have small, simple feelings and others have large, complicated emotions. Stresses of life tickle our emotions or act as fuses in a time bomb. Stress triggers emotion. Extreme stress complicates the wide range of varying emotional responses. Work is a stressor. Sometimes work is an extreme stressor.

If employees are not able to function because of emotional upheaval – for any reason – then there are fiscal risks that must be considered.

It is important to know what emotions are regular and what are irregular, abnormal, or damaging within the business environment. What happens if employees are engaged in emotional combat with other employees through gossip, innuendo, or out-and-out verbal warfare? And what if the entire company is in turmoil because you have a bully, who is like an "emotional terrorist" driving everyone bonkers? What if there is a disaster? What if? What if? *The business answer in terms of bottom-line thinking is that productivity is productivity. If employees are not able to function because of emotional upheaval – for any reason – then there are fiscal risks that must be considered. The human compassion answer, in terms of bottom-line thinking, is that employees need to be safe at work. Both fiscal and human compassion needs must be in balance for an organization to function well. Mixing the "oil and water" of fiscal concerns and human feelings at the workplace isn't something you can leave to chance.*

Employees today face the possibility of biological, nuclear, incendiary, chemical, explosive, or electronic catastrophe while, at the same time, potentially working in the same cubicle with someone ready to suicide over personal or financial issues at home. They face rumors of downsizing and outsourcing while watching for anthrax amidst rumors that co-workers are having affairs. A random joke makes someone laugh and makes someone else upset. Productivity can falter when the focus is on emotions and not on tasks.

Emotions run rampant in human lives and therefore at worksites. High-demand emotions demonstrated by complicated workplace relationships, time-consuming divorce proceedings, addiction behaviors, violence, illness, and death are issues at worksites which people either manage well or do not manage well. Annoyances, petty bickering, competition, prejudice, bias, minor power struggles, health variables, politics, and daily grind feelings disrupt productivity as well as taking up emotional or mental space. Add a bully to the mix and you have a recipe for disaster from the inside out!

In documents directed at Human Resources (HR) professionals, you may have encountered the term *emotional labor* to describe the requirement, in certain professions, for the worker to hide or manipulate his or her inner emotions, while displaying another set of emotions, in order to get the job done. The term was originated by sociologist Arlie Russell Hothschild (2003) to describe the need for workers in some professions to adapt the normal process of suppressing emotions for commercial purposes and its personal cost to them. Concerned for the long-term emotional health of the workers, Hothschild warned that this requirement to assume a mask or false emotional facade could be regarded as an "occupational hazard."

Use of the term *emotional labor* in recent years has moved away from Hothschild's original concerns, urging that the requirements of emotional suppression need to become a recognized part of the training of persons whose jobs require interacting with the public. We mention this concept in order to make clear that this book 1) shares Hothschild's concerns for the potential damage that can come from a policy of suppressing feelings at work and 2) does *not* advocate an approach of training workers to manifest artificial emotional responses. Rather, our purpose is to advocate the need to acknowledge, understand, and deal with strong emotions in the workplace in an honest, constructive, and healthy way in concert with fiscal responsibility.

Definitions

Emotions: All human feelings, those defined as positive and negative.

Spinning: Normal emotions that, for some reason, escalate and continue to develop an additional energy beyond the emotions of the original event. Emotional spinning occurs when a person, or several people, join forces with someone else to form a mutual or collective energy spin. The increasing collective emotional dynamic created by rampant, unmanaged, or poorly managed feelings.

Unintentional spinning: Being unconsciously caught in someone else's strong emotional process and temporary emotional repercussions or consequences associated with the effects of an emotionally charged event.

Intentional spinning: The intentional use and action of displaying and using emotions of self or others to control a situation or to accumulate territory – either literally or figuratively – using force through physical, mental, emotional, or psychological mechanisms of fear, intimidation, implied threats, or outright control.

Emotional terrorism: The use of emotional mechanisms and behaviors to force or coerce an emotional agenda on someone else with the intention or action of controlling a situation, or accumulating territory – either real, perceived, or symbolic.

Bully: A person who is habitually overbearing, especially to weaker people. Bullying is a form of abuse that attempts to create power over another group or person to create an imbalance of power through social, physical, emotional, or verbal coercion/manipulation; ***an emotional terrorist.***

1.1.1 Sometimes Emotions Get Things Spinning

Emotions can come and go. They can also gather speed and force like a tornado. At this point the emotional energy can take on a life of its own. Events as seemingly benign as a fully involved gossip chain or a computer upgrade can go away or they can lead to the exit of valuable employees. Each emotional charge can add energy to an emotional spin that can become a full blown disruption including time loss, recruitment nightmares, disruptions in customer service, additional management hours, remediation and trainings, consultation fees, health care costs, consultant fees, employee assistance program (EAP) dollars spent, HR time spent, administrative restructuring, and expensive and daunting litigations. What appears to be a simple case of "bullying" can turn into a homicidal or suicidal occurrence that can create a national media event that brings families and companies to their knees.

Companies that prepare in advance for the potentials of all emotions, the full range of emotions, and therefore emotional and fiscal risks – from minor annoyances to catastrophe, from daily stressors to a full-blown bullying and emotional terrorism nightmare – are better equipped to adjust to any emotionally charged event, small or large.

It is never a question of *if* something will happen to disrupt the flow of productivity, it is only a question of *when* and how large. No person and no company is immune. If you think you or your organization are bulletproof, *then* you are at higher risk because you have not been paying attention and you aren't living in the real world!

Emotions that ebb and flow are functional in the workplace. A healthy system should be able to manage the ups and downs of emotions. Emotions directly affect the continuity of production and services, customer and vendor relations, and essential infrastructure. Healthy emotions make companies accessible and user friendly. Unstable emotional infrastructure in the workplace disrupts business through such measurable costs as lost contracts, loss of goodwill, medical and mental health care, employee retention and retraining costs, time loss, or legal fees. Emotional continuity management, a conscious process that pays attention to and predicts and manages emotional ebb and flow at work, is reasonably simple for people to manage when they are provided the justifiable concepts and empirical evidence that the risks are real, along with a set of correct tools and instructions in their use.

What has not been easy until recently has been convincing the "powers that be" that it is value-added work to deal directly and procedurally with emotions in the workplace. Businesses have failed to see emotions as part of the working technology and have done everything they can do to avoid the topic. Now, cutting-edge companies are turning the corner. Also companies that have survived the horrors of an emotional disruption have attracted enough media attention to let others see the devastation. The secret is out: Emotions can destroy people and companies!

Significant emotions from small to extreme are no longer the sole domain of HR, EAP, or even emergency first responders and counselors. Emotions are spinning in the very midst of your team, project, cubicle, and company. Emotions are not just at the scene of a disaster. Emotions are present. And because they are not "controllable," human emotions are not subject to being mandated.

There are times when the management of emotions cannot simply be outsourced to an external provider of services. There are times that you – as an employee or manager – will face an extreme emotional reaction and find that you are on your own. Your job today includes acquiring the skills necessary to know when you can manage emotions yourself (your own and those of others), when you are way over your head, and when you need to call for backup.

In a perfect world, a system-wide approach to creating an emotionally spin-free workplace would mean all persons preparing themselves for potential emotional impact, thus lowering the risks of collective system-wide emotional spinning. This planning would prepare everyone for rapid recovery no matter the type, size or condition of the emotional event. Organizations that develop emotional continuity policy, procedures, practice drills, multiple resources, and management tools are more ready to withstand whatever comes along with a healthy, rapid-recovery mentality. And if your company won't create emotional continuity plans for you, do it for yourself.

> **Given the volatile nature of the world situation, you must begin first efforts to establish policies and procedures for managing emotions at the workplace.**

1.1.2 Thinking about Emotions

To start to think about emotions at work you will have to think about your own emotions first. You can start raising your emotional management grade point average (GPA).

Emotions are human feelings, sentiments, and sensations. Feelings are intangible, although the results of emotions and feelings can be quite tangible. Emotion is the stuff of love and hate, peace and conflict, music and poetry, art and madness, politics and principles, philosophy and religion. Emotions are defined and redefined, scientifically analyzed, researched, dissected, and sorted into bite-sized categories. Emotions are completely unfathomable and exquisitely human. Any attempt to define, much less comprehend, the emotional nature of human beings, for the purpose of mandating or controlling human emotional response, is whimsy at best, and dangerous at its worst. But we have to start someplace!

You cannot wait to be an expert to be the expert. Given the volatile nature of the world situation, you must begin first efforts to establish policies and procedures for managing emotions at the workplace. If that can't happen, you can start with yourself.

1.2 Sometimes Spinning Starts to Pick Up Speed

Okay, so you have started thinking about emotions. Then you are faced with an emotional incident. You see the emotion in yourself or someone else and know it is your job to manage it, but you don't have any tools. Then you see something that you think is bigger. Underneath the incident of the moment you see or feel or sense something else is going on. There is a subset of emotions that seem to have another dimension. This "something" seems to have a life of its own. *What you may be seeing is emotional spinning. It is bigger than you or any individual person. Now what?*

Emotional spinning is what happens when an employee or a group of employees experience what could be seen as normal emotions that, for some reason, escalate and continue to develop an additional energy beyond the emotions of the original event.

Emotional spinning can go on inside one person if something big is going on for them. Emotional spinning can also occur when one or more employees join emotional forces with someone else to form a mutual or collective energy spin. The secondary emotional spin itself begins to take form and shape and develop a life of its own. A spin may start as a simple feeling state and then escalate to interfere with work functions.

Emotional spinning can center on one person or can consume entire systems and whole industries. Emotional spinning can feel like a mob mentality or can be significantly more subtle. In fact, a subtle, scornful expression or undertone of disgust can initiate emotional havoc in a workplace quite effectively and extensively. A well-placed rumor can create cascading turmoil and emotional spin-offs that lead to deep emotional distress, leading to extraordinary fiscal carnage. A "soft" incident like a broken promise can turn into "hard" data of lost revenue. An angry facial expression can have more influence on feelings than words, as emotions fill in the gaps of meaning that lead people to make wild, emotional assumptions. Emotional spinning can take a regular workday and turn it into your worst management disaster nightmare!

1.2.1 Some Spinning is Contagious

Like a virus, **emotional terrorism** can spread between departments if the environment within them has vulnerable units. For example, a harmless rumor that might be laughed off by two healthy employees may be taken seriously by a dysfunctional member of the team. That same rumor, used by someone with pathology, could be the last straw for the vulnerable employee. It helps to know who the players are, so that an unexpected invasion, such as a rumor or disruption, can be anticipated and stopped in its tracks. Knowing or defining the players does not mean anything must be done other than determining the risk factors involved in developing situations.

FIGURE 1.1:

**Track the Movement and Contagion of an
Emotional Incident Through a System**

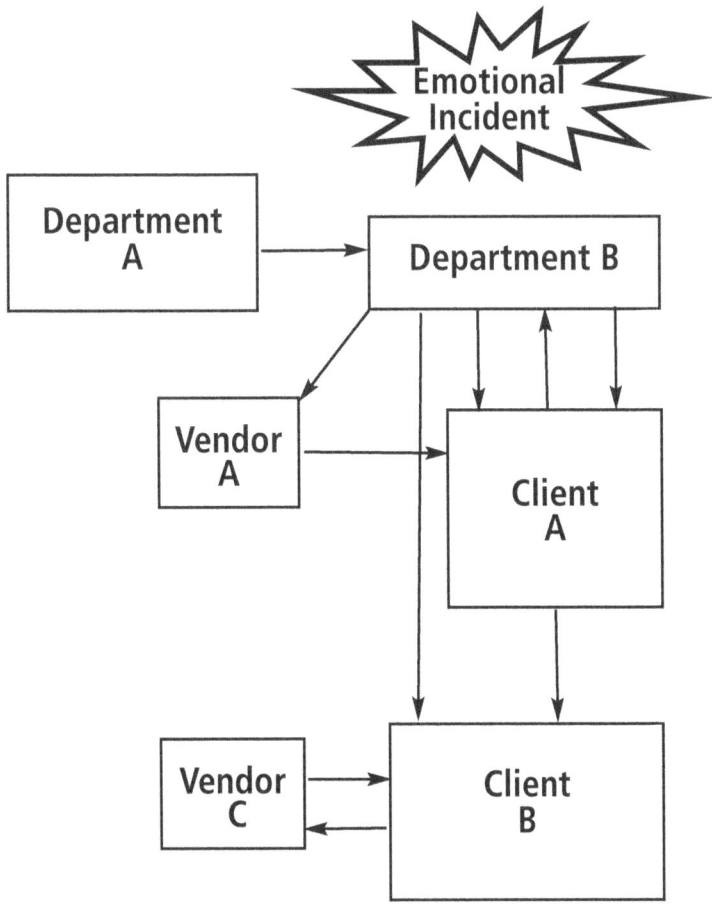

1.2.2 Some People Exploit the Emotional Situation

Bullies can act alone or in groups. Bullies can start an emotional spin that becomes a system-wide contagious event that can make an entire company swirl out of control. Bullies come in all shapes, sizes, genders, races, colors, creeds, philosophies, religions, shoe sizes, and levels of education and authority. A bully can be a boss or a custodian, a manager or a food service worker, a housekeeper or administrative assistant, a man or woman, old or young. Emotional terrorists (bullies) have only one agenda, chaos, which lets them feel more powerful. They can start a rumor, fuel it, and then step back and enjoy the insanity. Not nice people! Read on!

Bully Kids.... Bully Adults

There is a significant effort to educate children about bullies, because child bullies can become adult bullies. Look at this overview of recognition signs of children who bully and see how it is no different from adult behavior.

- Doesn't have empathy.
- Tries to dominate or manipulate.
- Likes feeling powerful and in control.
- Is a poor winner and poor loser.
- Gets satisfaction from someone else's fears or pain.
- Arrogant.
- Is good at hiding bullying from others.
- Is excited by disagreements or troubles between others.
- Blames others for his/her problems.
- Gets angry easily.
- Has gotten into trouble for behavior in the past.
- Is impulsive.
- Intimidates others.
- Is intolerant or prejudiced toward others or groups.

1.2.3 Emotional Spinning is More than Experiencing Our Feelings

Emotional spinning is not the regular day-to-day feelings that people experience and demonstrate. Emotional spinning is not the acute, short-lived moments of agitation or disturbance that are a reaction to normal challenges.

Emotional spinning is an effect, or process, which endures long enough to have consequences. Acute or short-term processes are like breezes; they come and go with a bit of a dramatic flair, but are not consequential, unless the breeze is carrying a contagious disease. (The consequences of a toxic-laden breeze may be quite collectively impressive.) When people get together day after day at work, tension happens and conflicts happen. Tension and conflict are normal breezy gusts associated with human beings that hang out with other human beings. People working together are going to find joy and annoyance as they associate with one another to create products and complete performance tasks. Human feelings happen and spin into all the nooks and crannies of human life, including the worksite, like simple breezes blowing across the face of planet Earth. No part of the Earth is untouched by the wind. This is a good thing. A bit of a breeze can move the dust of boredom around and create a sense of "fresh air" in a worksite. New ideas can come from a bit of fresh air. Normal human emotions are good. Emotional spins, however, are more like big winds, tempests, gales, storms, typhoons, hurricanes, cyclones, and batten-down-the-hatch-and-head-for-the-cellar tornadoes!

Many human feelings are the kind that can be described as positive, like happy, enthusiastic, hopeful, ambitious, energized, loyal, and so forth. Some feelings are the kind that can be described as negative like angry, fearful, gloomy, annoyed, tense, and so forth. Some feelings are comfy and some are uncomfortable. Both kinds of emotions, positive and negative, are normal, human, useful, to be expected, and are okay, even at the worksite. Most healthy adults can handle periods of joy and periods of discomfort without it interfering with their jobs. Even the bigger emotions that go with grief and sorrow, anger and disappointment can come and go. Most individuals and businesses can handle temporary periods of joy and periods of discomfort and even turmoil without significant risk or losses. Businesses that employ human beings should expect and be willing and able to handle the full range of human emotional expression without coming apart at the seams. If you, or your company, are made out of tissue paper and the wind blows, this is another discussion.

> **There are some very scary human beings in the world and in our worksites. Scary people have day jobs, too, you know!**

1.2.4 Sometimes Spinning Leads to Violence

Okay, so you agree that human emotions are normal. Even big emotions can be useful and creative. But emotions that escalate to conflict must be stopped long before violence. And what does that mean? When is someone having a bad moment, and when is someone being a bully or emotional terrorist? What are the rules? What is abusive? And what should you just ignore?

Violence and abuse does happen and it happens at work and at home. Women abuse men. Men abuse women. Men abuse men. Women abuse women. There are some very scary human beings in the world and in our worksites. Scary people have day jobs, too, you know! Bullies, battering spouses, child abusers, sex offenders, criminals, and even mass murders have jobs.

No one is immune to the potential dangers of abuse and violence, not even at work. Abuse and violence are not culturally, ethnically, racially, politically, socioeconomically, or in any other way limited to one group or another. Workplace spinning is an equal-opportunity issue. So is abuse and violence. It is necessary to learn how to recognize the difference between situations of normal conflict that includes big emotions, and situations of abuse or violence.

Some industries require their employees to be mandated reporters of abuse and violence. Health professionals, teachers, law enforcement personnel, and even day-care providers are required to take training on violence and abuse. You and your employees can opt to become mandated reporters of abuse violence toward other people and find a local or national educator to train your team. Abusers do not want you to have that information and will downplay the seriousness of their emotions and your efforts in order to create a deflection. The courts are becoming more and more concerned with bullies and domestic and child violence and *it is becoming more important for businesses to stop covertly supporting perpetrators, and to take positions of anti-abuse advocacy in their companies.*

If you suspect violence or abuse is happening at your worksite, or someone on your team is either perpetrating or suffering from abuse, check your employee handbook and follow your company's policies. If there is no policy, protect yourself first. As they say when you fly, "Put on your own oxygen mask first before you try to help others!" If you are not supported by your company, make certain you take care of you. Then if you need more help, go ahead and call Child or Adult Protective Services, a mental health crisis response unit, or 911. If you are wrong, it will certainly be embarrassing. If you are right, it will certainly be upsetting. If you are wrong, you might lose your job. If you are right, you might even lose your job. If you are right, you may save a life! If you are right and don't make the call you may read your name or that of someone else in the headlines tomorrow. Which headline would you rather read: "Joe Fired" or "Joe Murdered"? Up to you!

You may be in an abusive or potentially violent situation if you:

- Are frightened of someone's temper.

- Are feeling crazy because someone says you are the cause of the problems.

- Feel controlled by someone's actions, silences, moods, looks, gestures, voice, threats.

- Have the urge to rescue someone when he/she is in trouble.

- Apologize for someone's bad behavior.

- Make decisions about your activities, friends and ideas, according to what someone else wants or how they might react.

- Were abused as a child or in another relationship.

- Have been teased, pushed, ignored, slapped, chased, punched, tickled, thrown, hit, humiliated, or worse and that person has not responded to your needs for safety.

- Are forced to have sex, commit a crime, do something unethical or against your will, or are humiliated for refusal.

- Are forcibly isolated from others.

- Are afraid to express your feelings for fear of someone's response, or told your feelings were invalid, or that you were to blame for any problems.

- Are passive-aggressive and use silence and stonewalling to control someone else's behaviors.

▶ Blame others for your bad feelings rather than being accountable for your own moods.

▶ Feel like a poor victim most of the time.

You may be contributing to abuse or potential violence if you:

▶ Lose your temper frequently or easily.

▶ Drink alcohol or use drugs excessively.

▶ Are very jealous, sulk silently when upset, use silence as a weapon, use explosive behavior as a weapon, and have difficulty expressing your feelings.

▶ Criticize and put down people.

▶ Blame others for problems.

▶ Monopolize the free time of others.

▶ Have rigid ideas about roles and control.

▶ Have broken things, hit, shoved, kicked, tickled, punched, pushed, slapped, chased, humiliated, teased, physically controlled or worse, and blamed others for these behaviors.

▶ Frightened others with displays of anger or threats of danger to self, children, pets, property, or others.

▶ Were physically or emotionally abused as a child.

▶ Saw violence in your family home.

Questions for Further Thought and Discussion

1. Think about an incident that seemed to have everyone in your office unduly "upset." Now that you think about it, was that perhaps an emotional spin in action? What seems to have started it? What ended it? Were upper level managers ever aware of it? At what point do you consider an emotional spin something to take to your leadership?

2. What would be the risks in your company/industry if an emotional spin became contagious? Be very specific about the possible costs to your company in finances and goodwill. What level can your employees handle before they need intervention?

3. Under what circumstances would spinning that is not intentional need outside help? What would that help look like and how would you protect your staff?

4. Imagine you are having a difficult personal crisis of your own, and then you are faced with stopping a disagreement between two employees who are also experiencing personal crises. What would your strategies be for them and for your own self-care?

2

Some Workplace Spins Turn into Emotional Tornadoes

2.1 Defining Emotional Tornadoes

Just like a tornado of the weather variety, the outcome of an emotional tornado is often surprisingly destructive. The winds of these complicated forces can pick up you, beloved colleagues, friends, enemies, loved ones, communities, states, nations and in fact the entire world community and toss them about like a plastic cup. Reasonable, kind, hard-working individuals or entire systems can be relocated from a happy employment site right into an unemployment line with no references. A once vital person can be decimated and left languishing in a health care or mental health facility. Brilliant individuals can land in psychiatric or legal incarceration, alcohol and drug rehab, bankruptcy, divorce court, and even the grave. Emotional winds can swirl your co-worker into time-consuming child custody battles or a favorite boss into a fight for his or her personal or professional reputation. Emotional tornadoes can spin one person or entire systems. Just as the wind of nature isn't very picky about location, emotional tornadoes are not subject to specific places or industries.

Do this: Pay attention to emotional tornadoes to protect yourself and your company.

Don't: Assume emotional tornadoes will avoid you or your organization.

An emotionally spinning boss or employee who works alone or in isolation and is not in a position to do much damage to anyone else can usually be managed successfully. However, if an emotionally spinning employee starts to take over territory, moves into another area, or joins another spinner, the velocity and risk of potential damage escalates exponentially. With each addition of an emotional spin the stability of an entire system is at risk and becomes weaker as it becomes compromised. An emotional tornado can threaten infrastructure just as a real tornado can do untoward damage.

> **An emotional tornado leaves a swath of emotional rubble... Do you think your company is safe? Does it have the shelter of a policy to protect your people?**

One employee spinning is difficult enough to manage, but one in a key position is very challenging. When several employees gather forces, their collective energy is daunting. If the emotional tornado continues adding force, with or without intentionality, the consequences can reach "inconceivable" levels. An emotional spin that completely sabotages business productivity develops a life of its own while the office grinds itself into an emotional spin frenzy. Anger and sadness, indignation and rage, fear and jealousy, sweeping through a system may leave a trail of emotional carnage, chaos, and destruction with profound, immediate long-term requirements for reconciliation and repair. An emotional tornado leaves a swath of emotional rubble. The effects of an emotional tornado can be managed or left to chance. Do you think your company is safe? Does it have the shelter of a policy to protect your people? Do you think it won't hit your company? Think again!

Do this: Avoid emotional entrapments before they spin into large events that hold you hostage.

Don't: Try to manage large emotional spins alone. Some are too big to avoid, and secrecy and isolation are dangerous.

2.1.1 Quantifying Emotional Tornadoes

The effects of emotions in the workplace are significant and measurable. There is not a strong or long history of evaluating the effects of misplaced emotions in the workplace. Research is just beginning to ask the right questions. Feelings have been diminished in value to an extreme. Companies continue to spend millions of dollars evaluating tasks, performance productivity, IT security, competitive market strategies, ergonomic furniture, and customer service, yet they still spend little or nothing on how people are feeling at work. Eventually, research will catch up and prove its worth but, in the meantime, managers have to convince themselves and others that emotions are a risk that employers need to consider.

Evaluating workplace emotions and more specifically, emotional spinning in its overt and covert expressions, is no different than measuring other "intangibles" in the universe. The work begins subjectively and includes empirical data. Most scientific endeavors begin with a feeling, hunch, idea, hypothesis, belief, or partial observation that requires data to be complete. Only a few decades ago, scientists were unable to evaluate or measure many things we now take for granted. Evaluation starts when someone has a question and then gets an idea about how to measure it in order to answer the original question. Thus begins a rather tedious process of developing standards and practices, tests and measurements, assessments and evaluations. Although we are far from having an Emotion-o-Meter (thank goodness!), science has come to standardize other important life-saving information through thorough and thoughtful evaluations, tests, tools, measuring devices, and is now able to make some generally consistent predictions.

Only a few decades of science and advocacy has produced the wonder of measuring and assessing such variables as: (1) fevers, with a thermometer; (2) elevated blood pressure, with a sphygmomanometer; (3) earthquakes, with a seismograph; and (4) blood glucose, with a glucometer. But some effects of nature do not so easily lend themselves to physical tools and measurements so they have needed other means of measurement. Science is constantly evolving ways to effectively assess such intangibles as intelligence, learning, personality, anxiety, trauma, and joy. Other methods used to evaluate and predict visible and invisible effects are comparative scales and graphs. One such tool is used extensively in tornado evaluations. It is called The Fujita Scale.

Ted Fujita and Allen Pearson were scientists who wanted to predict and evaluate the activities of tornadoes (Fujita, 1981). Prior to 1971, weather experts used a variety of means to try to measure and describe tornadoes. Experts have used the Fujita Scale (also known as the Fujita-Pearson Scale) as a way of linking damage risks to wind speed. The Enhanced Fujita Scale is now available (Enhanced, n.d.).

It is an easy, simple and accessible tool to use for describing and categorizing tornadoes. Fujita and Pearson organized the size of tornadoes into original categories from F-0 to F-6, determined by the amount of their damage potential.

Now, translate that wind into an analogy to discuss emotional energy. What is an emotional dust devil? Gust? Gale? Tornado? How much emotional wind at the worksite will it take to create chaos? Carnage? What level emotional force can temporarily annoy productivity and what level can level it into rubble? What follows is my suggestion for how to rate Emotional Tornadoes on a scale from V-1 to V-6.

2.1.2 Dr. Vali's Enhanced Emotional Tornado Chart

V-1 Enjoy	Breezes and Good Circulation
Examples	Emotional issues breeze through the office but do not distract from productivity other than a few minor annoyances.
Business Outcomes	People are people. No violence. Creativity continues to thrive, and people feel part of a business culture. Co-workers generally enjoy their team and work well together.
Decomposition of Behaviors	No major complaints; life and work are managed and attended to in balance. Any difficulties are managed. General sense of well-being and "normalcy."
Interventions	Enjoy this time. Use it to create policy and make plans for potential changes, incidents, events, or intrusions. Do your homework, research, attend seminars, create drills, and educate staff. Create ECM Team

V-2 Educate	Brief Gusts with Moderate Disruptions
Examples	Stress is occasionally escalated. Disagreements with co-workers may become verbal disruptions, gossip, hurt-feelings, anxiety, and vague sense of unease. Petty annoyances are more open. Complaints are made.
Business Outcomes	Systems and productivity have small disruptions. Slight increase in EAP requests, absenteeism, and presenteeism (at work although sick). Slight decrease in morale and loyalties. Occasional outbursts with little or no damage.
Decomposition of Behaviors	Complaints are handled well. People still function, but continued V2 issues start leading the system to use more workhours to stabilize after each disturbance. Tension mounts.
Interventions	Use conflict resolution skills, affirmative attention, training, documentation, policy. Manage reports carefully, make EAP referrals, don't panic. Consult with ECM Team

V-3 Educate	Gales
	Disruptions
Examples	Overt behavior escalates. Noted office disruptions and upsets, outbursts, threats, storm-outs, sullenness, or pouting. Larger complaints, escalated language, more specific and person-alized complaints
Business Outcomes	Externalized anxiety now visible: fear, job concerns, rise in time loss and use of health care, requests for leave, turnover, and EAP referrals.
	More management time used. Meetings regarding "emotions" are now more frequent than production meetings.
Decomposition of Behaviors	Behaviors can be defined as "hostile" with threats, posturing, intimidations, complaints with focused energy, increase in emotional charge – a clear step away from "normal" business behaviors. Sense of diminishing control, a feeling of emotions being central to the situation.
Interventions	Document, report, formal supervision, EAP referrals, "Duty to Warn." Implement policies, do not minimize, do not over-react, inform security as part of procedure. Alert ECM Team

V-4 Escalate	Tornadoes
	Severe Disruptions
Examples	Head for cover! Multiple office upheavals, quarrels, verbal attacks in the open, possible assaults or threats. Can rise to injury, violence, crime.
	Significant complaints and time used in taking "sides."
Business Outcomes	Possible violent events with or without injury or damages, potential exists for life-threatening events. May or may not have national media attention, may have local media attention.
	Higher use of health/mental health care services, protracted absenteeism, increased turnover.
Decomposition of Behaviors	Specific complaints and directed forces of attention, threats, challenges to authority, litigations, violence, loss of control, disorientation, distortion of thinking and social behaviors that may rise to criminal levels.
Interventions	Involve leadership teams, management team.
	Consult Legal.
	Do what is necessary to stop behavior before it escalates another level.
	Use policy and offer full range of pre-staged interventions. Protect people first, provide post-incident support, call EAP, hire a crisis response team.
	## Full alert for ECM Team

V-5 Evacuate	Full Blown Hurricane Devastating Winds
Examples	Emotional infrastructure collapse, physical collapse possible (damage), death and/or casualties are potential, threats or acts of violence including suicide, homicide, hostage situations.
Business Outcomes	Local and perhaps national media attention. High rate of turnover, health/mental health utilization and stability, significant litigations.
Decomposition of Behaviors	Critical shift in thinking that moves from simple to complex survival and self-protection, with limited available options. Limited internal support and increased fear, terror, and paranoia. Likelihood of disordered thinking, may include a complete break in reality for some. Total destabilization.
Interventions	Self-care first. Protect yourself. Call 911 and everything and everyone available during and after event. Make use of full range of resources in an attempt to minimize post trauma effects (PTSD), use resources to stabilize people (employees first), then stakeholders, then business. Include ECM Team in post care support

V-6 Explunge	Unimaginable
Examples	Unimaginable
Business Outcomes	Unimaginable
Decomposition of Behaviors	Unimaginable
Interventions	Unimaginable

2.1.3 Calculating the Costs of Emotional Tornadoes

Startup Costs can include:

❱ Brochures on workplace violence.

❱ Training sessions for all employees.

❱ Training manuals on workplace violence prevention.

❱ Documentation costs.

❱ Private consultations and education seminars.

❱ Executive coaching on workplace violence.

❱ Management training.

❱ Posters.

❱ Media.

❱ Videos/DVDs.

❱ Events for team building a non-violent culture.

❱ Financial incentives.

V-1 Costs can include:

Everything in the previous list... PLUS:

❱ Management time to deal with small annoyances and daily grievances.

❱ Continuing education and trainings.

❱ Downtime for drills.

❱ Time spent planning upgrades for policies, planning, procedures.

❱ Teambuilding and micro-maintenance measures.

❱ Increased security devices and trainings, manpower.

❱ Supervisory time.

❱ Increased security and communications equipment and training.

❱ Time to build comprehensive communications with internal and external partners.

❱ Buy-in activities for top-down and bottom-up agreements.

❱ The unexpected costs.

V-2 Costs can include:

Everything in the previous list… PLUS:

- Continuing education for HR personnel, EAP fees and retainers.
- Training for staff, seminars, conferences on workplace violence.
- Consultations.
- Downtime for drills.
- Upgrades for policies, procedures, and staff information activities.
- Teambuilding for loyalty and stress reduction.
- Public relations.
- Structural changes, remodeling, upgrades to increase staff comfort, ergonomics, and general comfort to relieve chronic issues associated with stress (add vending machines, change furniture, lighting, upgrades of technology).
- Dispute resolution trainings.
- Increased security and communications equipment and training.
- Costs of absenteeism, and increases in "normal" cost issues associated with escalating tensions.
- Meetings with emergency and disaster responders.
- The unexpected costs.

V-3 Costs can include:

Everything in the previous list… PLUS:

- Signal alarms at desks.
- Radios or walkie-talkies.
- Sirens.
- Trainings.
- Security technology upgrades.
- External safety consultations.
- Advanced education.
- Hiring more security personnel.
- Making books available for staff.

- Redesigning office space.
- Remodeling.
- Replacing old equipment.
- Moving people or things to different locations.
- Adding luxury items for employee satisfaction and stress relief.
- Drug programs and rehabilitation for impaired employees.
- Increased health care costs.
- EAP sessions.
- Absenteeism and time loss from drug or alcohol use or abuse.
- Public relations (PR) management.
- Public goodwill losses.
- The unexpected costs.

V-4 Costs can include:

Everything in the previous list... PLUS:

- Public relations nightmares.
- Litigation for decades.
- Funeral costs.
- Ongoing mental health and health care costs.
- Remodeling, or relocation due to carnage.
- EAP and ongoing counseling.
- Critical incident debriefings and defusings.
- First responder fees in some communities.
- Rehiring and retraining of new employees under difficult circumstances.
- Family compensation payments.
- Lost production time, absenteeism.
- Consultations and trainings.
- The unexpected costs.

V-5 Costs can include:

Everything in the previous list... PLUS:

- Costs associated with losses from primary or secondary violence.
- Domestic violence.
- Alcohol use/abuse.
- Child abuse.
- Family neglect/abandonment.
- Divorces.
- Custody battles.
- Relocations.
- Housing losses.
- Exploitations.
- Looting.
- Scams.
- Property damage.
- Emergency management costs (anticipated and unanticipated costs).
- Retraining.
- Rehiring.
- Advertising.
- Long term costs.
- The unexpected costs.

V-6 Costs can include:

Everything in the previous list... PLUS:

- Unfathomable and unexpected costs.

> **Since September 11, 2001, people are struggling to deal with the adjustments to new language, terms, and concepts...**

2.1.4 Attributes of Emotional Tornadoes

Fujita and Pearson have helped wind scientists. But what can managers use to describe emotional spin phenomena in the workplace? What language speaks of evaluating emotions? Since September 11, 2001, people are struggling to deal with the adjustments to new language, terms, and concepts like homeland security, disaster readiness, critical incident stress management (CISM), trauma counseling, color-coded alert levels, and zero tolerance. Before the Columbine school shootings, the word "Columbine" was the name of a place. Now it is a noun and verb associated with disaster, death, trauma management, children, and national horror. Virginia Tech, Hurricane Katrina, The Gulf Oil Spill – businesses are going to require a new language about emotions at the workplace that include the small, non-dramatic feelings of everyday human life and the catastrophic terms associated with death and destruction. If managers are going to talk about emotions, the language is going to need to be technical, business friendly, and less "mental health" stigmatized. Human emotions must be discussed at least as well and at the same level as a discussion about ergonomic furniture.

The good news is that tornadoes have attributes and emotions do also. Tornado experts use terms like volume, speed, force, area (crossing boundaries), location, point of origin, range, level, frequency, and duration to discuss the attributes of wind. Using these same terms, managers can now begin to think in a new way about emotions in the workplace and consider how an emotional tornado could suddenly spin into a worksite. Consider the following tornado attributes and begin to apply them to human feelings and emotional spinning.

Volume: Volume is about the accumulation of mass that takes up space. A workplace spin usually involves more than one person or system and, if unmanaged, begins to increase in capacity.

Speed: Pace, rate, velocity, tempo. How fast is it going and is it getting faster because its own energy giving it more energy and momentum? Like a centrifuge or merry-go-round, the velocity of a spin increases its own speed. Emotional spinning is fast. It can pick up added speed that is self-generative. Small beginnings quickly gain velocity.

Force: Emotional energy comes and goes. If the energy gathers strength and cohesion it becomes a force. A force can generate creativity or destruction. When strong influences combine with other powerful energies a strong dynamic occurs. Hitler was a force. He started as a voice, with an opinion, and that energy combined with other influences to become a larger force.

Gandhi was a force. He started as a voice, with an opinion, and that energy combined with other influences to become a larger force.

Area (Crossing Boundaries): A boundary defines a limit to an area of domain. Putting up a boundary is creating a fence – real, perceived or symbolic – around an area. Putting up an emotional boundary, ideally, should be honored automatically and accepted by the recipient. One way a person can make an emotional boundary is to say "no" to an action that is offensive. Another way is to create protection by policies to define areas of control or domain. Initially, individuals may feel some loss or disappointment from what may seem like a limitation, but most regular, healthy, well-boundaried people adjust quickly to disappointment and appreciate some level of clarity. Spinning, like a tornado, does not like boundaries. Spinning does what it does, goes where it goes, and has its own agenda of spinning. Rules, policies, walls, boundaries, borders, guidelines, laws, limits, or definitions are counter-forces that define areas. Creating a no-spin zone, for example, is creating a boundary where spinning is not appropriate.

Location: Location defines where something is happening. It can also refer to its point of origin. Since workplaces are now global, the location, called "workplace," where a spin may start might include:

desks	transportation
cubicles	hotels
computers	business meetings
websites	restrooms
Facebook	hallways
Twitter	stairwells
social media sites	parking lots
cell phones	hotels
telephones	bars
lounges	elevators

Point of Origin: Where did the spin originate? Did the spin start in the middle of the system, from the bottom up, or from the top down? Did it start internally from an employee? Did it start externally from a vendor, customer, client, or other outside force?

Size: Micro: Small, minute, barely discernible.
    Macro: Large, obvious, visible.

Range: Emotional spins come in a fascinating assortment and array. The range includes:

Annoying	to	Deadly
Entry Level	to	Career Commitment
Amateur	to	Professional
Intermittent	to	Constant
Subtle	to	Blatant
Acute	to	Chronic

Levels: Ranking incidents is very subjective, but they usually fall between small with a small impact to large with a large impact.

Frequency: Most people can usually keep their emotions in line while working. They don't fall apart, have tantrums, or dissolve into lengthy crying binges every shift. If emotions erupt on a frequent or regular basis, the frequency of the reaction can indicated that something beyond the regular levels of emotional response is present. Something may be seriously wrong.

Duration: Most emotional crises begin some sort of resolution process within two to five days. They may not resolve ever, or may take years to complete to closure, but even tragedies and catastrophic traumas look quite different after the first few days. Strong emotions begin to give way to either a softening or a strengthening of other emotions, but the original set of feelings does not last for long. If nothing has changed and the force and volume remain high, something else may be going on. Critical incidents that come and go quickly, such as an accident, tornado, or earthquake, may have a different emotional impact on people than an incident that lasts longer, such as a hurricane, flooding, mass layoff, or long-term emotional chaos process. You can create your own chart to track emotions using the aforementioned attributes and the numbers 1 to 10 in order to document an event.

2.2 How to Recognize a Spin

To begin any discussion about people and their feelings, it must be said that there exist individuals who thrive on the emotions associated with light and hope, growth, and creativity. There are others who thrive on the emotions of despair and darkness, death and destruction. There are people who like to rain on everyone's parade, and there are people who like parading on everyone's rain. Some people seek transformation and others refuse to change. People are people.

An unwillingness or inability to adjust to necessary changes within a reasonable adjustment time frame is not conducive to workplace productivity. In truth, there is no correct timeframe for someone to adjust to change. Time is an artificial arrangement loosely agreed upon by socialized people and is not cross-cultural. Time demands in a competitive workforce suggest that people need to adjust rather quickly. Resistance can be a sign that a spin is starting. Recognizing the attributes of spinning takes some practice. Workplaces are not intended to be counseling offices, confessionals, churches, temples, cathedrals, mystical retreat centers or Aunt Sophie's kitchen table. Attending to every emotional problem is not emotional continuity management. Work is where work is meant to happen. Emotional continuity management is intended to increase rapid recovery as a necessary practice to keep things moving.

2.2.1 What to Look For

There are obvious and less than obvious signs of spinning. Resistances and extreme positions should lead you to a hunch that something in the movement of the energy in your system is not moving correctly or flowing smoothly. That is a clue. There is a scene in a movie about tornado chasers where the hero of the story, a former tornado specialist and scientist, suspects a twister is imminent. He doesn't confer with technology, like his counterpart the anti-hero who is presented as an unfeeling, human techno-robot bad guy. The hero has a hunch and smells the air. He notes the color of the sky. He picks up a handful of dirt and lets it fall between his fingers and watches how it falls to the earth. He closes his eyes. He hunches down and becomes quiet and still. He listens, smells, sees, touches, and attends to the signs, visible and invisible. He recognizes the early signs of a potential spin. He has a hunch first because he has seen spins very close up. He trusts himself. Do you? You need to backup hunches with data, but the best managers often start with trusting their own feelings first.

Do this: Pay attention to your hunches.

Don't: Use hunches as complete data. Hunches include bias and opinions. They are important as a starting point only when backed by data.

2.2.2 Early Warning Signs of Spin Risk

incongruent giggling	avoidance
malicious compliance	non-compliance
blame statements	eye contact
body language	no eye contact
littering	procrastination
gossiping	self projection
unsolicited opinions	avoidance of tasks
not returning phone calls	humiliation

excessive perfumes
unsolicited religious evangelism
invalidation
seductions
leaving tasks 1/4 undone
whisperings
nagging
ignoring
discrediting
partial lie
intimidation
disgust
jealousy
boredom
denial
criticism
intimacy
poor grooming
negation
poor hygiene
outbursts
offensive clothes
illegal activities
incongruent perkiness
non-completion of agreements
negative facial expressions
rebelling against dress code
loud stereos in quiet spaces
teasing
jokes
illicit love affairs
starting rumors
guilt language
cursing

inappropriate humor
trashing shared space
anger
minimizing
innuendo
raised eyebrows
dismissing
interrupting
partial truth
arrogance
distance
corrections
inattention
incongruence
unwillingness
questions
manipulations
compliments
poor boundaries
untreated health
drug/alcohol abuse
chronic irritability
sexual innuendo
demanding praise
gestures
mind games
power plays
manipulative silences
harassment
disrupt meetings
spreading rumors
false charm
shame language
exclusions/racism

2.2.3 Pay Attention to the Early Warning Signs

Most people do not see emotions until they leap out into the open. This is because most employees are busy working, and normal emotions will stay hidden, protected, private, or underground. Emotions can remain covert for quite a while picking up speed and volume.

Nobody want to spend their days in hyper-vigilance watching for signs of covert emotions. That sounds paranoid, right? What fun is that? Most people just want to do their jobs and not focus on the negative.

**Emotional continuity management
is risk management.**

To learn how to keep an eye out for signs of emotional spinning, raise your awareness levels and create a fine-tuned set of recognition skills. Managing emotions does not mean becoming a psychologist or a spy, although there are skills in these areas you must learn. Emotional continuity management is *risk management*. When everyone in your company becomes aware of the risk presented by emotional mismanagement, your company will have the upper hand in predicting, managing, and avoiding unnecessary emotional spin events.

Some folks complain that they are not showing faith in people if they are "on guard." Regular people don't want to appear paranoid. The *hard fact* is that emotional spinning does not care about your opinions or resistance to learning how to manage, because emotional spinning has a life of its own. Bullies don't care what you think; they have their own agenda. And *intentional spinners, like emotional terrorists and bullies, are counting on your resistance so they can take more emotional or physical territory.* Emotional terrorists are expansionists seeking new collections of people, places, and things to increase their empires. *Ask yourself if you really think it wastes company time and money, shows lack of good faith, or demonstrates paranoia to purchase a fire extinguisher? Then go have that discussion with a fire. Then go ask an arsonist.* If you are still worried about good stewardship over the corporate dollar, call five attorneys and ask them to give you their hourly fees for court appearances.

A Setup for an Intentional Emotional Spin Can Look Like One Of These

▶ Andrew starts a rumor about layoffs.

▶ Bryan tells Nora that his marriage is ending and asks whether she would be willing to listen to him later after work because he needs a special friend right now, someone who would understand and appreciate him like she does. He tells Nora she is special.

▶ Lonni cozies up to Desmond and tells him that she thinks it is a crime that Frank was given the assignment he wanted, and now she thinks that Frank might be having an affair with the supervisor. She tells him she is on his side if he wants to fight it.

▶ Gena repeats Jeanne's rumor, but adds her beliefs that it might have something to do with Bruce getting an attorney.

▶ Carl calls all his team members after work encouraging them not to go to the meeting with the new consultant, because he heard that he might be taping the meeting, and then would share that with the bosses.

▶ Krissy blows off the new training meeting and tells her co-workers that if they go they are just "kiss-asses" and that if they want to keep their jobs they should just let the manager know how absurd it is to keep on getting all this training when it doesn't help.

▶ Hanna tells the manager what Gene said with the additional information that "everyone is now upset" and that Jared, the assistant manager, mentioned he might quit over this.

▶ Karen has been trying to stir people up for years to keep her power and control base. She is in a union. The rest of the business is not union. She brings in union reps that start promoting their cause. She uses this information to terrorize people who are under-represented.

▶ Jorge is an anti-union manager who uses threats of lay-offs and bankruptcy to terrorize people against joining a union.

Questions for Further Thought and Discussion

1. How much can your company afford to spend on one employee who creates emotional spinnings that escalate into "tornadoes?"

2. What are the criteria that are in your policy for calling 911 or Security Services? Can anyone call at any time or does it need to have management approval? What is "enough" to justify a call to 911?

3. Under what circumstances would you report an episode of gossiping to your boss? What determines benign gossip as opposed to malicious gossip? What is the difference in terms of your policies and procedures for "hurt feelings"?

4. Can you list 10 reasons to call in your EAP provider?

5. Can you list 10 reasons to call in a Critical Incident Stress Debriefing?

6. Can you list 10 reasons to call in your Emotional Continuity Management Team?

3

Causes of Emotional Spinning

3.1 Life Consists of Change

It may be less important to have a deep comprehension of the causes of spinning than to appreciate that change creates reaction. A reaction is what a spin is at its onset. A research scientist terrorism expert, psychologist, psychiatrist, security specialist, or someone writing a book on emotional spinning, should have a comprehensive appreciation of the dynamics of change.

3.1.1 Spinning is Always a Reaction to Something Else

Some people are challenged by change, ascend to greatness and experience deeper calms and transcendent peace. There are people who have been in catastrophic situations who have gone beyond their own needs and moved beyond amazing circumstances to act in heroic ways. However, people who have had heroic personalities in one situation can also radically transform into less than heroic stances. Previously strong leaders can just as easily become completely incapable of functioning during crisis and the changes associated with a catastrophe. One small event can be the last straw in an already crumbling psyche. Kind and gentle folks can suddenly become monsters and fiends while just as unexpectedly, a former fiend becomes a saint.

Changes at all levels, from annoying adaptations to catastrophic upheavals, tend to bring out the best and the worst reactions and responses in people. A positive emotional spin of support, care, compassion, love, peace, and hope can easily be cancelled by a negative spin of abandonment, retribution, anger, rage, and revenge.

Do this: Anticipate that emotional spinning may happen in unexpected circumstances and create unexpected reactions.

Don't: Try to predict the unpredictable. Just be prepared for it to happen because life on life's terms is unpredictable.

> Life is change. And all businesses have changes.
> All changes create some loss... With either
> small losses or large losses, the human
> emotion that goes with loss is grief.

3.1.2 Change, Loss, and Grief

Life is change. And all businesses have changes. All changes create some loss. Even with gain there is loss through a change event. All loss leads to grief. With either small losses or large losses, the human emotion that goes with loss is grief. Elisabeth Kübler-Ross (1997) was the first to provide a good template to discuss the grief process. And although she focused on the extreme emotions of grief associated with death, she described a set of grieving stages, which can apply to all loss that comes from change, even small loss from small change. What most people who are not in the emotions industry do not realize is that these stages are not limited to physical death. It doesn't take a death to grieve. It only takes a change. Changes lead to the same feelings as if someone (or something) has died. The stages Kübler-Ross described are:

▶ Denial

▶ Bargaining

▶ Anger

▶ Depression

▶ Acceptance

Denial: The new manager instructed Annie not to use the company car until it was serviced, and to sign a new waiver before driving. Annie went ahead and used the car because she always had used it without having to ask permission. The manager reprimanded Annie. Her response was, "But this is how it's always been done."

Bargaining: When the manager repeated the policy, Annie said, "Well I'll just do it this way today, okay? And I'll pay for the gas myself."

Anger: The manager was consistent and courteously repeated the new rules. Annie reacted with, "Well this is pointless and annoying. I've always had free use of the company vehicle, and now you're telling me I have to ask 'mother-may-I' every time I have a client call me and I need to use the car?"

Depression: The manager explained the rationale for the new policy, which Annie agreed made sense. She stated, "Yeah, I can see that is a better policy for the organization, but it sure is difficult for me now that I have to re-think this entire logistics process for my project team. It was so easy before to just pop out on a client run without a bunch of paperwork and hassle."

Acceptance: The manager supported Annie by calmly listening to her as she went through the stages dealing with this change. When Annie seemed to be more in acceptance, the new manager complemented her on her history of teamwork, and suggested she review the policy and paperwork as soon as she had time, and offered to answer any questions that might come up. Annie responded with, "Yup, we're all in this new merger together I guess. I'll figure it out. Thanks."

Because the manager was aware of the stages of normal grief cycle, she didn't take Annie's resistance personally and was able to remain calm, focused, and supportive while Annie moved through the stages. The manager also tracked her own stages as she bumped into the resistance of Annie that was a change from her fantasy that everyone would just be easily willing to comply with her new authority. The manager noted her own emotional content, and put it on hold for the moment. She did not resist the resistance and did not counter it with more resistance and escalating emotional power plays. The resistance went away. The manager knew Annie to be a solid employee, and with the tool of understanding grief stages, actually facilitated Annie's adjustment to a rather small change. The entire transition took only a few minutes and did not evolve into an emotional spin.

> It is amazing to discover how much more receptive and non-spinning a person can be… when change responses are seen as grief responses and *not as emotional spins.*

Do this: Learn the stages of grieving and apply them to any change.

Don't: Make the common error of thinking that it takes a death to experience the stages of grieving.

The closer a change gets to threatening control over comfort, security, or mortality, the more serious it is perceived and the more loaded with spin potential.

It is amazing to discover how much more receptive and non-spinning a person can be, and how quickly they adjust, turn to teamwork, increase loyalty and respond with open communication when change responses are seen as grief responses and not as emotional spins.

Do this: See how grief plays into your relationships with clients or co-workers.

Don't: Assume that angry people are obnoxious when they just might be frightened.

Twelve people experiencing the same loss will go through the stages at different speeds and with different perceptions and responses. Some will resolve the loss quickly; some will take time and need additional support from co-workers, management, or from resources outside the workplace. Some people stay stuck in one stage or another and act from that emotional location for a long time. These individuals perceive their other experiences from a perception of loss that can be managed by understanding that their choices may continue to be predisposed to bargaining, anger, or depression. Moving between stages until resolution of one stage can seem to create endless spins of discomfort. Being stuck in one stage feels permanent. Finding yourself in a different stage than someone in the same situation can feel odd and is occasionally perceived as betrayal to the value of the loss.

The speed of recovery from a stage of grief is a variable. Rapid recovery through a change cannot be forced or mandated, but also depends on a willingness and ability to move through the grief work adequately. Avoiding the task does not help the process; it only delays it and leads it to becoming distorted into some other set of feelings. Most adults have experienced losses in their lives, but that doesn't mean they are efficient at moving through their grief in a healthy and efficient manner. Grieving can accomplish character building, or it can be the source of an emotional spin that can turn a person, situation, or business into emotional turmoil for the wrong reasons. Grieving is serious business, and business should take it seriously.

> There is no need for body bags and carnage to trigger significant and elaborate grieving states. Grief happens hundreds of times a day. Managers need to know that although most people adjust to grief, some do not.

Grief doesn't just happen when there is a high-drama event, terrorist incident, natural disaster, death, or traumatic episode. There is no need for body bags and carnage to trigger significant and elaborate grieving states. Grief happens hundreds of times a day. Managers need to know that although most people adjust to grief, some do not. Some people get stuck in one stage for a very long time. Have you ever known someone who was stuck in anger for a long time? Have you known someone who was stuck in depression for a long time? Have you ever bargained to try to maintain control of some difficult situation? Do you know anyone who is emotionally stuck in one stage of grief work? Are you?

Do this: Watch for signs of despair that may indicate that an employee is struggling with a personal challenge.

Don't: Invade the privacy of someone who is coping, but encourage him or her toward hopeful solutions.

3.1.3 Business Change

Business losses from change are emotionally loaded because work is so intimately associated with safety and survival. Work is associated with key perceptions about the self, ego, status, worth, value, money, and character. Something as simple as someone taking a parking spot that an employee has "territorialized" can lead to emotional grief and spinning behaviors.

Do this: Assume that everything matters to someone.

Don't: Forget to do your research! Don't neglect to ask everyone before a change. You don't want to find that someone you forgot to ask is disgruntled because you didn't anticipate that a simple loss might be catastrophic to someone.

Business changes range between very small and very large. Changes can be for the good, such as a multi-billion-dollar dream contract. Business changes can also be negative, such as an unthinkable, unpredictable publicly humiliating scandal and bankruptcy. Change can range between relocating the vending machine to catastrophic destruction of an entire facility such as the destruction of the two towers at the World Trade Center. Between these extremes lies a universe of small and large changes including business and personal changes that influence emotions. There are simple as well as wildly complicated changes. Some changes are short and instantaneous, and some take tedious decades to accomplish. Change isn't bad. Change is just life.

Changes in business are like changes in life. You will grieve them with a range from small to large. Any change can trigger emotional feelings, from small to catastrophic. Here are some examples of changes at work:

Examples of Business Changes:

Any Changes, Small and Large	New Administration
Moving the Pens	Illness of a Co-worker
Remodeling/Painting	Death of Loved One or Co-worker
Changing Letterhead/Logos	Suicide/Murder of Co-worker
Outsourcing/Downsizing	Rumors Of Changes
Re-Sizing/Layoffs	Marriages/Divorces/Affairs
Awards/Loss of Awards	Computer Upgrades
Losses	Natural Disasters
Personal Tragedies	Economic Changes
Catastrophic Trauma	Hirings and Firings
Organizational Change	Policy Shifts
Project Groupings	Local/National/International News Events
Furniture Arrangements	A New Custodian
Access to People/Information	A New Water Cooler or Vending Machine
Redefinitions of Tasks	Resizing

Bullies Exploit Grief and Change

Bullies are all about power and control. Bullies are seriously stuck and need professional intervention. Being a bully isn't about grieving. Although it may be true that a bully started his or her bad behaviors due to a childhood loss or significant life disappointment, by the time the behaviors have fixated or become rigidly mortared into a bully response, it will be necessary to work long and hard before those responses "become" soft and pliant again. That isn't your job. That is the job for a professional!

3.2 Main Causes of Emotional Spinning

3.2.1 Stress

Life is energy. When you know that all life is based on energetics, then it is relatively simple to remove all judgment from the challenges of dealing with human emotions. That doesn't mean it is easy to deal with energy that is out of control, but it does make it much less personal when a burst of human emotion comes your way. Emotions are energies, and in pure form they are neutral. The effect of various energies on systems can cause minor or catastrophic stress on a system.

Stress is energy placed on a system. Stress is neither positive nor is it negative. Stress is what keeps the body, mind, and emotions alive. Stress in the tensing of muscles against forces of blood and tissues keeps the heart beating. Without the stress in the system, the heart would not beat. What is key is the quantity and quality of stress on a system. Stress can be in too small or too large of an amount. Too much stress and the heart is overwhelmed. Too little stress and the heart stops beating. Stress in healthy doses can lead people to greatness. Stress in the wrong proportions can kill the body, disturb and distort the mind, and disrupt the spirit. Stress is experienced and defined internally. It is a very individual, personal, and subjective process. It may be spoken of in external terms, but it is registered individually from within.

> ...stress is very subjective and determined by the individual experience. One person's minor annoyance can at the exact same time be another's complete, catastrophic undoing.

While there are collective, current agreements on what constitutes a disaster, stress is very subjective and determined by the individual experience. One person's minor annoyance can at the exact same time be another's complete, catastrophic undoing. The reason for this is that people have different perceptions, even about the same thing. A familiar children's story explains perception. The tale is of the blind men (or blind mice, depending on the version) describing their perceptions of an elephant. One describes it like a hose, having only experienced the trunk. Another describes the beast as a rope, having only confronted the tail. One describes the elephant as a great tree, hugging one of the large legs. The moral is that even similar experiences lead to very different and distinct perceptions. These perceptions are then translated into beliefs, truths, laws, moralities, and judgment as the entire issue gets quite complicated and sometimes extremely distorted. In simple terms, people are different and thus perceive life events differently, including stress.

Human Life Factors That We Call "Stress"

Bills, Dandruff, Fabric Softeners That Get Caught In Your Socks, Loneliness, Phobia, Grief, Money, Guilt, Fear, Flying, Telephones, Flying Telephones, Procrastination, Low Self Esteem, Doubt, Jealousy, Envy, Money, Family Problems, Work Deadlines, Decisions, Shopping, Budgets, Lack Of Budgets, The Press, Idiots In The Office, Threats, Rumors, Success, Money, Failure, Rejections, Divorce, World Hunger, Childcare, Parenting, The Flu, Money, Separation, Work, Computers, That Woman With The Short Skirt, The Boss, The Boss' Mood Swings, Your In-laws, The Kids, Giving The Kids Money, Money, The Employee Who Just Never Gives 100%, The Employee Who Always Gives 198% While Singing A Chipper Little Song And Quoting Affirmations And Always Asks If They Can Help You Do Your Work Because They Like You So Much, Pets, No One At Home Understands You, Money, Everyone Feeling Like They Can Dump On You And Doesn't Anyone Care About What A Rotten Day You've Had And By The Way Is My Weight Going Up And What Do You Mean There Is A New Budget Cut Coming, A Child Off To College, Chronic Illness In The Family, Recent Death, Impending Death Of A Loved One, Divorce, Marriage, Pregnancy, Your Family Moving, Your Family Moving Next Door, Custody Battles, Tests For Cancer, Car Dies, Deciding To Stay Or Leave A Spouse, A Promotion With New Tasks And New Friends And New Enemies, Relocations, Political Correctness, Lack of Political Correctness, Travel, Office Politics, Performance Evaluations, Keeping Up With The Joneses, Being The Joneses, Starting An Affair, Ending An Affair, Divorce Of Best Friends, Having Horrible Parents, Miscarriage, Aging, Someone You Love Is Sick Or Drinking Or Using Drugs Or Addicted To Food Or Sex Or Gambling, Taking Medications To Manage Work And Home, Downsizing, Outsourcing, Natural Disasters, Terrorism, The Terrorist Attacks Of September 11, 2001, Train Bombings In Spain, The Iraq War, The Afghanistan War, The War On Terrorism, Privacy Issues, Mad Cow Disease, Global Warming, Holidays.

Bullies Exploit Stress

Bullies exploit stress because it represents a weak link in the chain of power and control. They can exploit stress in ways that range from either minimizing or over-exaggerating the situation. They will find a small loose string in the fabric and tug at it until it unravels. They won't let it go. And their stress is often compared dramatically to yours.

3.2.2 Burnout

Not all stress is bad. Some stress motivates and some stress causes difficulty. The amount of stress a human can deal with is absolutely individual and unpredictable. Burnout is a term that has become synonymous with the accumulation of too much stress leading to a maximum overload to the system. Common terms like running on empty, tapped, fried, dry, wasted are verbal clues that an employee may be reaching a stage of burnout, or is feeling a sense of personal threat which may lead to either a solo spinout, or group decay in productivity as determined by the position of the weary worker.

Signs of pending burnout can be feelings and demonstrations associated with:

- A sense of being held hostage, trapped.
- Having nothing more to give.
- Helplessness.
- Emotionally impotent, worthless.
- Depression.
- Seeing everything in terms of failure.
- Loss of power.
- Increased aggression, disappointment.
- Increased frustration over normal tasks.
- Suspicions and hostilities that are new.
- Memory losses.
- Forgetting details.
- Agitated or irritable, restless.
- Fatigue.
- Physical persistent illness symptoms.
- Increased desire for stimulants (alcohol, coffee, medications).
- Increase desire for depressants (sleep, medications, television).
- Social withdrawal.

Bullies Exploit Burnout

Burnout is like a flame that is on the edge of extinguishing itself from the inside out. A bully will toss water on that flame. Again, the weak link provided by someone in a burnout orbit means the bully has a place to blame, scapegoat, exploit, or leverage his or her agenda of control mechanisms.

Bullies don't rest until they are in control. Yes, bullies can have burnout also! Not a pretty sight.

3.2.3 Annoyances

Happy, healthy, well-adjusted people get annoyed. They get angry and they get sad. They experience a wide range of emotions. What makes them "well-adjusted" is that they have found methods to help them adjust. Healthy people emotionally self-correct to changes in their environment. If you are sitting in a chair and your leg feels a cramp coming on, you adjust your position to move your body away from the discomfort. This is a physical adjustment.

Emotional adjustments are the same. A brief discomfort, or even an extreme emotional pain, is managed by reorganizing an emotional position. With a minor leg cramp, most people do not need to call an ambulance or begin screaming hysterically. A heart attack is different and demands a different response. In the same light, most people do not go on crying binges at their jobs, throw chairs through windows, or become snipers if they have an emotional discomfort. They adjust. If a large or catastrophic emotional crisis occurs, adjustment may take longer. But well-adjusted people have methods, ideas, and support systems to help them adjust well.

Less well-adjusted people also have methods, ideas, and support systems to help them adjust. They just don't do it as efficiently or effectively. Where a well-adjusted person may reach out for a supportive word from a friend or a spouse, a less well-adjusted person may reach out for a pharmaceutical product. In terms of the workplace, both approaches to adjustment may keep people working and productive. The risks increase when either the well-adjusted person or the less-than-well-adjusted person cannot put his or her methods in place due to stress, interference, or interruption. What impedes or interrupts adjustment increases risk. As the capacity or ability to adjust diminishes, risk increases. Minor annoyances should require minor adjustments.

Do this: Get comfortable with emotions as part of your job. Stay calm. See chaos as an interesting feature of life and work.

Don't: Create a crisis inside a crisis.

Bullies Exploit Annoyances

Annoyances are often like small slivers or paper cuts, not life-threatening unless you get too many of them and bleed to death. How many is too many? It depends on the stamina and wellbeing of the individual. Bullies are annoying. Add that to a "regular" annoyance and you start to have accumulations of micro wounds that can add up to compromise your well-being.

3.2.4 Violence

Disclaimer: In reality, there is no final guarantee or absolute prediction of violence. Even the best of the best can't predict radical changes in behaviors. These are only guidelines, not rules, laws, or even grand truths.

When in doubt Call 911. I promise you that you would rather be embarrassed by being in error than seeing your name (or the name of a co-worker) in the headlines!

According to the FBI, workplace violence can be defined as "any action that may threaten the safety of an employee, impact the employee's physical or psychological well-being, or cause damage to company property."

Some individuals do not do well under even the most pleasant of circumstances. You may need to know how to spot the early signs of difficulty and trouble before they erupt into more severe incidents. News headlines of the most significant forms of violence and upheavals happening at the workplace are not uncommon. Workplace violence rarely strikes without warning. Recognizing those signs is critical to safety. Because violence at work is becoming more prevalent the Federal Bureau of Investigation (FBI) created a list of "red flag" behaviors and common warning signs, usually seen in potential offenders (Romano, S., and others, 2011).

These first early signs on the FBI warning list include:

- Mood changes.
- Recent personal hardships.
- Depression.
- Anxiety.
- Negative behavior (e.g., untrustworthiness, lying, bad attitude).
- Verbal threats.
- Past history of violence.

According to the FBI, workplace violence can be defined as "any action that may threaten the safety of an employee, impact the employee's physical or psychological well-being, or cause damage to company property." The FBI definition is a good place to begin a discussion, and the red-flags list is a good place to start paying attention to extreme emotional spins that may turn violent. However, this list is far from exhaustive or specific enough to be much help.

Violence can come out of the blue with absolutely zero warning. Zero. It can also be preceded by small noticeable changes that when connected to an event (a firing, layoff, death, divorce, reprimand, grievance, or other business change) could sometimes be predictive of a potentially violent episode.

Dr. Vali's "Heads Up List"

Disclaimer: None of these by themselves are a guarantee that violence will ensue, but then again, it's worth staying alert to these signs.

▶ Visible change in facial expressions (grimacing, scowling, frowns, blank-stare, rapid eye movements, biting lip or inside of cheeks).

▶ Change in voice tone or inflection (lower, higher, quieter, louder).

▶ Mumbling and denying (when asked what they said, they say something like, "Never mind it isn't important," "Nobody ever listens to me anyway," "Whatever," or some other non-response).

▶ Fist clenching (white knuckles, or squeezing).

▶ Jaw clenching (tapping or grinding teeth).

▶ Nervousness (leg bouncing, foot tapping, finger rapping).

▶ Sighing (loud dramatic sighs or deep, slow breathing that is audible).

▶ Uncharacteristic behaviors (loud whistling or humming, pacing, slamming, chair rocking).

▶ Disassociation (a sense that the person is really "somewhere else" if you are talking to him or her, especially in a potentially threatening situation, during a reprimand, or grievance situation).

▶ Personalized attacks (verbal attacks that are personalized, such as "You have never listened," or "John isn't a team player," or "The management here is against me").

▶ Sudden extreme silence (an abrupt silence that feels impenetrable followed by any of the other previously mentioned behaviors).

▶ Eye contact extremes (either very eyeball-to-eyeball in a threatening manner, or total loss of eye contact).

▶ Exit (a sudden exit from a meeting, or worksite, or threatening situation).

▶ Opposite behavior (pre-violent people can also act out in an oddly charming, ingratiating manner of sugary-sweet compliance and agreement that feels disingenuous or insincere).

Stress, survival, and violence: Sometimes violence erupts when someone feels as though his or her very survival is threatened. Severe stress can trigger the human responses for basic survival, including violence. When threatened, people have an organic protection system that is much like our ancestors. If you are interested in the why and how of threat reactions, research on the topic of survival mechanisms under circumstances of stress is plentiful from experts in physiology, psychology, sociology, and biology. If you don't have time to get an advanced degree in the socio-bio-psycho-physiology, it is probably sufficient to say that trying to survive threat is natural, and behaviors associated with the need to survive are rarely cozy and attractive. Most living creatures have a survival instinct that can be triggered by real or perceived threat. In fact, those who do not have that self-survival mechanism are clearly at risk.

Bullies Exploit Violence

Bullies can play "the victim" role brilliantly. Often if the bully actually sets the violence in motion, he or she will complain the loudest about their "injuries," as in Karpman's "drama triangle" (Karpman, 1968). He or she will use violence as an excuse for absenteeism, relocations, ongoing poor use of managerial time for attention, a personal entitlement event, unrelated legal actions, and more. What is daunting is to find out that the emotional terrorist has tipped the scale toward violence and then stepped back to watch a "blood bath." And then he or she will wail at the outcome.

3.2.5 Trauma

Prior trauma: Many people who get up and go to work each morning are survivors of previous traumatic incidents. Most people adjust to trauma without complications that impact their working performances. People are more likely to do well at work than at home if they have had a trauma. They tend to put on a "work" face and get by. People who have had prior trauma may however be more likely to perceive a threat in some situation than others who have not experienced a trauma in a similar situation. What this means is that because the effects of trauma may not be visible, some situations at work may trigger an old trauma. An employee who is your Rock of Gibraltar can suddenly fall apart at the seams or react with violence thinking he or she is protecting himself or herself from what feels like the "old" trauma. You cannot predict this. It does happen. It isn't something that happens very often, but you can add it to the list of unexpecteds that you might see. That way, it will be less likely for it to turn into an emotional spin or a gateway for a bully to gain a power advantage over someone who is temporarily in a weakened position.

Do this: Become knowledgeable about post-traumatic stress disorder (PTSD). Take a training course. Hire someone to teach you. Read a book on the topic.

Don't: Ignore this because it is more important and more prevalent than you would like to believe! PTSD might not get you, but what if it gets your ***teammate or partner?***

New trauma: Small or large stress reactions to crime, accidents, natural or man-made traumas and disasters are normal.

Showing no emotions is not normal. It means something else such as shock, denial, or perhaps something more sinister. This is when you call for backup. Not everyone experiences a traumatic event in the same way. Not everyone who experiences a significant event is traumatized. However, people who witness trauma or catastrophe may experience none, some, or all of the following:

Shock	Memory Changes
Terror	Disbelief
Blame	Disorientation
Anger	Confusion
Guilt	Increased Nightmares
Grief or Sadness	Lowered Self-Esteem
Emotional Numbing	Difficulty Taking Care of Self
Helplessness	Blaming
Unhappiness	Intrusive Thoughts/Memories
Loss of Normal Concentration	Worry
Difficulty with Decision Making	Feeling Unconnected

Past trauma survivors may have either a better or worse time dealing with a new trauma – that can be hard to predict. Be aware of the full range of possibilities and create a comprehensive list of providers to deal with small and large responses. Make sure everyone is okay – even those who do not show signs. Check back with them on a regular basis for several months. Better to check than to miss something brewing under the surface.

Bullies Exploit Trauma

Bullies can recognize weak people and target them. A trauma survivor is not a weak person, but bullies can often find the small niche in the person's armor and work it and work it until the victim has a meltdown. Then the bully can cry "foul" and manipulate the situation.

3.3 Examples of Spinning: Spin Stories

Note: All names and other identifying information have been changed to protect anonymity.

Note: The real-life narrative examples below have been provided to give you a sense of the types of situations I have encountered in my work with organizations like yours. For some of the stories, I have given the solution that was arrived at to resolve the situation. Some have been left open-ended and others have a less than happy ending. These are for you to think about (and possibly discuss with others who are reading this book at the same time) and to enable you to explore how you would apply the information in this book to defuse the particular situation.

Story A – Shifts in Job Status, Shifts in Loyalty

A consultant company is hired to increase efficiency within a major, science-based industry. It is told that its agenda is to create a process that eliminates "dead weight." There are over 700 people in the company. One group of 40 is engaged in a project that cannot be disturbed, so they will remain exempt from the process until the project is completed. The company creates a new process, with a buzzword called Re-Focusing. Each employee must now reapply, Re-Focus, for his or her position. The reapplication process takes approximately 3.5 days to complete at an average expense of $100.00 per day of salary ($100.00 x 3.5 x 700=$245,000.00). Work stops during this process. Each employee is then either rehired or let go depending on his or her eligibility and qualifications. 12% of the non-exempt workforce is not rehired. The other 88% is reassigned new positions. No employee is in his or her original job. Employees that had been with the company for decades and developed expertise in their specialty are now in new positions with no expertise. The experts, who are in the exempt group, are not available for mentorship. The experts who mentor the exempt group are not available now either. Previous mentors are now learning new jobs. Tension and anger is elevated. One employee becomes incapacitated from the stress of the situation and loses several days of work. While decisions are being made as to who goes and who stays, loyalties shift. Stakeholders become acutely aware that they are expendable. The exempt team finishes its project. They are now required to go through the Re-Focus Project. They have been out of the collective company loop and are now thrown into it somewhat after the fact. Some employees are given a large bonus with the explanation that they will be given the dollar lump sum amount "as if" they had been promoted and given a raise. However, their status in the company will not be elevated, so that their social security and retirement benefits will not reflect that change. Some employees begin to seek work elsewhere. Several employees, who are within a few years of retirement, shift loyalties away from a company to which they have given decades of service. Their interest in projects begins to wane. They seek support outside the company.

> "We lost employees during [this director's] reign…We lost a top-notch executive secretary, three comptrollers, and a development director. We lost Board members."

Story B – The Dictatorial Director

Dear Dr. Hawkins Mitchell,

I wanted to share with you a story about my previous job. We had a very dictatorial director for just a year. He would call people into his office and ream them out. For the women he would pull out a box of tissues when they started crying. There were ample counseling costs because employees had a great need to talk about it. We didn't hire a new director for another year, and throughout that time people were compelled to talk about their awful experiences with him.

The replacement director was there for about six years. He had a very bad temper and would just explode. We lost employees during his reign, although he went through at least one anger management program. We lost a top-notch executive secretary, three comptrollers, and a development director. We lost Board members. When another company was interviewing this director, he asked us, his current staff, to put in a good word for him and to "be kind." We were afraid to tell the company the truth because we desperately wanted to get rid of him; I believe that is how he keeps getting jobs!

Story C – The Unwritten Grant

In a higher education setting, one individual responsible for writing a million dollar grant repeatedly assured people that the work was progressing when, in fact, the person and the process were paralyzed. Close to the deadline, the individual's supervisor discovered that little had been accomplished on the grant. An organization-wide effort completed the grant at the last moment. The one-week effort to write the grant cost the institution $12,000 in lost salaries in addition to a week's disruption of five other projects. In jeopardy were services to over 800 students, over a million dollars in grant funds, and four staff positions.

Story D - The Boss with the Trashy Office

Dr. Bleuer trashed his office at the university. His students had to climb over papers, books and objects literally a foot deep. No one complained because he was a "nice guy and a good teacher" and his office hours were short. Contact with him was at a premium. His secretary, Linda, was miserable trying to keep things in order in an effort to answer business calls and manage his schedule. Early on in their association, she had assumed it was a temporary situation and that he had just been too busy. She asked him how she could help him organize. He verbally attacked Linda and warned her not to interfere with his important work with her frivolous requirements and apparent need to control him. She was embarrassed and confused. When he began dumping his garbage on her work area, she was afraid to ask him not to do that. He now controlled both his and her space with his clutter. She tried to work around it to the best of her ability. Dr. Bleuer had established his intentionality from the beginning. It was not negotiable; he believed he was entitled to trash his and her space. The secretary lasted eight months.

The next secretary, Connie, found the situation exactly the same. When she appropriately asked Dr. Bleuer how she could help, he repeated his offensive behavior and raged at her. Connie laughed at him and was not intimidated. Dr. Bleuer laughed also and gruffly gave her permission to "figure it out and leave me alone! I don't have time." Connie spent the next five months carefully designing a system of baskets and boxes and shelves to manage the multidimensional chaos of Dr Bleuer's creative mind and chaotic style. The professor would run through the door and toss his papers at Connie. She would then toss them into one of the many baskets or containers sitting around the office. After a while she noticed that he would toss them into the appropriate box or basket. On Secretary's Day, Dr. Bluer brought Connie flowers and tossed them at her. Then he asked her if it would be okay with her if he moved all the baskets into his office since it was now too hard to come out to her office to retrieve the papers he would throw on her desk. She gladly moved those baskets into his now much more well-organized office space. The flowers looked better on her tidy desk without boxes.

Story E – The "No Smoking" Policy

Max had just quit smoking. It was his first week at work without cigarettes. He was doing well and felt good about himself. At the weekly staff meeting, it was announced that the office now had a no smoking policy in effect immediately. A few people cheered, a few grumbled, and there was light-hearted banter and friendly ribbing to those who were the smokers. The policy included an EAP series on quitting smoking, a special smoking area away from the building, and a non-judgmental atmosphere about the change in policy.

Max took it personally and felt defensive. He felt shame and anger about his years as a smoker and now he felt angry that smokers were being judged and scorned by the administration. It made him jittery and angry. He wanted a smoke. He knew he was detoxing and wanted to quit, but now he wanted to defend his smoking friends. He remembered how glad he was that he was a non-smoker now, but felt angry for the other smokers. He wanted to rescue them. He didn't know which side he was on. It reminded him of his experiences with his family of origin. When his parents found out he was a smoker, they were disgusted. He remembered getting caught behind the garage by his Dad and how small he felt and afraid to show his Dad his temper. He didn't let on how he felt at work either, and so he hid his feelings. It made him feel like a small child again. He started pacing about the office grumbling and complaining. His resolve to not smoke crumbled. He went outside for a smoke with a friend. They grumbled together. Max went back in the building and fumed all day. Toward the end of the afternoon, he went into the restroom and smoked. The manager came in to the restroom and reminded Max about the new policy. Max blew up and stormed out of the office in righteous indignation. This time he wasn't going to just take it like a child; he was going to do something about it! He took his old childhood anger at his Dad out on the manager. Before he even knew what was happening, a full tilt emotional spin was launched.

Lee had just quit smoking. It was his first week at work without cigarettes. He was doing well and felt good about himself. At the weekly staff meeting, it was announced that the office now had a no smoking policy in effect immediately. A few people cheered, a few grumbled, and there was light-hearted banter and friendly ribbing to those who were the smokers. The policy included an EAP series on quitting smoking, a special smoking area away from the building, and there was a non-judgmental atmosphere about the change in policy. Lee felt relieved.

Story F - Co-worker's Dysfunctional Drinking

Jay was a social drinker. Over time his drinking behavior escalated into dysfunctional drinking. His co-worker, Kevin, thought there might be cause for concern when Jay would show up on Mondays obviously slammed from the weekend. On occasion, Jay would have a few drinks at lunch. His use of mints and cologne did not hide his using behaviors. Jay missed a few workdays here and there, and a few times these were during critical project crunch times. He began getting disturbing phone calls from his wife on Friday afternoons, and Mondays were a waste of time after each bad weekend.

Kevin had always liked Jay and they had worked together for many years. Kevin had considered Jay a work buddy and didn't want to make waves or cause any trouble, but did not know how to address this distressing behavior. After all, it was not really disturbing his production too much and he could cover, but it seemed to be getting a little worse and that was unsettling. Kevin decided to live and let live and figured that it was none of his business what Jay did and tried to focus on his own work.

One Friday afternoon, after Jay had taken an extra-long lunch, and returned with alcohol and mints on his breath as well as slurred speech, the boss sent a fax from the main office stating that he wanted Jay and Kevin to deliver some key data to the next city that was about 85 miles from their location. Road trips had strict policy and procedures including the proviso that the senior man would drive. Jay was senior and management assigned Jay a company car as the driver. Now Kevin had to get in the car with an obvious drunk or make a critical decision.

Story G - Sexual Preference Issues

As a heterosexual, politically correct, educated, compassionate white woman, Ami was working on her personal growth and examining her attitudes about life, including being politically correct on the topics of racism and homophobia. Recently divorced and raising children alone, she felt vulnerable and worked very hard at her new job. Her worksite training had included diversity and racism training. Her boss was a lesbian. Her work partner, Syleena was also a lesbian, a woman she admired greatly. The office had several women of color in key positions, and Ami was excited and felt positively obligated, challenged, and inspired about exploring her inner world and developing a more sophisticated and worldly life experience. She eagerly attended trainings on diversity, conflict resolution and gay and lesbian issues.

During her employment at the center, Ami occasionally worked with another lesbian, Diane. Ami didn't really like or respect Diane as a person or professional. She just didn't feel comfortable with her style at work or in person, but she wanted to be a good employee and made an effort at professionalism. Diane wanted to be close friends with Ami and invited her to socialize frequently. Diane continued to engage her in conversations about non-business topics and things of a personal nature, such as clothes, dress, dates, and so forth. Every time Ami resisted a personal relationship, Diane protested with statements about Ami being a closed-minded white woman, homophobic, and how hurt she felt. Diane would follow Ami to lunches and even came to her home uninvited on several occasions. Ami was trying to develop a new social life and so was trying to include all her new acquaintances and workplace colleagues into her life.

Diane suggested that Ami was discriminating against her because she was a lesbian and that she should make more of an effort to "come around" to "reality thinking." Ami was concerned that Diane might be right. After all, what did she, as a heterosexual, white, divorced woman know about real life? She decided it might be her homophobia acting up and that she was indeed a bad person by discriminating. She really didn't know what to think. She agreed to go out for lunch with Diane to "try to get beyond it." She worked harder, read more books, attended more training sessions, and asked questions.

Diane became more demanding and continued to complain that Ami was discriminating against her because of her sexual orientation. This was very stressful to Ami, who really did care about human beings and their oppressions. Ami tried to socialize with Diane, and it just never seemed to be enough or correct. Diane insisted that she go with her to a local gay bar if she really wanted to know about the lifestyle. Ami felt a lot of pressure from Diane. On one occasion, after a period of soul searching and frustration she finally took the risk to confide her difficulties to Syleena. Ami explained, with some embarrassment, that she just couldn't figure out how to move forward in this endeavor of being professional and appropriate to women with a homosexual orientation. She blamed herself and said that Diane often encouraged her to "try on the shoes of being a lesbian so she could have some compassion and really understand her world." Ami told Syleena that Diane suggested to her that her husband left her for another woman because she was probably really a lesbian. She said Diane had offered to help her get more physically comfortable with "the real truth of her feelings" by offering to have sex with her.

Syleena immediately reassured Ami. She told her, "This struggle you are having with Diane is not because she is a lesbian, and it's not because you are a lesbian. It is because Diane is inappropriate and may actually be a sexual predator. This behavior is completely inappropriate both personally and professionally, and it isn't about homophobia. Let's go talk to the boss together."

Where Ami may have easily tossed off male aggressive predator behavior, she was blindsided by Diane's "we're just girlfriends" intimate hugs and touching. Syleena and her boss mentored her and explained that within the lesbian culture, just like any other culture, there are good people and less than good people. It had never occurred to Ami that she had been attacked at her workplace by someone who used the issues of diversity and human rights to offend.

Story H – Loss of a Window

Gary loved his workspace window. It allowed him to stay on top of his claustrophobia. He used to take medications to manage his anxieties over this, but he was doing well in his new job and discontinued the prescriptions. Management decided to upgrade the office and move desks. Everyone agreed and was excited about the new change. Gary did not want anyone to think he was weird or trying to hog the window and he became anxious. He felt stupid and weak. He couldn't express his preferences to management because he felt humiliated about his anxiety and that a small window meant that much to a grown man. His anxiety escalated and led to other self-defeating thoughts and behaviors that he had put away long ago. His production diminished. His marriage became strained. He felt like he had failed when he went to his doctor for more medications.

Story I – Memories of Childhood Abuse

Chris had an abusive childhood and managed long-term recovery with the help of a therapist and a support group. When the office changed a procedure, Chris had trouble making the adjustment and consistently forgot the new procedure. After making a number of minor errors management called Chris in to find out what was going on, and followed it with a reprimand. Chris apologized and felt horrified and ashamed, which was reminiscent of childhood abuse feelings. Chris felt helpless and lost confidence. It took a number of extra therapy sessions to address this shift, and his performance evaluations suffered in the meantime. Chris lost an important promotion. A new employee cost the agency significantly more than promoting internally.

Story J – Cancelled Counseling

Bill was frantic. As a Gulf War veteran, he had been successfully dealing with his PTSD issues with weekly counseling sessions. The company decided to change health insurance providers to a managed care system that did not include mental health provisions. Bill had to decide how to handle this because he could not afford the counseling sessions out of pocket, there were no other counselors in the area that specialized in PTSD, and he knew that he needed ongoing care to manage his feelings of anger and betrayal. He started transferring his emotions toward the company that seemed to betray him. He knew this was not appropriate thinking and that his PTSD had been triggered. He didn't know what to do.

Story K - The Noisy Neighbor

Elijah was annoyed. The woman in the next cubicle ate all day long. If she wasn't snacking on hard candy and opening little crackling wrappers, she was eating apples, or popcorn. He couldn't see her over the cubicle divider, but he could hear her. She shuffled about all day long as she worked, hummed little tunes, and made noises associated with either eating or preparing to eat something.

Do this: Take a few moments to remember some of your personal spin stories.

Don't: Forget that you have survived lots of spins already and are now ready to be an expert on the management of emotional spinning.

3.4 Other Emotional Responses May Look Like Spinning

There are responses that look like spinning but are not. Reactions originating from the following list may increase vulnerability to workplace spinning, but of themselves, they should not be considered emotional spinning. These emotional subsets may respond surprisingly well to simple, positive management, affirmation, mentorship, a kind word, support system, training, an educational pamphlet, or brief EAP intervention.

Emotions that may look like spinning include:

- People grieving the death of a significant family member, beloved friend, pet, or co-worker.
- People who are separating or divorcing.
- Parents who are in the middle of a custody issue or other legal challenge.
- Grandparents who are peripheral to a grandchild's custody issue.
- Abuse survivors, male/female.

- People with physical illness (self or loved ones).

- Adult survivors of childhood sexual assault.

- Previously diagnosed mental illness that has usually been well managed.

- Changes in medication.

- Adult children of alcoholics.

- People living with active addicts/alcoholics.

- People dealing with issues about their aging parents.

- Addictions (active or in recovery).

- Diagnosed serious illness of a loved one.

- Undiagnosed physical illness (self or loved ones).

- Ethnicity or cultural differences.

- Local or national tragedy or catastrophic event.

- Stress.

3.5 Healthy, Dysfunctional, and Pathological People

As you begin to differentiate between how to deal with the variety of emotional responses, it is valuable to see them along a continuum in their level of functioning in the world. Use the following analogies to begin getting more comfortable with the continuum:

What are healthy, dysfunctional, and pathological cars?

The Healthy Car Analogy

If you want to take a trip, and actually get there while also enjoying the scenery, you want a car that is *healthy,* a car that is functional. It gets you from here to there.

- A high order healthy car just needs fuel and an occasional window washing. Driving this car is a delight.

- A middle order healthy car needs regular oil checks, tire rotations, and an occasional wiggle of the spark plugs. Perhaps the glove box gets a little stuck. It still gets you where you want to go without much effort.

> ▶ A low order healthy car is one that requires frequent replacements of spark plugs, extra oil on a regular basis, needs to warm up before you drive it, the third gear sticks and must be wiggled just right, the outside mirrors wiggle out of place, and you never think about leaving without a spare tire. But you still get there without major concerns and you get to enjoy the scenery on the way because regular maintenance will generally keep the car functioning adequately.

Some healthy vehicles look cosmetically perfect. Some look like they just came from a wrecking yard. You don't really need to worry.

The Dysfunctional Car Analogy

Dysfunctional cars might get you to your destination and they might not get you there. They need occasional or constant support to keep running. Even with constant help there is no guarantee that the dysfunctional vehicle will make it through the journey. Even with all the preparation and maintenance, it is a risk. Unfortunately, over the long haul they are vulnerable to break-downs.

> ▶ High order dysfunctional cars usually get you there, but you have to take a few spare parts in the trunk, check the oil, watch the gauges and be on alert for random strange sounds.

> ▶ Middle order dysfunctional cars need more care and attention and the glove box doesn't even close. You are pleased if you get somewhere, and not surprised when you don't.

> ▶ Low order dysfunctional cars break down every few miles and there is no time to watch the scenery out the window. These clunkers rarely make the trip worthwhile or enjoyable due to the high level of maintenance required to micro-manage every detail.

The dysfunctional car starts incurring costs. You may have to join a towing membership club, keep a cellular phone available for breakdown, or hire a mechanic to ride with you to help keep it going. Some dysfunctional vehicles look cosmetically perfect. Some look like they just came from a wrecking yard. You worry.

The Pathological Car Analogy

Pathological cars don't get you there safely, if at all. They tend to catch on fire under the hood and may explode before you even see much smoke. They may randomly swerve into oncoming traffic. The brakes may fail as you are going around an important curve and the windows don't open if it plunges into the river. The head gaskets crack under any sort of pressure. The rubber comes off the tires at 55 m.p.h. The engine might not start no matter what you give up in the process. In fact, these cars control the entire vacation and take up your time looking for ways around the delays. You spend time seeking other modes of transportation while hoping the vehicle suddenly turns into something functional.

- High order pathological cars sometimes have an interesting capacity for crime. They are the stolen cars that run well, but are on their own agenda. They may be confiscated before you get to your destination. And you might unknowingly become an accessory to the crime. They may appear very powerful or very calm – just before they kill you with carbon monoxide.

- Middle order pathological cars are wannabe soapbox derby cars with no motors. They have the flash but not the power.

- Low order pathological cars are usually easy to spot. They may barely be recognizable as vehicles. Or they are the lemon cars that someone else traded in that looks good, but have been involved in a fatal accident or cleaned up after someone committed suicide in the front seat.

They might look very good cosmetically, but under scrutiny do not measure up. They may look shiny in the driveway and make you look very cool, but don't put your kids in the backseat and head for the Grand Canyon because no one would survive.

3.5.1 Levels of Functioning in People

Healthy
The shaker and the mover.
The capable and the helpful.
The well intentioned and the steady.

Dysfunctional
The present and accounted for and troubled.
The present and troubled and needy.
The randomly absent, troubled, and needy.

Pathological
The criminal and the manipulative and ill and brilliantly successful.
The criminal and manipulative and ill and needy with less success.
The incapable and removed from society.

Bully or Emotional Terrorist

This is a separate and distinctly specific type of individual that is not one of the previous, although may have attributes of all. While a healthy employee who is dysfunctional and pathological can be managed at work with the right tools and skills, the bully or emotional terrorist cannot. A bully or emotional terrorist will generally either leave or go underground when detected.

Healthy people are eager to find ways to make their lives easier. Regular people like assistance. Healthy people may fuss a bit because they perceive themselves as competent and want that acknowledgment from others. But again, healthy people adjust quickly. On the other hand, dysfunctional people and those with pathology have a different response to needing or receiving help. They resist. Resistance is interesting.

Resistance usually indicates you have bumped up against something that creates some kind of a threat, real or perceived. People who resist opportunities to make their work easier and to feel better are giving managers a sign that something is in the way of good and healthy responses.

Healthy Employees

Healthy employees can have their feelings and continue to be productive. Well-adjusted employees generally tend to have the following recognizable traits. It is reasonable to transpose these traits into opposite terms to suggest what traits less-than-well-adjusted people might demonstrate:

Traits of well-adjusted employees include:

- Let go of past grudges easily.
- Assume the best from one another.
- Seek outside feedback carefully.
- Do not participate in emotional drama.
- Do not initiate emotional drama.
- Put clients first.
- Maintain a good attitude even during challenging times.
- Use the chain of command to effect change.
- Use policy format to offer complaints.
- Do not hide memos or information from some staff and provide it selectively to others.

- Strive for cooperation.
- Verbally appreciate help given.
- Show respect for each other.
- Model appropriate business site sense of humor.
- Do not participate in humor that includes inappropriate innuendos (sexual, racial, socio-economic, political, gender bias).
- Model flexibility.
- Offer examples of personal truthfulness.
- Show personal accountability.
- Give and receive forgiveness.
- Offer clear communication.
- Demand and offer equality.
- Perform the highest work ethics.
- Complete and follow through with assignments.
- Do not engage in second-hand gossip.
- Do not spread or encourage rumors.
- Participate actively.
- Show consideration for others.
- Stand by confidentiality standards.
- Act professionally in the presence of clients.
- Give more than just the minimum.
- Work with cooperation between hierarchies.
- Show courtesy in all situations.
- Listen and respond to feedback.
- Compromise and contribute to positive dispute resolution.
- Stand behind own opinion, yet open to negotiation.
- Use non-violent communication methods.

Do this: Start watching people to see if you believe they fall in the healthy, dysfunctional, or pathological categories

Don't: Be afraid of misjudging at first. Remember that the key is to not tell anyone or act on your judgments – just observe and categorize and say to yourself "Isn't that interesting," or "Maybe that's why that is such a difficult person for me to deal with."

> **Now is not necessarily the right time to confront the person because, for now, you are just going to watch.**

3.5.2 Recognizing Levels of Functioning

You observe a behavior that makes you wonder if "something is up" with the employee. It makes you wonder if the person is indeed in the healthy employee category. Now is not necessarily the right time to confront the person because, for now, you are just going to watch. Use the "What's Up" Questions Checklist below to begin evaluating observable, emotional behaviors or begin thinking about feelings in the worksite. Do not ask "Why?" questions at this point in your exploration. Ask the following action questions first.

3.5.3 The "What's Up?" Checklist

What, where, when, who, how, which, how many, how often?

- Is this behavior due to a new circumstance?
- Is this behavior temporary or has it been ongoing?
- How long has this behavior been observed?
- Exactly when did this behavior begin?
- Is this behavior consistent or intermittent?
- How many people have seen this behavior?
- How many people have seen this behavior and not mentioned it?
- If this behavior escalates what might happen?
- If this behavior de-escalates what might happen?
- Does this behavior cause harm to anyone or anything?
- Is there a specific place, person or thing that is associated with this behavior?

▶ Is this behavior consistent with your sense of the employee's personal style?

▶ Has this behavior happened before?

▶ Is this behavior in any way associated with an anniversary of some previous incident?

▶ Has this behavior been influenced by outside forces or inside forces?

▶ Is this behavior due to interactions with people or equipment?

▶ Which performances or tasks does this behavior impact?

▶ Who has this behavior influenced?

▶ Is this behavior in any way life threatening?

▶ If you confront this behavior, what might you anticipate as a response?

▶ Is there any way this behavior could be helpful to a creative solution?

Now you know about emotions and spinning and how these impact healthy people. You have begun to think about how other people who may be in the dysfunctional or pathological ranges might deal with emotions and spinning differently, and you have seen how bullies exploit situations to create spins. In the next section, we'll look at bullies and extreme bullies in greater depth.

Questions for Further Thought and Discussion

1. After reading this chapter, can you identify some things that you are currently grieving? And if so, can you identify the stages of grief for each item?

2. Can you think of some situations you have observed in the workplace that would have been good stories to add to the ones in this chapter? To what extent would you say the upsets (or grief) involved were normal and to what extent were they a sign that one or more of the persons involved needed assistance?

3. How would a bully in your company threaten the bottom line? Can you imagine a bully's reaction to a disaster situation? What would you need to consider?

4. What strategies can you think of that would positively influence an employee who is operating dysfunctionally? What about someone who is significantly dysfunctional or moving into the range of pathology? How can you retain and empower all levels of employees, even though they may have different levels of emotional capacity?

4

Bullies and Emotional Terrorists

4.1 Emotional Terrorists: Extreme Bullies

Because emotional terrorism is domestic terrorism that uses human feelings for ammunition, nice people don't want to think about it. Assuming that you are a nice person, the reason you need to read this chapter is to address and absorb the reality that there are employees who have an agenda to destroy the well-being of others, using emotions as weapons. They are prepared for you, and you need to be prepared for them. They are getting better at what they do, and you need to be better at recognizing them while protecting yourself and others. They hope you don't get this information. They will discredit this topic. They will distract you and encourage you to be nicer. You need to read this chapter because emotional terrorism is real, and it isn't going to go away anytime soon.

> Emotional terrorism... has eluded or been ignored by business leaders for a long time. This subset of actions and emotions is at first illusive and intangible... a specific blend of human behavior that seems to go beyond the normal definitions of disruptive employees.

4.1.1 Emotional Terrorists and Bullies

If you have ever worked with or for a bully or what I call an emotional terrorist, you already know why you want to read this chapter – for validation. No, you are not crazy; that person you thought was dangerous to your mental health may indeed have been trying to make you go mad. If you have never worked with or for an emotional terrorist and survived, consider yourself lucky. You will want to read this chapter for self-preservation for the long-haul span of your career. If you are an emotional terrorist, you will want to read this chapter to find out if someone is on to you – because someone is! And eventually you will have to move on and find another place to be seriously annoying!

Emotional terrorism is an emotional and behavioral phenomenon in the workplace that has eluded or been ignored by business leaders for a long time. This subset of actions and emotions is at first illusive and intangible. Business writers have made attempts to deal with the visible or overt nature of these phenomena by writing about jerks at work, or angry employees, or other references to people at work who are difficult. Managers have read books, gone to countless workshops, talked secretly to each other, consulted psychologists and therapists, and have found themselves unable to wrap their minds around a specific blend of human behavior that seems to go beyond the normal definitions of disruptive employees.

Why Dealing with Emotional Terrorism is Difficult

At closer scrutiny there are three reasons why dealing with the phenomenon of emotional terrorism has been so difficult:

1. Emotional terrorists do not fall into the range of regular to dysfunctional people and need a separate category;

2. Most employees are nice people; and,

3. Emotional terrorists count on nice people to struggle with the definition and use that discrepancy to gain emotional territory.

Staying good, nice, and friendly is what most human beings do. The majority of people do not like to upset other people. Emotional terrorists have a different approach to life. They actually seek and find pleasure in the discomfort of others. As workers, managers, and administrators have been concerned with productivity and not offending anyone, emotional terrorists have crept into workplaces and felt right at home.

If Steven Spielberg did a scary movie called "The Emotional Terrorist in the Workplace," managers could see it on the big screen while eating popcorn.

Such a public validation would create a forum for discussion. It would be out in the open. As it is now, emotional terrorists at the workplace continue to stir up emotional chaos and are getting away with it on a daily basis. It is time to put some light on this and make it less possible for people with an agenda of destruction to have their way.

4.1.2 Emotional Terrorism

▷ *Emotional terrorism:* "Domestic terrorism that uses human feelings for ammunition" (Hawkins-Mitchell, 2007).

▷ *Bully:* A person who is habitually overbearing especially to weaker people. Bullying is a form of abuse that attempts to create power over another group or person to create an imbalance of power through social, physical, emotional, verbal coercion or manipulation; an *emotional terrorist*.

Emotional terrorism is everywhere. It can be found in homes, churches, synagogues, shopping centers, parent-teachers association meetings, city council meetings, and anywhere that people live, work, and play. Emotional terrorism at work is a significant risk. International and domestic terrorism are now factored into business risk management. Emotional terrorism must also be seen as risk.

The fact that international or domestic terrorism has emotional roots (someone is very, very upset about something) should immediately translate into the awareness that emotional terrorism is a constituent of these other forms of terrorism. Perhaps one way to discuss emotional terrorism at the workplace is to describe it as *big terrorism's little cousin*. Nevertheless, the agenda of either *big* or *little* terrorism is the same: control through the use of terror. All terrorists have a common agenda: to create fear, chaos, havoc, terror, and destruction in any way possible in order to have some sense of control, make a statement, divert attention, or call attention to something.

Mean, evil, bad, horrible, icky, intentionally dangerous, unconscionable, criminal, vile, scary, seductive, dangerous people exist. *And they work with you.* One very simple and horrifyingly daunting statistic may convince you. It is a statistic that is hidden from public view because of its nature and implications: *the exact number of registered sex offenders in this country!* The reported number, depending on the site, is daunting. One site says 600,000, and another says more, or less, but more than can be even considered without pause. And many are missing and don't continue to report (Child molester statistics, 2005). This statistic represents only the ones who are registered. What makes you think they do not work with you? Or go to church with you? Or shop at the local market with you? Or sit with you at a PTA meeting? They do. And some of them are reading this book. *If this does not get your attention, nothing will.*

Knowing a statistic like this just is not enough. Protection of the vulnerable from the inherent risks of such dreadful behavior demands much, much more attention. Knowing that this statistic is a reality makes it difficult to continue making good management decisions that are based on a belief that "people are good" and kind. Instincts must be challenged. Nice and trusting instincts do not work when dealing with a sex offender. Their thinking process is completely different from regular people who would never consider harming a child for their own gain. *Regular instincts do not work with emotional terrorists either.* Their thinking process is completely different from regular people who would never consider harming a co-worker for their own gain. Terrorists do not operate by the same rules as regular people.

> **Emotional terrorists... have an agenda to destroy the well-being of others using emotionally loaded information, behaviors, innuendoes, direct assaults, inferences, rumors, and language to establish either disruption or decay within a system...**

4.1.3 Emotional Terrorism at Work

Businesses and managers need new language to deal with the ranges of terrorist challenges at work. A disgruntled worker who arrives with a gun is obviously a workplace terrorist. The employee who systematically disembowels someone's reputation through gossip and innuendo is no less destructive. One workplace terrorist will make the nightly news. One will not. Both have far-reaching consequences.

Emotional terrorists are people who have an agenda to destroy the well-being of others using emotionally loaded information, behaviors, innuendoes, direct assaults, inferences, rumors, and language to establish either disruption or decay within a system with no regard to the emotional well-being of others and to the benefit of a personal, albeit private or collective mission of control. Instead of hand grenades and weapons of mass destruction, they use emotions, vulnerabilities, implications, innuendoes, gestures, rumors, subtlety, victimhood, deflection, games, and power plays to take territory and cause harm. These are not regular, healthy, well-adjusted, or nice people. If you consider the statistics of active sexual predators, criminals, addicts, or untreated mental illness, it must make sense to you that statistically you will meet these charming folks at work! Emotional terrorists do not live in isolation, nor do they wear black hats to identify themselves. Emotional terrorists have taken some of the least pleasant human attributes, dysfunctions, and pathologies and turned them into an art form.

Do this: Know beyond a shadow of a doubt that emotional terrorists are counting on your denial to keep their secret.

Don't: Let emotional terrorists hold you or anyone else emotionally hostage. Shine a light on them so they can scurry back into the shadows and play nice with everyone else, or go somewhere else.

Emotional terrorists maintain control over people by holding them hostage inside their own illusions of power and control. Terrorists do not feel obliged to live within the framework of regular society. Think about how someone might hold a company hostage emotionally.

Do this: While maintaining your kind heart, find a way to temporarily put your "niceness" aside in order to stay safe. Learn the difference between being nice and being compassionately smart.

Don't: Put yourself at risk.

As a malignant tumor that does not respond to chemotherapy may require removal, the only rational option for an emotional terrorist who does not respond to appropriate, nice interventions that would get the attention of nice people may be amputation: removal through termination. Transferring the employee simply moves the malignancy elsewhere as a stopgap. Eventually the disease will appear elsewhere in the system.

Some powerful religious organizations and churches have recently become aware of how a simple, logistical relocation of a priest who has sexually exploited children does not end the problem. Moving an offender to a different diocese worksite is a stopgap response that is ineffective when someone is an offender. That person's behavior goes with him. The same is true with even a less severe representation of emotional terrorist. There comes a time when it does not serve the company to keep a malignant person employed. Managers must be the ones to track the effects of one employee on others.

4.2 Attributes and Behaviors of the Emotional Terrorist

There are at least seven primary attributes of emotional terrorists. The difficulty is that as soon as a perpetrator reads these, that person is quite capable of rearranging the criteria for his or her own purposes. Emotional terrorists are experts at using information to deny accountability, manipulate a vulnerable person or situation, educate others in their ways, groom new victims or recruits, litigate to gain position, or defend their own threatened innocence. That is the bad news. The good news is that the following attributes are impossible to disguise over time. A persistently neutral, businesslike, pleasant, courteous, and boundaried approach to an emotional terrorist just drives the person nuts. If the emotional terrorist cannot control a situation, he or she can adapt, migrate, or change.

1. Entitlement

Most healthy and dysfunctional people work at growing and evolving appropriate self-esteem to a point where they can realize that they are good and indeed deserve good things in life. Emotional terrorists take that normative behavior and escalate the healthy idea of deserving to another level. They not only deserve, they are entitled well and beyond anyone else. Where the idea of "I want and deserve good things" can lead to appropriate self-care and compassion to others, entitlement leans toward justification and rigid self-aggrandized thinking, which affords permission to "take from" someone else in order to get the deserved or entitled goal, object, or outcome.

Entitlement is subsidized by a sense of personal victimhood, real or perceived. Entitlement rationalizes the accumulation of property, territory, or rights from someone else as perfectly correct within the context of its own motives for control. Entitlement thinking creates a cause-and-effect thinking structure that does not include external data. For example, an emotional terrorist will not consider the needs or wants of someone else because his or her agenda, cause, or motives are a bit, or a lot, more justified. Victimhood is increased and entitlement leads to increased accumulation needs. This sort of victimhood may begin with a real event or loss, but it is perpetuated and increased beyond the realm of true victims. Some individuals or groups actually work out contrived victimhood for litigated dollars. It is not unheard of that someone with a whiplash injury may not truly be injured. In certain parts of Asia in the 1970s, it was not unheard of for locals to throw themselves in front of automobiles of Americans and then claim entitlement to life-long financial support. Opportunists are not victims.

True victims are people without choices. Someone who is hit by a car is a victim. If you were molested as a young child or adolescent, you were a victim. This kind of victimhood is nonnegotiable because children do not have the power to choose. People and survivors who are true victims generally make every human effort possible to move away from victimhood status, away from self-entitlement and the identification of vulnerability.

Example of differences in motives for wanting a day off:

Wanting: I want a day off, because I have worked hard.

Deserving: I deserve a day off, because I have worked hard.

Entitlement: I work harder than anyone else does; so I am entitled to time off. I have special rights. I'll get my manager to let me have next Tuesday off. I don't care that Susan is at her mother's funeral that day. Who takes care of me? After all, didn't I bring donuts last month? What did I get for that?

Emotional terrorism entitlement: I don't deserve this treatment. Why should I do all the work when I can get Mary to do it for me and I'm out of here? I'm entitled to extra time off, and since I have Mary under my control, I think while I'm at it, I will make it look like she isn't working as hard as I am. So, she can work for me and take the rap for me later. And if the manager doesn't give me the day off, I'll start telling people he's having an affair.

2. Bulletproof

Being *bulletproof* is an interesting term that finds its psychological origins in topics of addiction. Addicts are said to be "bulletproof" when their disease has taken the normal course of decay to the point where they have a belief that they can do anything without consequence. Addicts who are reaching advanced stages of their disease might think they can drive under the influence and not get caught because they are too smart, or are safe from reproach due to their "cleverness" and ability to "handle their liquor" or know when to stop. Such behaviors are typical of those used by people who are operating with a sense of entitlement. The distorted thinking suggests to them a level of immunity not held by "normal" people. Somehow, they become outside the laws of social norms and even nature.

Being bulletproof in its most nonproductive form typically shows itself in the later stages of addiction, criminal activity, and emotional terrorism. A somewhat milder form of being bulletproof is seen in first responders who think they can survive what "normies" or civilians cannot even handle on TV. They run into burning buildings, take down violent thugs, clean up blood and guts off highways, and leap buildings in a single bound. In this career, it is necessary and useful to have a level of this thinking to act and survive out in the field of their "worksite." This overlay of capacity is called image armor. Cops and firefighters carry a lot of it. They are allowed!

Bulletproof is something different. Bulletproof is when people, including those with image-armor, push that thinking too far, to a point beyond which they take risks that are not reasonable to take. Bulletproof people believe they are beyond the domain of what "regular" people must accept. Law enforcement and fire service professionals with image-armor survive in severely risky situations. But if they see themselves as bulletproof, they may put themselves and others on their team at risk.

At the workplace, bulletproof employees are somehow mysteriously special, unique, and above all, unquestionably correct. They truly believe they are untouchable. For example, a bulletproof employee might blatantly steal and brag about it. The employee is so convinced of his or her unique status that he or she will try to eliminate anything that does not fit into his or her picture. Anything that threatens that picture or threatens his or her sense of being bulletproof, is suspect and dangerous, and must usually be eliminated. Bulletproof employees are beyond the scope of social behaviors, morals, taboos, expectations, guidelines, laws, and the other rights and comforts of others humans. They do not really think that the rest of the universe is much of their concern. Bulletproof people consider themselves untouchable and are completely surprised when consequences arrive.

The term Greeks used for bulletproof thinking was *hubris*. Hubris is an inappropriately escalated level of pride that precedes a mighty fall to humiliation. When employees start thinking they are bulletproof, immune, safe, or untouchable, trouble is not far behind. Most regular human beings know they are mortal and fallible and are concerned and thoughtful when taking dangerous risks. Someone who is bulletproof has a different approach to risk.

The early signs of emotional terrorism can start with a small level of hubris. The lowest level of hubris belongs to people who are just simply obnoxiously arrogant. These people are not emotional terrorists unless they impose non-consensual agendas on others based on their sense of entitlement and arrogance. Emotional terrorists evolve the level of their hubris to risk taking. Over a period of time they will take increasingly bigger risks. They may start with verbalizing more entitlement, rising to a sense of not caring how their behaviors impact others, until they see themselves as more and more omniscient and omnipotent, and begin to carry an odd sort of rigid new rules about themselves which allow them to do things that are over-the-top. At first, the behaviors may possibly look brave and useful. Then, as the behaviors become more rigid, the individual is less approachable, less malleable, and less willing to be "managed" by anyone else.

Examples of Workplace Bulletproof Behaviors

▶ An active alcoholic or addict who drives a company car while under the influence.

▶ A cyber-hacker who keeps at it, thinking he/she won't be caught.

- Having an affair with a co-worker, practicing unprotected sex and hoping not to get HIV or that it will affect working conditions.
- Coming to work intoxicated.
- Using a work computer for pornography.
- Using company resources for personal gain and assuming no one will know.
- Assuming terrorism only happens to the other guy.

> Passive-aggressive behaviors are antagonistic... finding people who are vulnerable and pushing them a little bit until they are just slightly emotionally off balance. Antagonists then shrug their shoulders and say, "Gee I didn't know you were so sensitive."

3. Antagonistic

Antagonistic behaviors are the natural consequences of conflict between forces or tensions, a pulling apart of substances where that pulling diminishes one side. Antagonism is hostile. Emotional terrorists create an atmosphere of tension and conflict that is almost palpable, even when hidden behind polite behaviors. In fact, an overlay of polite on top of a depth of antagonism is standard fare for the emotional terrorist. Home ground is overt courtesy with an undertone of something miserable and angry.

Passive-aggressive behaviors are antagonistic, a bit like a game to an emotional terrorist. It is the playing field on which people are vulnerable. Set up an antagonistic dynamic and watch the fun! An antagonist especially enjoys finding people who are vulnerable and pushing them a little bit until they are just slightly emotionally off balance. Antagonists then shrug their shoulders and say, "Gee I didn't know you were so sensitive." Or they tease someone and say, "Oh, I'm just kidding, that was a joke. Don't you have a sense of humor?" Or they like to stir up anger in a group, tease someone, belittle, or just act in an edgy sort of way that keeps the general tension up. This makes it much less boring for the antagonist. They have an amazing capacity to keep conflict going, even in the midst of peacemakers. They use direct or indirect methods, whichever work best.

Antagonism is often directed at management. This is different than normal whining and moaning about management. An emotional terrorist will use antagonism to stir up the emotions of others. Claiming that someone else has to be the "problem" causing all the tension in the office will effectively deflect accountability away from himself or herself and onto someone else. It is a good trick. When people are suspicious and nervous, the terrorist has taken some ground. "Antagonists are individuals who, on the basis of non-substantive evidence, go out of their way to make insatiable demands, usually attacking the person or performance of others. These attacks are selfish in nature, tearing down rather than building up, and are frequently directed against those in a leadership capacity" (Haugk, 1988).

4. Entrenched

Emotional terrorists do not quit. They do not back down. They dig their heels in for the long haul and take a position that is fixed and unshakable. Flexibility and negotiation are not the domains of emotional terrorists. They are deeply rooted in their positions rather than shared interests. Whereas individuals may be narcissistic, selfish, self-centered, or egotistical, emotional terrorists go beyond these personal interest behaviors. They take such self-indulgences and raise them to a level of "cause." In international terrorism, individuals have been known to participate in suicide or homicide in the name of a particular cause. Emotional terrorists at the worksite symbolically mimic this in their willingness to sacrifice others for their rigid belief system – and to see themselves as martyrs in the process.

Entrenchment is easily recognizable in a discussion. You may be offering ideas and concepts for negotiation, and someone who is entrenched in his or her position will not budge. In fact, that person will not bend. In mediations, the entrenched person will rarely even see that there is a workable solution for all. This is not a concept that fits within the realms of entrenchment. Entrenchment is more all-or-nothing, win-lose, with-us-or-against-us thinking. Most healthy people will eventually apologize, open up, bend, flex, leave, cry, stop, laugh, move on, or adjust in some way. In other words, they will make movement. Emotional terrorists will move only to regroup their agenda and hit it from another angle. Emotional terrorists do not let anything deter from their goal of control of something, someone, or somewhere.

5. Multi-talented

Managers need new ideas, new tools, and new ways of seeing people because emotional terrorists are always thinking up new ways to create chaos. International and domestic terrorists like to catch people who are asleep on the job or not paying attention. Emotional terrorists are no different. They will create, re-create, and turn themselves inside out to achieve their agenda. Emotional terrorists have to be multi-talented, with many diverse skills to accomplish their mission. This is why as a manager you need to be more talented than the emotional terrorist. Look at the following list of tools and techniques available to an emotional terrorist, and consider what you might have to have in your toolkit or emotional arsenal to manage these workplace challenges. The annoying thing about preparing for terrorism of any kind is the necessity of having to see things through their eyes. Knowing that ethical people cannot see through unethical eyes any more than a sane person can see through the eyes of someone who is mentally ill, managers must still begin the tedious process of thinking beyond their own niceness to find creative solutions and risk preventions.

Tools and techniques of an emotional terrorist:

- Lying to a supervisor or co-worker.
- Dramatic victimhood.
- Tampering with files or documents.
- Harassment.
- Use or misuse of company resources.
- Knowledge of schemes or practices that take advantage of the company.
- Requests for confidential information.
- Sharing and withholding information.
- Access or control over proprietary information.
- Rumors and gossip.
- Contributing or withholding support to individuals or key team members.
- Time card reports falsified or inaccurate.
- Inaccuracies.
- Inappropriate acceptance of gifts, gratuities, entertainment.
- Manipulation of data.
- Security tampering.
- Overt theft.
- Manipulated expense reports.
- Failure to follow through.
- Incomplete tasks.
- Abandonment of tasks.
- Selling or marketing business practices.

▶ Conflicts of interest.

▶ Substance abuse.

▶ Insider information abuse.

▶ Unethical recruitment practices.

▶ Downplaying public safety.

▶ Unnecessary trainings and time-consuming meetings followed by consequences for tasks not finished.

▶ Maintaining only minimum legal or code compliances.

▶ Inappropriate responses to reports of danger, whistle-blowing, or common knowledge.

▶ Poorly managed customer relations.

▶ Corporate spying, losses of security, disclosure of security information.

▶ Accepting or making inappropriate political contributions per industry standards.

▶ Price fixing, gouging, hoarding.

▶ Ignoring laws about immigration.

▶ Not abiding by drug laws.

▶ Avoiding tax laws.

▶ Corruption of public officials or private individuals.

▶ Dangerous sexual practices.

▶ Using company technology to further addictions, crime, or sabotage.

▶ Antitrust violations.

▶ Creating pressure that leads to the misconduct of others.

6. Able to attract innocent supporters

Emotional terrorists count on innocent, nice people to further their causes. They use their many skills, tools, and techniques to accomplish this. Emotional terrorists are sometimes seen as heroic to the naïve. They become the gallant spokespersons for the truth, often seen as brave activists, guides, or gurus. They project themselves as victims, and innocent people are often gullible to this line and are hooked into the martyred cause for justice. Anarchists, fascists, and dictators have used this ploy throughout history to get other people to do their dirty work so they can remain the pure heros or heroines. Some people have personalities that lead them to be followers who cannot or will not think for themselves. Others are afraid, passive, lack imagination, short sighted, or bored. Some people follow leaders without question. Other people join emotional terrorists to create a spin and have no idea that they have been exploited.

Emotional terrorists have a talent for recruitment by making their followers feel special, entitled, and eventually bulletproof. Of course, it is the emotional terrorist that maintains control over the one flak jacket, parachute, or life ring, but does not hesitate to volunteer someone else to step into the line of fire, jump first, or swim through the sharks first. Thinking how people respond to group energy explains how emotional terrorists can be contagious and – symbolically, as well as occasionally literally – fatal to the follower. The emotional terrorist does not mind sacrificing the employment or reputation of someone else to maintain his or her own job. If a manager is a leader, emotional terrorists may not hesitate to do whatever they think is necessary to erode that position of authority. Emotional terrorists can act "injured" or "defensive" and expertly play the victim role.

7. Charismatic or tragic

Two powerful methods that emotional terrorists use to attract supporters are the demonstration of charm and sadness. Charisma calls on the weak by suggesting a special luckiness if the charismatic person accepts their presence. Luck will somehow rub off and special good feelings are assumed a next small step away. Disenfranchised employees will seek strength from anywhere if they feel the ship is sinking. *Managers need to find ways to be attracting and appealing leaders to counterbalance the exploitive, charismatic appeal of emotional terrorists.*

> **Emotional terrorists take people and workplaces hostage... The worksite is a perfectly constructed container for chaos because no one can leave.**

Tragic or sad performance from emotional terrorists appeal to helpers, lost nurturers, co-dependents, and the need-to-feel-needed people. The charms of an emotional terrorist who drops a head, sighs, tries to talk and doesn't finish a sentence, sits a bit apart from the group, rubs a forehead, leaves early, asks questions that have no clear answers, raises his or her hand to ask a question then, when called on, says, "Never mind, it wasn't important," and generally appears sad, are compelling. These and other behaviors draw energy toward the emotional terrorist. Remember, an emotional terrorist does not really want to share, partner, or collaborate. He or she may appear to be inclusively charismatic or inclusively needing constant help, but the purposes behind these activities are self-focused and exploitive. Charisma and tragic behaviors are extremely deniable by the emotional terrorist. Charisma denial is characterized by "I was just helping" and tragic denial is characterized by "I just was trying to get some help." The word "just" is the tipoff. A sentence that begins with "just" is usually associated with either entitlement or denouncement of account-ability.

8. Hostage takers

Emotional terrorists take people and workplaces hostage. When people are held emotionally captive at the worksite because they have to be there from nine to five, the risk potential for emotional terrorism elevates. The worksite is a perfectly constructed container for chaos because no one can leave. Emotional terrorists will use this captive audience to pull off an emotional incident, after which they will sit and watch the consequences unfold like a soap opera they are writing themselves. Think of this as an "emotional drive-by shooting" where the victims cannot even call for help or run away. And tomorrow it may happen again because that emotional terrorist is going to be at the worksite again.

Hapless employees in this drama may not even know the roles they have been assigned until they are given a script from the emotional terrorist. When the cast assignments of good guys and bad guys, heroes, heroines, and villains are written by the emotional terrorist instead of the manager, then it becomes a question of who is the director of the show. Who is writing the script in your department? Who is running the show? Can anyone get out of the worksite hostage environment long enough to get a new perspective? Are doors open?

4.2.1 Warning Signs

- ▶ Intangible feelings, hunches, intuitions, sense, or opinion that something is "going on" with no specific data to confirm or deny.

- ▶ Grooming: a systematic, unnatural approach to relationship control that appears upon close scrutiny to be contrived and gainful.

- ▶ Contact escalations: interactions get more frequent.

- ▶ Early spinnings: small emotional events increase.

- ▶ Covert works: reports of trouble without evidence.

- ▶ Rejection of approach: suggestion of problems met with resistance, denial.

- ▶ Early signs of entrenchment: rigidity.

- ▶ Overt signs: visible tensions and emotional reactions with no real data.

- Accusations: blame statements or inferences.
- Side attacks: indirect blame, accusations, complaints.
- Overt visible behaviors: demonstrations and activities, documentable data.
- Gathering of forces: small or large groups spending time processing issues.
- Direct attacks: specific demonstrations, behaviors and complaints.
- Ultimatums: provocations, challenges.
- Threats: intimidation, pressure, bullying, coercion.
- Repetition: continuing or repeating any or all earlier signs, even with increased risk, in order to demonstrate a willingness to continue for absolute control.
- Gotchas.

"Gotcha"

The *gotchas* are verbal clues that an emotional process is going on in your midst. Traditionally, managers are trained to see the obvious signs of annoyance, discomfort, dissatisfaction, and outright trauma or catastrophic emotional incident. The emotional terrorist is also trained or aware of these, and finds it more useful to work "under the radar" with more subtle language. The language of emotional terrorism is easily deniable with an innocent laugh, distraction or direct lie. Remember, emotional terrorists do not hold to the same accountability as the regular employee; so a lie is not an issue if it will further their cause. Lies come in all languages and in many forms, shapes, and sizes. The gotchas are lies with strings attached. The strings are a leftover feeling of guilt, shame, discomfort, and confusion often attached to a need to defend or attack. Even the so-called positive grooming statement has an edge of something sticky that just does not hold true.

Gotchas:

- *After all, you are my new best friend.*
- *Ha! Ha! I caught you in an error.*
- *You are the most special person in the world.*
- *Everywhere I go, people don't get it.*
- *I won't stop until I get what I want.*
- *What will it take to get you on board?*

▶ *I'm watching you no matter what until you fail.*

▶ *I'm an expert, and you are not.*

▶ *I'm a victim of all this.*

▶ *You aren't going to share this with anyone, are you?*

▶ *I was just joking; what's wrong with your sense of humor?*

▶ *Can't you take a joke?*

▶ *Maybe you're too sensitive.*

▶ *I have the ear of the boss and can tell him what you want.*

▶ *I thought we were close friends, but obviously not.*

▶ *Promise you won't tell anyone this.*

▶ *If you tell anyone this, I'll get fired (you'll get fired).*

4.2.2 Mis-informants/Liars

Just about everyone has told a lie at some point in his or her life. Some lies are socially acceptable and appropriate for a situation. "Please don't tell the lady in the next office that the purple dress really makes her look fat." Just as there are pathological liars, there are pathological "truth-ers." Bullies can hurt you with lies and with truths.

Balance is the key. Emotional terrorists don't like balance; they like chaos, and they like to have power. They prefer manipulating truth and manufacturing lies for their own agendas. Emotional terrorists use different levels and styles of lies, as do non-terrorists. However, emotional terrorists use a very different intentionality and purpose for their lies. And, they become very good at it. Take a moment to consider the levels and styles of lies used by sex offenders, bank robbers, and serial killers. They adopt comprehensive lying strategies that are beyond the imagination of healthy people. Addicts develop an increased capacity to lie as their disease progresses. As the disease progresses, the lies may become very elaborate and transparent. These are lies that fall into categories of dysfunction, pathology, and emotional terrorism. The "little white lie" about the lady's purple dress isn't this kind of lie, unless the lie is being used to have power over her or in some way to coerce her. These "bad-bad" lies have a purpose, an agenda or intentionality to self-protect or do harm.

Kinds of lies:

- Trivial matters, false excuses to spare a feeling, flattery.
- Harmless or inconsequential.
- Lies to children about Easter bunnies, Santa Claus, the tooth fairy.
- Deceptions to make a person feel better.
- Inflation, exaggeration to make something sound better than it is.
- False praise, false encouragement, false support.
- False recommendations: intentional incorrect or incomplete answers.
- Fake resumes, false credentials.
- Lies to protect a boss, a colleague or client.
- Lies to liars.
- Lies to enemies.
- Not quite exacting, half-truths, soft-soaps.
- Lies in a crisis when innocent lives, health, and safety are at risk.
- Lies for no apparent reason.
- Lies for the sake of lies.
- Lies as games and manipulations.
- Terminal lies.
- Cover-up lies.
- Brainwashing lies.
- Corporate lies.
- Accounting lies.
- Political lies.
- Seduction lies.
- Addiction lies.
- Agreed-upon group lies.
- Criminal lies.
- Lies about lies.

4.2.3 Time Bullies

Time is a precious commodity to us all. Time is Money. To most adults, time is sacred. An *emotional time terrorist* messes with your time. Such people have many ways to accumulate, control, or dispose of your time. They work either actively or passively to manipulate the clock. Bullies use time to control people. Being late or early or demanding with your time puts you in a position to have less power.

Look at the following list and think if you know any time bullies:

- **Time tyrant:** So demanding about punctuality or deadlines that it is difficult to think straight under the pressure. A minute late is too much, no flexibility or patience, judgmental about other peoples' time.

- **Time thief:** Procrastinator, or gets to arrive late, or asks for last-minute details at the end of the day. Uses work time for e-mail, personal calls, video games, dating set-ups.

- **Time hoarder:** Won't do anything extra, as if time were his or her own domain, saves up leave and uses it at inopportune times, demands special time with managers and administration, asks for extra meetings.

- **Time addict:** Rigid attention or non-attention to time, unchangeable time habits no matter the situation or circum-stances, works only out of a day planner, no flextime, no breathing space, Type A people, every moment used, must be "on" all the time.

- **Time miser:** Makes everyone wait for him or her, late to meetings because of his or her other meetings, demands that everyone work on his or her clock, Scrooge-like control of other peoples' time.

- **Time victim:** Always behind or ahead of time, but it is never his or her fault.

- **Time gambler:** Takes risks with projects, or deadlines, or lunch breaks, or holiday scheduling. Does not take time seriously, his or hers – or yours; time is a game, bulletproof.

- **Time saboteur:** Will distract or employ manipulations to make himself or herself central in the middle of a time crunch, late to meetings, interrupt meetings, work during meetings on other projects, sidetrack other employees' time making others late.

Some Typical Tools And Weapons Of Time Bullies

Unclear Language
Distractions
Red Tape
Unresolved Conflicts
Poor Ethics
Poor Authority Chain
Indecision
Poorly Managed Fatigue
Clutter
Poor Listening
Gossip
Lack of Accountability
Unreasonable Expectations
Blaming Others
Arriving Late
Needing to be Central

Procrastination
Grandstanding
Victim Attitude
Low Moral Standards
Untrained Staff
Unnecessary Travel
Mistakes Without Learning
Changing Deadline Mid-Task
Disorder
Disorganization
Ethical Violations
Won't Clean Own Messes
Poor Self-Care
Arriving Too Early
Avoiding Participation

4.2.4 Bullies Resist

Here is one way to look at resistance. An ill patient comes to a doctor with symptoms, and the physician diagnoses the disease and prescribes antibiotics. Most patients are interested in taking the medications if they are truly interested in health. What kind of a patient would resist the medicine? Resistance suggests sabotage, fear, or a need to control something. When patients are noncompliant about medical treatments that are simple and meant to help, and then return to the doctor complaining that "things are not better," the clinician has to take time to explore the resistance. Resistance is a force that is used to control something.

Don't immediately take it personally. Stop and think, and slow the process down a little. If you resist the resistance, you will create conflict and possible spinning. Before you try to "fix" the apparent problem, first evaluate where the threat originates. The threatened person may try to suggest that it is you or your idea. This is not usually the case. Someone who is not threatened can simply say, "No." Someone threatened will resist and create force to control.

Most healthy employees just want to get their work done and get on with their lives. Others, like bullies, may have other agendas.

Questions for Further Thought and Discussion

1. Why do you think people don't want to address issues associated with bullies, emotional terrorists, and extremely difficult employees? What is the resistance to this topic and how would you challenge it?

2. Examine a personal experience working with an emotional terrorist. Was the person your supervisor, co-worker, someone who reported to you, or someone outside your office whom you dealt with occasionally? How did you handle it? How did it make you feel about going to work? If you were in the same situation now, how would you handle it? What would you advocate for someone having their first "run-in" with such an individual?

3. Do you think it is ethical to warn people about emotional terrorism in the workplace? Why? Or, why not?

4. Under what circumstances would it protect the company's bottom line to bring the topic of emotional terrorism to the forefront and create plans to manage these individuals?

5

Tools for Emotions: Managing Your Feelings and Dealing with Bullies and Emotional Terrorists

To manage your feelings, you need to know yourself and take care of yourself first. In my article, "Taking Your Own Pulse: Self Care Protocols" (Hawkins-Mitchell, 2007), I discuss why and how you need to learn to take care of yourself first. The best way to manage all feelings, yours and the feelings of other people, is to know yourself, your strengths and limitations, and become an excellent manager of your own life. Healthy people do this. Dysfunctional people can't or don't, pathological people avoid or blame, and bullies are too busy creating chaos. To stay in the game you have to take excellent care of yourself first. That is job one! Then it is important to have an understanding of how to deal with the full range of emotions that you may have to confront as you deal with others. Some emotions are simple to manage and others may demand you have 911 on speed dial.

5.1 Starting Out: Preparing to Deal With a Bully

In recent history the awareness of bullies has – unfortunately — escalated. For a long time I was ringing the warning bell, but no one wanted to listen. I don't blame them. I often felt like I was "Debbie Downer bringing a dead rat to the Party." But now, after tragic events that we all can recall, we know. Emotional terrorists exist and can bring ruin. And yet many people still do not believe that the consequences of the actions of a bully can cause a full range of problems, from simple to complex. Perhaps you still aren't ready to consider the topic of emotional terrorism at work. I don't blame you. Nice people want to think the solution is simple. Nice people want to think it is something that will just go away. I know better. I assume if you are reading this book, you know better also and are not one of the people who are putting their fingers in their ears and singing, "La la la la la la!" But you may not be quite ready to jump on board with the entire topic yet. So we will move forward slowly. If you want to start out slowly, you might first look at resources directed toward teaching young children about bullies. Countless resources are being developed by educators for young children who are at risk. Much information is available on the web and elsewhere on topics related to bullies. Two good sources you can go to right now are:

1. Stop Bullying Now

A well developed government site for teachers, parents and children (Webisodes, n.d.) will provide you with an abundant set of images and ideas to consider. It is designed for children, but if you take a few moments you can easily translate it to work for adults.

2. Mental Health America: Bullying and What to Do

Another excellent source is a posting by Mental Health America, which was formerly the Mental Health Association (Mental Health America, 2012).

Please… go to your internet and search "bullies."
Turn on the Light… Get Help.

> Sharing feelings at work is a human privilege
> in a unique community. Do it well, and it
> won't be a problem. Do it poorly,
> and it can become a hazard.

5.2 Understanding Feelings

Let's start the discussion with something safer than emotional terrorism and bullies. First we will consider generic "feelings" as we ease into looking at the dark-side of human behaviors. Feelings come in all sizes and shapes. Both small and big feelings are okay. Making good choices about how to act out those feelings is important. Adults have choices. Having feelings at work is okay as long as they do not interfere with functioning. Sharing feelings at work is a human privilege in a unique community. Do it well, and it won't be a problem. Do it poorly, and it can become a hazard.

Some tips for understanding feelings:

- Establish a quiet and safe time separate from business to discuss feelings.

- Don't start a feelings discussion with complaints.

- Think out your feelings and write them out.

- Take your time.

- Remember that emotions do not make people weaker.

- Use your energy wisely. Pace yourself.

- Feel your emotions without the aid of anesthesia from drugs, alcohol, food, sex, overwork, gambling, or other numbing devices.

Some feelings feel different from other feelings. If we put 37 people in a room (I just like the number 37, it has no particular meaning) and ask them what they are feeling, you might get an interesting view of "feelings." Someone will say "fine." What does that mean? What does it mean to say, "I'm fine!" And if 37 people said, "I'm fine" it would mean 37 different things.

Here are just a few specific "feelings" to consider:

5.2.1 Tension

There are many ways to cope with tension. Some ways are healthy, some are dysfunctional, while other ways can be dangerous. Avoiding tension through the use of anesthesia is an overwhelmingly simple, accessible, and eventually pointless process. Numbing oneself with the anesthetics of illegal or prescription drugs, alcohol, gambling, sex, shopping, eating, exercise, work, or other activities delays the process of experiencing genuine and authentic feelings and ultimately complicates resolution. In the long run, the continued use of anesthesia makes tension much worse as the system begins to consider the anesthesia as normal and requires more to maintain the status quo. There is no such thing as "the first one is free" because the long-term costs significantly outweigh the value of the first dose. Even if the first dose is amazing, there are diminishing returns over time. Dependency leads to addiction and addiction is not a tension antidote.

The most remarkable antidote for managing tension is to not resist it. What you resist persists. In its earliest phases anxiety is simple tension. If you can just go ahead and feel the tension and do some minor adjustments, it often just goes away. Tension that increases or turns to anxiety may be something other than tension.

There is a phrase that is useful in psychology that lets the therapist know if it is a simple event or a more complicated incident: "If it is hysterical it may be historical." What that means is that if the feelings go beyond a normal range of experience into bigger and bigger emotions, it is likely that it has tapped into some old belief system, bad experience, trauma, or memory stored in the brain. Regular daily grind tension should dissolve rapidly with a few deep breaths, a coffee break, a walk around the block, a phone call to a support person, a minor complaining, or a yoga sun-salutation. In other words, normal tension is normal. Try first to get creative with your own tension and turn it into an ally. Find out first about yourself and your style of taking care of tension. Let the energy of tension rise and fall like a wave in the ocean. If it continues rising and rising like a tsunami tidal wave, it may not be tension. This is also true for your employees. You can help them "ride the waves" or pay attention to see if they are falling off their surfboards and drowning. Translate the idea of tension into a metaphor of surf waves of energy. Then you may be able to try one of the following techniques to "play" with the energy of tension at work:

- During a high-tension project invite everyone to wear Hawaiian shirts to work.

- Laugh at tension and sweep it out of your mind.

- Give tension a first name or character image.

- Take your tension out for ice cream or sugar free yogurt.

- Have an annual "Tension at Work Day" in your office with awards.

- Come dressed as your favorite fantasy drama triangle character – "victim," "rescuer," or "persecutor" (Karpman, 1968).

- Have a "Biggest and Smallest Tension of the Week" bulletin board (that spider, the power outage, the day 49 people called in with the flu, current events, broken vending machine).

- Play with your tension. Buy it a toy. Buy it a blanket. Make it a paper hat!

- Hire tension experts to give anti-tension trainings.

- Create a tension support group.

- Delegate someone on your "anti-tension team" to come up with a tension motto, logo, or mascot (put small bungee cords on name tags on "Fight-the-Tension day," make a poster depicting a room filled with long-tailed cats and rocking chairs).

Do this: Accept that tension is necessary to hold things together.

Don't: Let tension rule the day, but don't call it something it isn't.

5.2.2 Boundaries

A boundary is a feeling of a real or perceived edge, limit or border between yourself and someone else. The boundary can be physical, such as a fence, wall, or cubicle. It can be emotional, such as not sharing a personal story; it can be mental, as in protecting your intellectual properties. A boundary can be spiritual in the sense that you can allow someone to share a religious opinion, or not. We place boundaries to protect and enhance our lives. Boundaries can frame good art or keep an invasion from your sacred ground.

When you give someone a boundary, it is quite reasonable for them to ask if you meant it. If you repeat your boundary one more time – clearly, calmly, and sincerely – a healthy person will accept that as your truth and not press forward, risking a potential crossing of your boundary. If the person asks again, and he or she is told no, then that person should move on and accept no as meaning no. When a boundary is not accepted after three clear messages, it is possible you are dealing with a dysfunctional or a pathological employee. This is an excellent early warning sign for spin potential.

When boundary-crossing behavior continues, it is important to give another quiet and clear message to establish the firm reality of the boundary. Establishing a boundary more clearly does not mean louder. Clearer means being very specific and simple. There should be no need for detail or explanation. No means no. If the demands or behaviors escalate, you may need help in getting your message across. This can be a good time to have a policy in place.

For example, if an employee makes a personal advance and asks another employee on a date, and there is no policy against it, this is not necessarily a boundary crossing. It may be an exploration. It is not necessarily inappropriate to ask. However, if the answer is a clear "no," the exploration ends.

The reply message requires neither violence nor volume. If it becomes more challenging or difficult to maintain or hold the boundary in place, this is significant information. The ease or difficulty in establishing clear boundaries indicates the agenda of the person crossing the boundary. The key to a verbal boundary is this: Yes means yes, no means no, and maybe means maybe. The answer must not have a hidden giggle, nod of the head, or shake of the head that is incongruent with your words. If you don't know, say, "I don't know; please get back to me later."

Do this: Have good boundaries.

Don't: Put up walls that are not necessary. Don't take down walls that are necessary.

> Most people can keep their emotions in line at the workplace. They don't fall apart and have tantrums and crying binges all day... But even normal, healthy, well-adjusted adults have bad days.

5.2.3 Acute Stress Reactions

Most people can keep their emotions in line at the workplace. They don't fall apart and have tantrums and crying binges all day. If they do, it is clear that something is seriously wrong and they have too much stress or tension in their life. But even normal, healthy, well-adjusted adults have bad days, and suffer from acute episodes of stress and tension. Ideally, people should not fear this, nor should businesses fear these events. Normalizing stress as part of the human experience takes a lot of pressure off of everyone. In fact, it is usually a bonding process between "survivors of stress" to share tension and stress stories which often increases team loyalties, somewhat like fox-hole buddies. "We did it! Good for us!" Normal tensions should come and go like waves and a good management team can support their people by handing out the surfboard wax, or hollering a rousing "Surf's up, gang!" cheer. Normal, regular, run-of-the-mill emotional spins are not a problem, and, in fact, can add color to a dreary workplace. But if spinning does not rapidly resolve, or becomes a repetitive cycle something else is happening.

Do this: Let feelings and reactions come and go like sneezes.

Don't: Sneeze on other people (eeeewwww).

5.2.4 Grief

There are five stages, identified by Elisabeth Kübler-Ross, considered by many to be the expert in the field of grief-work, that people go through with losses through death: *denial, bargaining, anger, depression, and acceptance* (Kübler-Ross, 1997). Other losses necessitate we go through the same stages in either an abbreviated form or equally as pronounced. The level of loss is self-defined and based on the individual's perception of the value of the loss. No one can ascribe value or lack of value to another human being. Values are self-validating and supported by personal experience.

Mental health professionals will attest that, although there is no absolute standard way anyone goes through the stages of loss, moving through all the stages would define grief work as accomplished and minimize the risk of being stuck in a stage for a protracted period. Moving through grief is like moving through a tunnel. Feelings inside the tunnel can be viable, fluid, erratic, weighty, vague, explosive, quiet, energized, controlling, vacant, passive, and aggressive. There is no one right expression of these feelings. It takes moving through the tunnel to get to the proverbial "light at the end of the tunnel."

What is often missed is that all change creates a loss. Change can offer gain as well but always with a price of loss. If you choose one path, you will have to lose the other path either temporarily or permanently. You may gain the value of the chosen path and lose the value of the lost path. There may be no judgment of right or wrong in this, but the choice necessitates a loss of some sort. With every loss there is some level of grief work. The entire process of going through the tunnel to adjustment may last five minutes if it is a small loss. It does not take a death to have a loss. It does not take a death to go through the stages of loss.

Example:

I lost my pen! It is a favorite pen. I am a writer. I will need my pen to continue writing my poetry.

1. **Denial**: This is the "as-if" stage. There is no awareness that the pen is missing; so I continue my life "as-if" it will be there when I require it. I go about my business. I plan to write this afternoon with my favorite pen, and I have no concept that my pen is gone. I naturally act "as if" my pen still exists where I left it in my mind.

But the pen is gone, and this thought does not change the facts.

2. **Bargaining**: I go to my studio to write. Wanting my pen now, the energy of that desire begins to stir within me. I move from a rather blank thinking place to a more active thinking place of, "I

want my pen now!" Energy moves toward my goal, and I begin to work my thoughts in order to create the end I desire. I am trying to anticipate and control the outcome. I want to shorten the gap between me and my pen. My bargaining thoughts continue: "When I get my pen, I will keep it close to me or on a string around my neck so I won't have to look for it like I am right now." "When I find my pen I will write all the time, go to church, be nicer, etc." I may even engage others in my attempt to control by asking someone, "Will you help me take care of my pen?"

But the pen is gone, and this thought does not change the facts.

3. **Anger:** Now the energy increases as bargaining, the earlier control mechanism, did not control the situation or produce the pen. This energy must go somewhere. The first place it goes is outward, toward anger. The loss cannot belong to me; therefore, it must belong to someone else. The energy now begins to sputter, spurt, or explode outward away from the self into forms of blame, shame, anger, rage, accusations, defiance, attacks, and rebellions. I may shout angry accusations like: "Who took my pen?" "You were supposed to help me. You are a jerk." "You hated my writing."

But the pen is gone, and this thought does not change the facts.

4. **Depression:** The energy production, still unsuccessful in producing the pen, now makes a U-turn and blame, shame, anger, rage, accusations, defiance, attacks, and rebellions are now directed away from others and toward self. In depression, I may believe: "I'll never write again," "I was never any good anyway," "I picked the wrong person to help me protect my pen."

But the pen is gone, and this thought does not change the facts.

5. **Acceptance:** Acceptance does not mean joy and celebration. Acceptance is the arrival at a clear awareness of the situation. The loss is real. The loss has meaning. Gains are seen, losses are absorbed, and gradually there is a return to a more stable energy. I come to believe, "My pen is gone. I liked that pen a lot. I will live through this loss, but I will remember it each time I write or see a pen like the one I lost."

But the pen is gone, and this thought does not change the facts.

However, life has moved on. And so shall I.

Once such a minor grief is completed through the cycle, it will recycle again and again, usually in smaller doses and briefer cycles. A reminder of the loss may trigger the residue from a past stage. But eventually, the recycling resolves more quickly. If the loss is severe, the stages may hold the same energy and strength, but usually they are more fluid, less fixed, and less likely to become locked. A loss that is perceived as small, although it must follow the same stages, has less depth and usually resolves more quickly. The cycles may come quickly at first but with less force over time.

> **Move through the stages of grief: denial, bargaining, anger, depression, acceptance. Remember that avoidance of any stage only postpones the inevitable.**

The frivolous example of losing a pen is useful to explore grief work because most people can discuss loss if it is about something as inane and common-place as a pen. Most adults have experienced losses in their lives. That does not mean they are efficient at grief work. A person can be in one stage of grief about one loss, while in another stage about another loss, or change. You can be in anger about your pen and acceptance about your receding hairline or expanding waistline. You can be in bargaining about your receding hairline or expanding waistline and pitch an anger fit because your favorite pen is missing. Humans go through countless changes and losses and gains on a daily basis. Two people experiencing the same loss will perceive its value differently and may be in very different stages at the same time.

Move through the stages of grief: *denial, bargaining, anger, depression, acceptance.* Remember that avoidance of any stage only postpones the inevitable. It is okay to stay in one stage as long as necessary; just don't move your furniture into any particular stage. It is also okay to move back and forth between stages for a while until you are emotionally equipped to complete a stage. This takes some time.

5.2.5 Avoidance

Avoidance can be called a "non-feeling" feeling. It is an anti-feeling of feelings that accumulates emotional slush that can become fixed and rigid over time. Avoidance is not the same as denial. *Denial is unconscious. Avoidance is a choice.*

Healing means being willing to go through all the stages several times and then repeating the whole process again. It is like going through a tunnel and coming out the other side, or going around a baseball diamond until you get back to home plate. Each time this is accomplished successfully, there is potentially more compassion, wisdom, and meaning to the loss. By going through the process again, the person finds it becomes more familiar and less threatening.

The degree of energy in grief is related to the inherent value of the loss. Grief levels can be determined only by the person experiencing it. This level is determined by their perceptions alone. Outside perceptions can influence this determination, but it remains very personal.

Work is an appropriate place to express feelings of loss within some appropriate guidelines and boundaries. It is not necessary or healthy to pretend loss does not exist. Neither is it healthy to express grief constantly or make it central in the workplace. It is helpful to find an honest, open, and measured balance in the workplace. If that balance is lost, there should be no shame, although it may be appropriate to take time to rebalance feelings. An old measure of correct grieving suggested by Native American tradition is that the only way to release sorrow is to tell your story 1,000 times. Silence does not serve the grieving process. Find safe listeners. Create safe places to share grief stories.

Do this: Learn how to grieve.

Don't: Avoid grief. It is human.

5.2.6 Inflexibility

Growth can be annoying. It is uncomfortable. People don't like to be uncomfortable. But without that struggle, they can become fixed and rigid. Many conflicts are born from people who have lost their flexibility, either temporarily or permanently. Inflexible people become positional and become used to, or become comfortable in the position they pick. They may forget that they began a project with a group shared interest. They become fixed in their thinking, and now they have a new goal, a new agenda: themselves. Inflexible people take a deeper positional stance, and their opinion, rather than being a place for discussion, creativity, or group brainstorming, becomes a personal Holy Grail. They fear losing ground or territory and feel compelled to fight and to defend their place. They begin to see their only choices as fight or flight. Standing ground is tough work.

> Flexible people are less likely to develop into emotional terrorists... Helping inflexible people to get back on a safe track... moves people away from fear and back into faith.

An effective manager must discover why an inflexible person has become positional in a conflict situation. If the inflexibility is situational, the manager may assist that person in restoring or remembering the original goal, thus reclaiming flexibility. The manager must assist him or her in refocusing on the original shared interest.

Flexible people are less likely to develop into emotional terrorists. Inflexibility is often triggered by a perception of fear or loss of control. Helping inflexible people to get back on a safe track into shared interests can restore their faith and hope, limit potential isolation, and be a first step in successfully resolving rising tensions, conflicts, and disputes. It moves people away from fear and back into faith. Good faith resolutions are the product of moving away from rigid positions toward shared interests and goals.

5.2.7 Neutrality and Groundedness

Neutral: *impartial, not taking sides, disinterested, non-aligned.*

Grounded: *steady, firm, sturdy, balanced, whole.*

Remaining neutral and well-grounded in the face of spinning is the only effective position. Employees should just step away from the spin, and defer management to managers. Managers should carefully gather information, evaluate and synthesize data, reevaluate, and gather more data while keeping an eye on the big picture of the organizational mission.

An effective manager becomes a bit like Switzerland. Switzerland maintains its neutrality partly due to the fact that it is a very powerful country with an extremely well trained and expertly prepared military power to back it up if necessary. Unless it becomes necessary to defend the country or attack someone else, the country will just remain neutral and operate from the observation deck. If Switzerland did not have a powerful army as a contingency, it would be more difficult to remain neutral. If management does not have the backing of effective policy and solid, supportive CEO or administration, it is very difficult to remain neutral in a battle against regular conflicts, much less the more derisive and distorted conflicts associated with workplace emotions and emotional terrorism.

Standing ground and remaining neutral in the face of conflict is a learned skill and can become an art form. Like all skills it takes a willingness to learn. Unfortunately, many adults think they have learned it all. It is uncomfortable to be new at something. Remember, most people don't like being uncomfortable. Conflict is uncomfortable, and managing conflict can be quite uncomfortable. Managing conflict in the midst of personal discomfort takes energy and life force, plus it takes being a neutral grownup.

Remember that growth can happen in the presence of conflict. The seed must be in conflict with its hull to germinate. This is life. Without life, growth stops and decay begins. Decay is evidence of the end of life force. When growth stops, death is not far behind. Effective managers need to keep up their own personal life force to manage the rigors of managing other peoples' life force. Then they take all that energy and turn it into grounded neutrality. This is daunting work. Not everyone is cut out for it. Managers have to balance great self-care while being in the presence of a range of things that most people only read about or see on television.

Maintaining effective neutrality is particularly difficult when managers have been promoted from within ranks. Perhaps someone is a brilliant nurse or administrative assistant. This does not mean that the person has had *any* management training. Such training must be attended to for good management to take place. Spend training dollars to let managers learn how to manage. This is a brilliant investment! To stay neutral, try to see the bigger picture of the system in working order. Use self-care models and transformation ideas to find your own central core.

5.2.8 Conflict

Conflict can mean tension, struggle, and even war. It can be managed readily when people want to be out of conflict. Here are some quick tips for managing conflict or threatening emotions:

▶ Communicate limits ("I won't allow you to scream at me").

▶ Share your personal feelings ("I feel upset when you raise your voice").

▶ Exit. Leave quietly without explanation and refuse to join conflict.

▶ Identify how the conflict may be something you will need to address, but that you are not the conflict. The person escalating owns the conflict.

▶ Breathe, relax, breathe, and stay calm and quietly grounded. Think of the conflict as a set of burning boats trying to port in your harbor, but you do not let them tie up on your dock. You will watch these burning boats sail away into the sunset.

▶ Keep your office doors open when in a conflict situation.

- Remember that conflict is a temporary condition. Conflict can be turned creative.

- Soften your voice while continuing to speak your truth.

- Do not use escalating language, gestures, body language, or make threats.

- If someone crosses your boundaries emotionally, it may be necessary to enlist assistance.

- If you ask someone to stop a behavior and the behavior continues, you may need to ask twice. If the person does not respond after two requests, it is appropriate to exit the situation. You may inform the person that you will continue this discussion at a later date, but that the emotional content is too loaded at this time.

- Document your experience after the fact, not during the event.

- If someone crosses your boundaries physically, call 911, security, or scream for help.

- If you are male, screaming for help in a dangerous situation is appropriate. Many men are needlessly attacked because they assume they can "talk themselves out" of an escalating situation and think it isn't masculine to seek help. There is nothing un-masculine about needing help if someone is threatening your well-being and you are isolated.

5.3 Managing Emotions at Work

There is no universal standard to emotional continuity management. The following list consists of guidelines and not rules. Start here, but create your own personal list!

5.3.1 Guidelines for Managing Emotions at Work

- **Calm thoughts create calm actions.** You can handle this; you are a grownup and not a child. There will be a beginning, middle and end to this incident.

- **Picture it.** Visualize a calm place where you feel safe. Do this for as long as possible before responding. Even five seconds of a calm image will help your brain respond with calming chemicals rather than anxiety chemicals. The brain is a pharmacy and you give it the prescription for anxiety or calm.

- **Breathe, breathe, breathe.** Deep slow breaths through the nose and down to the belly. Release the breath slowly to the count of five. Begin again and repeat until settled.

- **Do a body check-in.** Are you sweating, chewing your lip, tapping your foot, pacing, breathing shallowly, and talking rapidly?
- **Pacing exercises.** Pace yourself with a walk, writing, drawing, a trip to the restroom or water cooler, a moment outdoors, stretching, or resting quietly alone for a few moments.
- **Big Picture.** Remember your big-picture mission and the fact that you decided to be a manager, so you are not a victim of this moment, it was and is a choice.
- **Remember.** Feelings matter mostly to the person having them. Honor this unless you are physically unsafe. If unsafe, call 911.
- **Listen.** People usually escalate their emotions when they believe they are not being heard. There is one theory that violence is simply extreme communication.
- **Calm voice.** In a duress situation, do not use a fake calm voice. That behavior may be perceived as condescending and create more stress. It can also imply that there is some other "secret" information that you have that the others do not have. However, try to soften the edges of your voice tone and slightly decrease the volume to model calmness.
- **Gestures.** Move a bit more slowly, with less movement and gesturing. Some people read gestures as threats and may misinterpret your body as an attack.
- **Know your resources.** Know your resources!
- **Don't be bulletproof.** Do not put yourself in an isolated, dangerous, unprotected, or risky situation or location.
- **Postpone.** It is very appropriate to postpone discussions when they get too hot or overwhelming. The trick to this is to state clearly your intention to continue and define the exact time that continuation can occur if both parties are open that time.
- **"No" is okay.** Saying "no" is okay. Saying "no" is a complete sentence. No means no. Saying no twice is still okay. If you are forced to say no again to make your point, the situation is escalating.
- **Take care.** Do good self-care after an *emotional continuity management process.*

> If you are a target, you are simply the emotional terrorist's target of the moment – their current squeaky toy, blue-plate special, soup of the day, or "victim du jour." It probably is not about you.

Some Quick-fix Tools to Manage Emotions: When emotions start spinning, employees need support. And they may need that support immediately to stop a spin. Emotional zingers, guilt trips, shame language attacks, verbal innuendoes, and outright attacks can hit even the most stable employee sideways when least expecting it. Emotions that are subtle or profoundly upsetting can come on suddenly and out of the blue and, in most universes, these forces hit the most available and vulnerable target of the moment. If it isn't you then you might have a chance to do a quick-fix to stop the spin.

Emotions matter to the person having those feelings. If the emotions are coming from an emotional terrorist, it is important to recognize that, if you are a target, you are simply the emotional terrorist's target of the moment – their current squeaky toy, blue-plate special, soup of the day, or "victim du jour." It probably is not about you. You may have contributed to the environment of emotions, or triggered some feelings for someone else, but feelings come from within and are always a response to how someone puts meaning into an experience. Someone who has had previous trauma or abuse may have a tendency to turn an emotional content into a personal event. The emotions of someone else do not originate inside of you.

It is important to make an effort to not allow your emotional response to be part of a spin process, small or large. Your emotions matter also, but mostly to you. Take your feelings to an appropriate source of support, which could be a friend outside the office, partner, spouse, family member, EAP provider, counselor, clergy, journal, or yoga class. Take care of your feelings without engaging in the agenda of someone else.

Go Neutral: Healthy emotional variances come and go. Emotional terrorists do not want to spin out of control themselves; they want you to do that for them so they can control the emotional situation. Remaining in control allows them to justify their reality, make you the "bad guy," and walk away clean. It is a very powerful control mechanism. The trick with this is to just go emotionally flat. Do not engage. Do not agree or disagree. Respond to their device with a neutral, "Oh," or "I will take that into consideration," or "Why do you ask?" or "I will get back to you on that later," or "I was just heading to the restroom – I'll get back to you."

Step Away: Literally move back a step, and then redirect your progress or energy to an entirely different place. If you are stuck in a corner, cubicle, or office space, take one step back and stand firmly grounded on two feet with arms at your sides in a relaxed manner, visualize yourself moving backwards and away from the emotional debris, or make a position change in your chair that suggests you are changing the situation. Taking a break reorients the energy flow. It can be useful to say, "Can you just hold that thought until I return from the restroom?" Excuse yourself and come back to the room and position yourself in a neutral way.

Silence: There are times when silence is the perfect response to aggressive behavior. Breathe quietly and wait quietly and see if the person you are dealing with either escalates or de-escalates the situation.

No Eye Contact: Although making no direct eye contact or too much eye contact is a favorite mechanism that emotional terrorists use to control or invalidate you, you can use it also. Use your eyes to hold a position as you step back and exit from an uncomfortable situation.

Boundary Gestures: Raise one hand, palm forward, in a "stop" gesture, with a very clear neutral phrase, such as, "Not here, not now," or "I need to be elsewhere; could we take this up later if it is important?" or "Thanks for your input on that, and I will have to move on with what I was doing," or "Oh, I understand what you are saying, so let's stop here for now," or "This sounds important to you, and I'm just on my way to the copy machine; perhaps we/you/I should discuss it with the supervisor," or "This does not sound like business to me; it sounds like emotions, and so we will need to establish a different venue for this discussion."

Closed Phrases: Closed phrases are more socially acceptable ways to say, "No." They end the conversation without being extremely abrupt while leaving no room for discussion. They can sound like, "This is certainly a good topic to discuss with the boss," or "Since our anti-terrorism training, I have decided to not even start to go there with anyone," or "Now that I understand how rumors get contagious, I am sure being careful with what I discuss with people. But I hope you bring that up at the next staff meeting when everyone is present."

No Spinning Allowed: If you recognize an unavoidable spin coming your way, take a moment to get grounded. Take a few deep breaths, and brace yourself for the blow. Know this is temporary. Know that you can survive more readily if you don't go spinning off with the emotions of someone else. See yourself as well grounded and safe. Let the emotional tornado blow itself out, and then use the proper hierarchy process to report any danger if necessary. Make every effort not to add to the spin when reporting the spin. Make good choices and try not to be manipulated by the grand or subtle spinnings of others. Let dust devils go by. Report tornadoes. Pay attention to dust devils that gather speed and force.

Take Care of Your Feelings: If someone attacks you emotionally, you may have a wound that needs care. Your feelings count, but usually not to the person who attacked you. Honor your feelings, and give them reasonable attention and care. Take it to a trusted friend off the site. Write in your journal. Share at a 12-Step meeting. Call your spouse or sister. Do not dump on others any more than you would lift the edge off of every bandage to show someone the goo of your skinned knee. It's yours. You are responsible to take care of it. You are grown up. If you need help, get it. If the attack is big then feel no humiliation in seeking more significant help. Even little boo-boos deserve a nice bandage. Big wounds require bigger bandages, and sometimes more gauze. Unless you are completely taken out you need to take care of your own feelings. When you are recovered and secure, report the attack forward through the appropriate grievance procedure rather than random venting to co-workers that may injure them or start other spins.

Take Care Of Yourself Because You Are Valuable

Important: if you do not feel safe, these tips are not recommended. Put this down and call 911 immediately.

Temporary: Know that storms are temporary. Some of them are nasty even if they do have a natural, very brief, lifecycle. Remember, problems can be fixed and issues can be resolved. If there is no life-threatening situation, time is not an enemy and can be used for healing and resolution.

Stand on the Observation Deck: Do whatever it takes to stay neutral in your observations. For example, you can pretend to be standing on the observation deck of a spacecraft. You are surrounded and protected by a force field. You see an alien approaching you. It speaks through a translator device and has a human form. You know it is not really human because you have been in this part of the galaxy before. You listen. The alien spews emotional content your direction. Because you know it is alien-speak you can offer a courteous remark from your safe perspective and then get back to the command post to carry on with your own mission. Later you may think to yourself, "Wow, that was an emotionally agitated alien walking around here; I wonder who let it loose? Oh, well, I guess they'll let anyone work on this ship."

Pretend: As you stand on your observation deck you can get through a lot of minor emotional spins by playing and pretending. No one else needs to know you have created a fantasy to survive your worksite chaos. Keep it to yourself and smile pleasantly in the face of chaos.

Captive of Witch: After all, you are royalty who is being held captive and must weave sticks into gold before 5:00 p.m. The evil gremlin king who is trying to distract you from your work has been sent from the evil witch's castle to try to keep you from your release. You cannot let on that you know; so you politely turn him away with a regal phrase and return to your weaving.

Secret Weapon Goalie: Or, no one knows that you are the secret weapon goalie on the Olympic hockey team, and your coach has planted you in this office to learn skills in deflecting the emotional hockey pucks. You know your task is to avoid being hit in the head by the puck, but also to drop it back into play. You don't own the puck, but you must keep standing as it is being hurled at you at 599 mph. The crowd roars!

Act Out a Little (a Little): Be a little silly and slightly whimsical in a way that no one else will notice. It is useful and healing to shake off the "nasties" with a dose of humor that causes no harm. Keep a small toy in your pocket. Collect jokes in your day planner. Wear your socks inside out. If you get a paper cut, put a cartoon character bandage on it and send yourself a get-well card. In Oscar Wilde's play Lady Windermere's Fan, a character comments, "Life is far too important a thing ever to talk seriously about." Keep your humor about life to yourself. After all, someone may be doing very important work, and your whimsy could cause harm. This is small whimsy you do to entertain yourself.

Overact*: Sometimes it stops someone in their tracks to react to an overreaction with another overreaction. Be careful and make very good choices, but it can be very powerful to provide a fun-house mirror reflection back to someone. For example, someone comes to you with a rumor. Listen politely. If you suspect that the person is trying to make a spin, offer the reminder that spinning isn't appropriate, and if it is a real problem, the person should use the chain of command. This is supportive to someone who is in distress. If, on the other hand, this is an emotional terrorist who demonstrates that he or she is not really interested in problem-solving, and if you think you can get away with it, throw your hands in the air, or fall down on the floor and pretend to weep uncontrollably while raving about the potential ramifications of this rumor to yourself, your unborn grandchildren, national security, global warming, the ecosystem of lint, the spiritual wellbeing of the Maharaja LeBlommbia's Quest for Interplanetary Peace and the migratory status of Canadian Geese in the Northwest. Then stand back up, quietly dust yourself off, and say, "You are right; this is so important that I think we either need to tell our manager, write a formal grievance, or would you just like me to spread this around the office with your name on it?" Again, although this is a theoretically sound process that has been used in therapeutic settings for decades, you must be very careful with whom you use it in the office. **Note: Do not use this method in the presence of violence.*

Seek Beauty: Go to the window and look for beauty. Go outdoors for thirty seconds and take a breath of air. Even a cement walkway is beautiful if you take a moment to consider its texture, solidity, how it came to be there, the humans who put it there, the water that was used to mix it, and how it came from the sea and the clouds, the sun and wind that dried it that leave each day and return at dawn, the feet that walk across it that were once the feet of small children with sweet innocent smiles, and the ants which scurry across what must seem to them a rugged terrain in a never ending cycle of life. Emotional terrorists hate beauty and grace. Appreciation for beauty does not support the agenda of destruction. Beauty is life-affirming and not life-alienating. The power of beauty dismantles negativity. Take a beauty break to regroup your emotions on a regular basis, and always do it after a brush with anything that is anti-beauty.

Develop a Personal Practice: Develop a personal recovery practice, and do something wonderful for your body, mind, emotions and spirit on a daily basis. This will keep your emotional immunity in top working condition. Develop your own sacred recipe for self-care, joy, beauty, persistence, whimsy, connection, and peacemaking.

Discover Your Inner-Self: Listen to an emotional terrorist closely from your observation deck to discover your own vulnerabilities. Learn more about your own fears by seeing the reflections off the mirrors of others. Each experience we have either takes us forward or moves us backward. Life is about moving forward. You started this life in perfection and innocence, and this is your true nature. Find out how this applies to you now and how it applies to you at work. No matter how many times you have been dropped on your head by people and situations, you are an adult and you have the choice whether to use life for life-affirming or for life-alienating purposes.

Building a Toolkit for Managing Emotions

The best tools to facilitate strong employee revenue are those that will be efficient for the entire range of human emotions from daily annoyances to catastrophic trauma. Although different tools should be used for the variety of issues and problems at work, managers should consider tools that match incidents throughout the entire recovery process. Be good consumers. Many trendy and faddish hot items are available in the emotional continuity management marketplace. As you are developing your emotional continuity management plan, it may be helpful to think of your plan as a recipe box or well-stocked toolkit. Emotional continuity management plans should contain essentially the same foundational ingredients. Review the list below as you develop your shopping list. As you get more advanced and creative, you will want to explore other tools and create your own.

Minimum ingredients of an emotional continuity management toolkit:

- Conflict resolution methods.
- Communication methodologies.
- Systems education.
- Diversity training and cultural norms of emotions.
- Icons, slogans, and banners for quick recognition.
- Team building strategies.
- Grief work education and practice.
- Control and management strategies.
- Personal values tools.
- Humor.
- Emotional terrorist information.
- Tools for new employee orientation.
- Normal and abnormal psychology basics.
- How to recognize signs of traumatic stress.
- Emotional self-defense.
- Ventilation models for debriefing and defusing.
- Adjustment strategies and practices.
- Stress management tools for the life span.
- Physical, mental, emotional, and spiritual health practices.
- Resistance and creativity training.
- Memos of understanding with external vendors.
- Bibliographies.
- Other resources.
- Corporate models for emotional continuity management.

Your toolkit should also:

▶ Provide emotional tools that generalize across occupations.

▶ Provide a full range of emotional tools for the entire range of human emotions.

▶ Provide emotional first aid and have arrangements in place for more serious emotional requirements.

▶ Generalize to small and large organizations without significant adjustments.

▶ Avoid trends and fad solutions.

▶ Be gender and ethnically sensitive.

▶ Be cross-cultural.

▶ Work equally well for the diverse needs of executive, management, and line staff.

▶ Offer simple, understandable, and practical tools for use both inside and outside the work setting.

> **Emotional continuity management is a life-long learning process. People grow and develop over their lifespan and do not stop that process at adolescence.**

5.3.2 Learn How to Be In The Presence Of Emotions

How do you manage the emotions of yourself and others? Emotional continuity management is a life-long learning process. People grow and develop over their lifespan and do not stop that process at adolescence. Adult learners can use the following steps to become more effective in finding comfort and pragmatic means to be in the presence of emotions in the workplace or anywhere else:

1. Know Yourself and Your Feelings

How you feel in a situation contributes to how an emotional communication works or does not work. As a manager, you need to be on top of your own emotional game and not let the feelings of others take over the situation you are managing. Allowing room for feelings does not mean that feelings run the show. Feelings need to have their say in a situation but need not overwhelm it. Even big or huge feelings can come and go if they are well-managed. Remember that managed does not mean controlled. Managed does not mean denied or exploited. Your emotions matter also, but mostly to you. If you know your own feelings in a situation, you can do self-care during or after the emotional situation has been resolved.

One of my favorite mentors, a psychology professor, taught his students that if they were not aware of their own feelings when they were conducting a counseling session, then they were not doing it correctly. He taught that these inner feelings are excellent tools for both empathetic listening and informative response. If you feel anger, fear, embarrassment, curiosity, satisfaction, or any other feeling, you can access this to discover more about the speaker and more about yourself.

2. Approach Emotions with Empathy

Probably the best term to express how a manager manages the feelings of others is the word empathy. According to Marshall Rosenberg, considered by some to be an expert in non-violent communication, empathy can be defined as a "respectful understanding of what others are experiencing" (Rosenberg, 2003). If you begin a management situation with empathetic listening to your own feelings and those of another, you begin with respect to all parties. You first allow yourself to respect your own emotions to increase understanding of your own experience. Then, find appropriate ways to listen and seek understanding about what others are experiencing. Empathy is respecting both sides of the exchange.

3. Flow with the Motion

Your feelings are on one side of a divide, and the speaker is on the other side. This chasm must be crossed for communication to be successful. This separation between you and "them" creates the necessary gap to be present in any discussion of emotions. That gap is a safe place, the demilitarized zone, and the neutral ground where something will happen. It is a breathing space when feelings are big or strong. The gap should not be filled with a wall or attack language. Let the opening occur naturally. Do not rush to close the gap, even in the discomfort of a time when there is no understanding. The gap is an open place in which feelings can be safely exchanged. Think of a figure eight moving between two people. Imagine the flow moving easily and calmly between the two individuals.

Conflict starts when one of the individuals places a wall between that empathetic flow or begins to attack. Empathy does not imply agreement, suppression, control, or co-opting to a feeling that is not on your side of the figure eight flow. A manager is open to the flow. Great managers encourage it.

4. Avoid Judgment

In emotional situations, there is a natural tendency to judge the feelings as good or bad. If you do not agree with the emotion or the details of a situation, you may want to control it by making a judgment of its value. Hold your ground and let the flow continue. If it gets personal or attacking, rather than calling it bad or a failure, see that the need of the person communicating is extreme and that they are expressing fear that their needs will not be met.

5. Express Needs and Wants

One of the most important clarifiers in a difficult and emotional conversation is to determine the difference between needs and wants. Needs are require-ments and are therefore nonnegotiable. Wants range between slight preferences to extreme desires. Needs and wants are emotionally charged feelings depending on the degree of requirement or preference. We need air. We prefer good smelling air. We need food. We prefer gourmet fare. We need clothing. We prefer comfortable clothes. We desire elegant and expensive labels. We need money. We want a raise. We need money to feed our children. We need a raise.

6. Validate

Validation confirms and authorizes that a situation is within acceptable boundaries. A validating statement sanctions it. Again, this does not mean that you agree or accept the truth of the statement or feelings expressed, but that you, as a leader, authorize its presence in the discussion. By neutrally reflecting back to the speaker that he or she has been heard, the speaker feels validated. In many cases of conflict or emotional content, the sense of being heard is all that is necessary to solve what may seem like an irresolvable problem. Validating that company policy defines emotions as okay within certain parameters allows the feeling to be ventilated. Ventilation is movement. And movement means change. Such change may bring up other emotions, but it does not reflect intractable stagnation in a system.

7. Express Hope and Gratitude

Current scientific research is confirming that positive language changes molecular structure. Words of positive expectancy and appreciation do not close the process. Managers who fear the flow of emotions in a process will usually place a wall here. Individuals who feel the need to control rather than manage emotions, will use language that stops the flow. Someone who wants to be a tyrant or autocrat, or perhaps even an emotional terrorist, will take the opening and exploit it. Stopping emotional communication does not stop emotions from flowing; it merely moves the flow from one place to another.

If you want that flow to move elsewhere and create unknown consequences, create a dam. If you want to be in the loop as the manager, then you need to keep the flow open by establishing a sense of future through hopeful language and gratitude. Hope-related words like trust, anticipate, wish for, and looking forward to, create a sense of future. Future suggests life. No hope and no future imply death. Death is the most emotional thing that humans experience.

8. Pause and Reflect

Unless there is a life-threatening situation, in which case you would immediately call for backup, dial 911, or implement your emergency plan, a pause to reflect and consider is a very useful tool for managers. Pauses do not imply stoppages. Pauses are bookmarks to return to later. Pauses are brief moments to catch your breath so you are not spun up in someone's emotional tornadoes. When you take a break, define it clearly and honor that time frame. Tell your employees that you are going to take five minutes and will be back to them. Make sure it is within five minutes when you return, or trust will be broken – emotions will stir up again and will include feelings of an additional betrayal. You can also tell someone that you are going to sleep on it, take 24 hours to consider it, or bring it along to the next meeting in two weeks. What is important is to express it as a pause and not an end.

Reflection on an emotion is not critical thinking or evaluation. Reflection is lighter and gentler. It is a pondering, a consideration, contemplation or musing about something. This is not the time to move into cognitive, intellectual, or brainstorming problem-solving. Rather, this is a time to let the feelings settle down into their most clear form so that what is important stands out. Emotional energy can be chaotic, loud, spinning, and confusing. During a reflection time, you may discover that only one important or critical feature was being expressed, perhaps fear. Most negative emotions sift down to fear. If you can discover through gentle reflection what the fear may be, you are well on your way to begin problem-solving, because you will be addressing the real issue that created the emotion.

9. Move to Problem Solving

If you have followed the steps, you are now ready to move your thinking into problem-solving strategies. This is when you can implement a style you are familiar with if it works, or do a transformation activity that will move the problem into a new light. Many managers try to problem-solve by approaching the conflict, running from it, creating a distraction, or using total avoidance. These behaviors are all about fear. *Manage your own fear first before trying to manage the fears of others.*

One surprisingly interesting way to problem-solve that you may never have tried is to write poetry about the concern. Poetry writing, besides being therapeutic, moves the thinking from one part of the brain to another location in the brain. You have access to many brain locations. How many do you use? Perhaps you are a manager who goes back to the same old brain location hoping to find a new trick. The standard definition of insanity is to keep doing the same thing while hoping for different results. You will still have to come back to the problem using appropriate business and industry-standard approaches based on policy and procedures. But before you move into that place that is familiar, you can explore alternative problem solving strategies that add another dimension to the information.

Perhaps you want a new role model for problem solving. Study the lives of successful problem-solvers to learn how they did it. Pick someone you admire, real or a fantasy character, and explore how that person's style could be included into yours.

Keep in mind the difference between problems and issues, and remember that problems can be solved.

10. Follow-up

Check back with all participants to make certain there are not lingering emotions that may spin into tornadoes.

11. Value

Using the artificial technique of reflecting back to someone what you think you are hearing may, at first, feel awkward and "techniquey." That's because until it becomes natural, that's exactly what it is. Nonetheless, it is crucial to communication that you express something about what you heard and give the speakers an opportunity to clarify and simplify the message they want heard. If you hear people correctly, according to what they want you to hear, emotions that charge the situation will begin to decrease. Being heard allows people to feel validated and valued. Being not heard leads to increased emotions and violence. It has been said that violence is simply extreme communication. If emotions are escalating, someone is not hearing.

> Think about your favorite person. How would you combine the attributes of these people into a composite "you" who is the innovative management professional?

12. Explore Options

It is usually not helpful to problem-solve while emotions are being expressed. Problem-solving or fixing a feeling denies the value of the feeling. Exploring options is about trying to find a way to define precisely what is required or desired in order to address the specific feeling. When people are engaged in strong emotion, language tends to become vague and falls into words of extremes and demands as the emotional person is struggling with control. Gently helping the speaker to express specifics during this portion of the exchange is validating that you are listening and interested in the person's needs and wants, will help the person move into a more calm and rational part of the brain where problem-solving can be seen as an option, and find real actions to solve real problems.

Transformative people see things differently. They see the small detail and the big picture. They find a way to combine science, art, and action in ways that inform and affirm. Einstein suggested that all that science really consisted of was everyday thought that had been refined. Refining, transforming, fine-tuning, adjusting, and creating new ways to solve old problems is the hope of the global consciousness and subsequently the global marketplace. M.K. Gandhi is attributed with saying, "We must be the change we want to see in the world." Think about your favorite manager. Think about your favorite person. How would you combine the attributes of these people into a composite "you" who is the innovative management professional?

Know Your Responsibility in "Duty to Warn": Some professionals are required by law to report violence or threats of violence. They are called "mandated reporters" and must, by law, call professional agencies to report even a suspicion of threat risks. You may voluntarily become a mandated reporter by deciding you will take the risk to have someone upset with you if you are overly concerned in error.

The state of our world today suggests that you are sometimes best served by overreacting rather than underreacting to your intuition. You will not have to make the final judgment that someone is at risk. You can call in the experts. Mental health professionals, law enforcement, child protective services, or other appropriate agencies need to be called in if you ever are concerned about violence. The rule of thumb for managers is that it is better to err on the side of being overly concerned than it is to read a name of one of your employees on the front page the next morning after you did nothing. Memorize the phone number for your local crisis hotline. You can always call them for advice and let them make the decision if you are overly concerned. That is what they are trained for and will be available for 24 hours a day, 7 days a week.

(The following two lists should in no way be considered absolute, complete, or anything more than a general guideline. Always consult a professional, a security person, and never hesitate to call 911).

Listening For Suicide Risk

▶ A direct statement of the intention to commit suicide.

▶ A specific plan.

▶ History of attempts.

▶ Vague statements about suicide or his or her own funeral.

▶ History of depression.

▶ Hopelessness or recent losses.

▶ Alcohol or drug use.

▶ Ill health.

▶ Impulsivity.

▶ Stressful events.

▶ Adolescent or elderly.

▶ Access to or availability of weapons.

Risk of Homicidal Behavior

▶ Direct threats.

▶ Access to or availability of weapons.

▶ Substance abuse.

▶ History of past acts of violence.

▶ History of explosive, persecutory, paranoid, suspicious, angry, hostile behaviors.

▶ Verbalized a plan to do an action.

▶ Verbalized an identified victim.

▶ Apparent unwillingness to collaborate during a conflict.

Make an emergency phone list and put it by your phone, not in a notebook: crisis hotline, mental health, EAP, law, and fire... Remember that the number for 911 in most places is "911."

It is easy to remember for a reason.

5.4 Become Fluent In a New Way of Communicating

Communication models are not one-size-fits-all. Finding a style that fits your personality is important to competency and confidence. Whether you study Rosenberg's model of "non-violent communication" or your grandmother's "be-nice-to-everyone" model, that is up to you. There are styles that are more functional at the workplace, especially when dealing with difficult people, bullies, jerks, and emotional terrorists.

> If everyone on your team is on the same page, the emotional terrorist... [will] eventually lose control, lose interest, and either become compliant or move on to the next target.

5.4.1 Karpman Drama Triangle

The approach developed by Stephen Karpman is a model of communication within a psychological model called *transactional analysis* that efficiently removes the power plays from any interaction (Karpman, 1968). Karpman's drama triangle is described below. If you see an interaction a bit like a game model, the three roles in the drama triangle would be victim, persecutor, and rescuer – taking on any of these roles is a dangerous position. As the roles shift quickly from one to another, anyone playing this game will be caught in a veritable unending spiral of emotional conflict. Moving away from any of these three roles will lead to neutrality and a position of clarity that will move any discussion away from emotional content to business content.

Managing the creative attributes of emotional terrorists takes calm, quiet, non-emotional persistence. In the face of tornadoes at work, you are the calm place, the shelter, the cellar, or the quiet serenity model for your staff. If you spin, all will be lost. If you get into anger, fear, or blame, all will be lost. If you take on any one of the drama triangle roles – becoming a victim, a rescuer, or a persecutor – all will be lost. If you are tranquil and persistent over time, that will become the tone of your leadership and the higher ground that your team will go to when under duress.

If everyone on your team is on the same page, the emotional terrorist will not have a place to spin or create chaos; so they eventually lose control, lose interest, and either become compliant or move on to the next target. I have found that once managers get the hang of this, they truly enjoy the refined, professional power of being in a neutral position. The pressure is off, and they are able to access their own opinion, ideas, intuitions, and creative ideas. I have seen them sit up a little taller, have softer expressions on their faces, laugh more frequently, and relax in the knowledge that what they have been doing is actually very, very hard. They give themselves some permission to feel a bit proud of their work. Good managers are a brave lot!

A suggestion I give managers who are trying for the first time to experience neutrality is to think of themselves as Switzerland. I remind them that Switzerland, as a nation, maintains a politic of neutrality. This is not a weak position in the world. In fact, Switzerland is where the Geneva Convention was held, where Swiss bank accounts are considered the safest, where there are Swiss Army Knives and the best chocolate. The Swiss have a very powerful and well-trained army. They know they have the capacity to defend and attack, but choose not to do so. In that choice, they have remained world leaders and safe haven as neutral ground. They do not participate in the drama triangle sorts of politics of the rest of the world. After I explain Swiss neutrality as a model of strength, I remind them of the chocolate part. It is obvious to me that after any enduring challenge of remaining neutral in the midst of conflict, chocolate is indicated. This is not carte blanche for a binge feeding frenzy, but rather honoring the tradition of many warriors to finish a battle with a "wee bit of chocolate."

Master the Drama Triangle: *I would like to thank Stephen Karpman for supporting my use of his wonderful model. Others copy it, or change the words of his original work and call it their own, but the original works well – so why change it.*

Karpman's drama triangle is a model for communication drawn from the psychological theory of transactional analysis (TA). The model can be used to look at human interaction like a game with three players:

▶ The Victim,

▶ The Rescuer, and

▶ The Persecutor.

As the game is played, no one wins. The roles are exchanged and repeated in a vicious cycle of exchange that moves each player into the other role to maintain the game. As the game continues, the Victim attacks the Persecutor for "crimes" and thus now becomes the Persecutor through the use of blaming. The Persecutor now is the Victim. The Rescuer may step in to offer assistance to the Victim, which threatens the Persecutor, who is now the Victim by way of the Rescuer. The Victim may join the Rescuer and both may now attack the Persecutor, who becomes the Victim by the attack and uses it to justify another attack or to hook another Rescuer *and the game continues until someone steps out of the cycle and becomes a Non-Player.*

The Non-Player, although seen as a player by the others, can remain in the setting but will take on a neutral, nonparticipating role. This may be seen as a rescue, an attack, or a martyr (victim) stance, but if it is maintained over time, players will either end the game or move on to solicit new players.

5.4.2 When is it a Game and When is it for Real?

There are real victims in life. If you are hit by a car, attacked by a terrorist, molested, assaulted, and so forth, you are a victim. (The victim in the Karpman drama triangle, however, puts adhesive on the back of his or her wrist and attaches it to his or her forehead in an ongoing "poor me" position).

There are real persecutors. Terrorists, offenders, and criminals are not playing. They are dead serious.

There are real rescuers. Law enforcement, nurses, fire fighters, EMTs, teachers, counselors, social workers, and other "good guys" are not playing the triangle game, but must watch that they aren't rescuing people who do not want to be rescued.

Individuals in the drama triangle are playing roles that are not real – they do it for the game itself. If you stop playing, eventually they will move on because you are not playing. They may up the ante, or raise the stakes significantly to entice you to continue being a player, but if you move away from the triangle, you will eventually feel better and be more useful.

An old classic drama triangle is seen in the melodramatic scene of the sweet and innocent heroine tied to the railroad tracks by the evil villain as the handsome hero rides in just in the nick of time. This is endemic to our collective sense of theater. Hollywood knows that the archetypal evil-doer must kidnap the helpless victim so that the hero as Agent 007, Superman, martial arts expert, or even cartoon figure sweeps in to save the weak and to save the known world for the betterment of humanity.

The drama triangle is everywhere, but that does not necessarily mean we have to play it out at the worksite with theatrical dimensions. Even if your company is part of the industry that promotes or supports the drama of victims, rescuers, or persecutors, it doesn't mean your workplace has to replicate the soap opera within the work environment. Watch a soap opera or CNN to see how the triangle plays out. Now watch your worksite for how you may be unconsciously playing.

I often meet resistance to the topic of managing emotions at work. I am no longer surprised when someone verbally attacks me or my ideas. Some people just do not want to deal with the soft-sided emotional contents of business.

Often, they are themselves dysfunctional, afraid, threatened by their own humanity, or just plain mean. I understand. But when I run into someone who seems to be on a mission to make me look bad, I find it interesting. I use my tools and move into a non-spinning zone of neutrality to avoid taking it personally or getting worked up into someone else's emotional frenzy. Then I teach the drama triangle. Difficult people are now surrounded with individuals who know that it is relatively easy not to participate in collective chaos. This is a good moment for me when I see an entire group of people relieved to stop spinning. It's a great moment for them also because, from this point forward, they have a portable tool to avoid the chaotic agenda of someone else. They are now equipped to identify those people who want to contribute to the team and those people who would rather stir up emotional sabotage.

5.5 Understand What It Takes to Manage or Deal with a Bully

If you are not safe, put down this book and get help. Contact security, call 911, reach out for support, don't deal with it alone! If you suspect a bully or emotional terrorist is in your midst, you are probably not just making it up, but it may be difficult to get support. Often people are afraid to admit their own fear of a bully to others – and this gives the bully more power. *Do not confront an emotional terrorist alone.*

Tool #1: Recognition and Validation

Tool #2: Excellent Self-Care Tools and Use Them Daily

Tool #3: Have Smart Resources and Support

Tool #4: Tip-toe Away in the Other Direction When Possible

Tool #5: Use the Karpman Drama Triangle and Become Neutral

Tool #6: Have More Tools and Skills than Anybody Else

Tool #7: Know the number to 911 is 911

Tool #8: Don't Do it Alone

Tool #9: Get More Tools (Call Dr. Vali for more tools!)

Don't: try to "fix" or "save" emotional terrorists unless you are a professional. Like sharks, they are not necessarily something to be judged as "bad" but on the other hand, where do you want to swim? Me? I'm a goldfish, so I need to be thoughtful! I need to be a very, very smart goldfish if I find myself in a shark-tank. So I tend to swim the other direction as soon as I notice where I am. So far, so good!

What I have found to be the simplest first tool to deal effectively with an emotional terrorist or bully is validation. I can't tell you the countless number of times I have described the attributes of a bully to someone and their eyes light up with recognition and relief. This awareness that bullies are real and exist takes a tremendous load off the person who has been bullied. They often can then muster their own inner strength to deal with it, or ask for appropriate support. Part of what a bully does that is very effective is to make you second-guess yourself.

If you have become aware, or been made aware, that someone under your management is a bully or an emotional terrorist, it may eventually become necessary for you to interact with the individual. These are guidelines you can follow, but not rules or laws of the universe. In other words, you will have to find your own way through this process using your style – within the context of the situation, and the size and culture of your company, and the style of your industry. The interview process below offers some good suggestions for how to avoid obvious pitfalls and traps of working with someone who does not follow the same guidelines as you do. Being clear about what you are doing, where you are going, and how you are going about it, will give you the upper hand. That upper hand will give you the sense of presence necessary to manage someone who is cunning, baffling, tricky, subtle, upset, chaotic, manipulative, angry, frightened, controlling, or in some rare cases just plain "evil."

You may be the first person to ever contain and lid an emotional terrorist. (See the "Snakes in the Schoolyard" example below). They usually don't like that. Planning for the worst, but expecting the best is a good beginning. Using a bit of humor, you might think of yourself as an animal trainer who likes the critter, but you don't want it to chew up your slippers. You may not need to train, punish, or eliminate the beast. The simple act of you taking your hierarchical authority and letting the emotional terrorist know that you are the alpha leader of the pack may settle things down immediately.

Sometimes the challenge for control or power can be dissolved easily with a silent presence that originates from a feeling that is fearless. We have all heard expression "Never let them see you sweat" and "They can smell your fear." This is true when you are dealing with emotional terrorists. You need to understand your own bottom line without question – your own strengths, your own weaknesses, your own available support systems, and your own deep, abiding faith in those systems.

Once you have faith in something, you will not so easily slip into fear. Of course, if you survived the Titanic, you might not have absolute faith in ships and may find yourself slightly hesitant to get on board another ship. In the same way, if you have come up against an emotional terrorist in your past, you might wonder if the effort to deal with all of this management process is worth the work. Although this is a valid thought, it is also a doorway to fear. This is why it is essential throughout the process of managing to decide and re-decide if you truly want to be a manager. If you do not have faith in your decision to manage, you will not operate from a position of strength. Emotional terrorists smell your fear and will dive deep into that fear with a variety of unique or custom-designed "gotchas."

Do this: Remain calm in the presence of an emotional terrorist. Remember that you are the good guy. Do your best!

Don't: Worry if you feel shaky or get tricked. Remember, these men and women are well practiced at this. Don't forget that it isn't about you. You are just the "victim du jour."

5.5.1 Managing an Emotional Terrorist: Snakes in the Schoolyard

Management and terrorism have a number of common denominators. The words include *concepts* and *actions*. Both words imply that there are rules and policies to follow, work within specific procedural activity formats, a level of predictability, and consequences that affect others. What is different about the two is that most managers, unless they are terrorists themselves, work inside the lines. They respect authority, work within the chain of command, operate through guidelines and principles, and adhere to generally accepted norms. Terrorists count on this and employ their imaginations to work within and around all these normative boundaries.

A story from a manager of a small company brings this difference to light as she was trying to out-think an emotional terrorist in her workplace. She had been working with other managers for months trying to teach them the necessity of creative management of difficult employees, and during a spin-free workplace consultation, she came up with a way to teach the value of "out-thinking" the problem makers and managing emotional terrorists.

Snakes in the Schoolyard: A Metaphor

Delores was a senior manager in a private school. One early spring morning a staff member came running into her office reporting that there was a big snake in the schoolyard. Delores quickly assessed, to her discomfort, that as a manager it might indeed be her responsibility to remove the snake to protect the children and staff. So, she proceeded to go out into the field with an ax. Just as she was about to destroy the snake, she felt dozens of little eyes and big eyes on the back of her head. She turned around to see little noses pressed against windows and staff faces with worried expressions. They were all wondering what she was going to do with that snake! Delaying her initial organic disgust of snakes, she stopped her homicidal intent, returned to the school, got a bucket, and proceeded to go through the emotional and physically difficult challenge of catching the snake alive. She wanted to do it without causing the children or staff to be unduly upset and without doing harm to herself. To her surprise, she found that she no longer wanted to harm the snake. She just needed this threat gone. She succeeded, with some help from another brave staff member. This strategy later became a written policy, the "Snakes in the Schoolyard" Policy.

Snakes in the Schoolyard Policy:

1. At least two (2) employees with gloves approach the snake. Snakes squirm toward the easiest direction to escape, the path of least resistance. With two people, the snake has no escape route. The snake catchers must not fear snakes. But gloves are required for better performance.

2. Whichever employee grabs the snake must immediately toss it into a bucket with a lid. One of the employees must then immediately secure the lid. The real trick to snake removal is the lid. Without the lid, the snake escapes and you must do it again. Spending your time catching the same snake over and over is not efficient and is not good business practice.

3. Once you contain the snake you must take it into the school, let the children see that it is not hurt. This step is important because children have imaginations and like to see even crawly things cared for correctly.

4. Later, transport the snake elsewhere, off the premises, a long way away from where you work, and dispose of it.

5. If the snake is toxic, call in a professional.

The Outcome? Generally, everyone is happy: the managers, the staff, the children, and – if done well – even the snake. The manager did disclose privately, "Of course, you know, Dr. Vali, that if this type of snake came to my house, I'd just chop its head off, but workplace snakes are different."

The manager... removed the word "snake" from the policy and developed a procedure for her team that they understood.

With that comment, the manager arrived at the concept of how to manage a workplace terrorist. She removed the word "snake" from the policy and developed a procedure for her team that they understood. The company had recently been challenged by a workplace emotional terrorist in human form, and after the snake incident, the manager was able to show her staff how to protect the company, clients, themselves, and even the emotional terrorist from harm.

Do this: Learn what snakes are toxic and what snakes are harmless.

Don't: Assume that all snakes must be removed. Some snakes can do very well with micro-management if they have solid and well-defined boundaries (lids).

Do this: Step up to the task of managing emotional terrorists at work.

Don't: Try to handle this alone! Get help!

Snakes in the Schoolyard can apply to bullies: Snakes in the Schoolyard is based on a true story of an organization that had a problem with snakes. By extension, it can be a potent metaphor to use to teach a compassionate method to deal with something or someone toxic at a company. You need not kill the snake to protect others. You simply need to let the snake be the snake somewhere else. We will explore this metaphor further by reviewing how this might work for a company.

5.5.2 Applying the Snakes in the Schoolyard Model to a Business

1. At least two (2) employees with gloves approach the snake. Snakes squirm toward the easiest escape direction; the path of least resistance, and with two people, the snake has no escape route. The snake catchers must not fear snakes. But gloves are required for better performance.

   a. A manager, with the support of his or her manager, approaches the employee in question. The manager creates an environment that has appropriate boundaries, an office, a meeting room, and a safe place that is clearly a workplace environment. The manager informs the employee that she/he is operating in association with her/his manager and may even include another person to take notes of the meeting. The manager has prepared himself/herself in advance to manage personal emotions, and plans a post-meeting self-care activity. If the manager has fear, it is essential to have someone else present. Preparation is essential.

b. At least two (2) employees approach the emotional terrorist. Emotional terrorists head toward the easiest escape direction, the path of least resistance; however, with two people, the emotional terrorist has no escape route. Managers must not fear emotional terrorists, but support is required for better performance.

2. Whichever employee grabs the snake must immediately toss it into a bucket with a lid. One of the employees must then immediately secure the lid. The real trick to snake removal is the lid. Without the lid, the snake escapes and you must do it again. Spending your time catching the same snake over and over is not efficient and is not good business practice.

a. The meetings should not dally around conversations or other personal and potentially emotional data. The manager must grab the content of the meeting first and describe the issue in clear statements that are non-emotional in language. The employee will respond immediately to language of attack or blame. Accountability is the key, and the manager needs to clearly state the situation first, before there is an opportunity for the employee to squirm out of the situation by counter-attack using justification, entitlement, charisma, or tragic language. Inform the employee about policy. Describe adminis-trative position that affirms that policy. Settle into the process of repeating the information quietly and calmly if the employee attacks or defends. The employee will test the lid to see if it is held in place.

b. Whichever employee connects with the emotional terrorist must immediately define the boundaries. Managers must then immediately secure the lid of boundaries with clarity. The real trick to emotional terrorist removal is the lid. Without the lid, the emotional terrorist escapes and you must do it again. Spending your time catching the same emotional terrorist over and over is not efficient and is not good business practice.

3. Once you contain the snake, you must take it into the school, let the children see that it is not hurt, because children have imagina-tions and like to see even crawly things cared for correctly.

a. One technique that is very powerful after such a meeting is to walk quietly back to the employee's workstation with the employee. Carry your posture straight, place a pleasant expression on your face, and escort the employee back to his or her cubicle while quietly discussing non-emotional content, such as a new contract in the future, a company picnic, the state of the technology advances in the company. Stay neutral. If that is not possible, stay quietly pleasant. Always leave your door open after such a meeting to let other employees feel as though you are not hiding, fearful, or did something that you feel ashamed about. It is a powerful option to walk quietly about the worksite and do some small task that shows other employees that you are calm, to model calmness for them. If the difficult employee acts out at this time, the other employees will be able to observe that behavior and remain more neutral themselves. After you leave the area, people will try to discover what happened. They will have to make their own assessment of the situation, but you will continue to model your openness to inclusion. If the difficult employee continues to act out, it will eventually become apparent that you are not the source.

b. Once you contain the emotional terrorist, you must allow it to stay in the company so that the other employees can see that it is not hurt. Distressed employees have imaginations and like to see even an emotional terrorist cared for correctly.

4. Later, transport the snake elsewhere, off the premises, a long way away from where you work, and dispose of it.

a. If the problem has not been solved you may need to call the employee back into your office and reiterate the policy and to encourage the employee that this is a time for him or her to show personal commitment to the policy by not stirring up the emotions of other employees, because that would be a considerable distraction to the workplace. You may assign the employee some EAP intervention, set the employee up for a personal training, or give the employee a small amount of time away from the job site to reconsider his or her behavior choices. Such time away could be an extra hour for lunch, a ten-minute break, a day off with or without pay, a probation period, or temporary suspension. If the choice is suspension you will have to communicate clearly to the rest of the staff how to support the employee. One of the biggest mistakes a manager can make at this point is to get defensive or secretive.

b. Later, manage the relocation of the emotional terrorist elsewhere, off the premises, a long way away from where you work, and establish closure.

5. If the snake is toxic, call in a professional.

a. If the employee is not able to manage the emotional boundaries of your company, a number of low-level interventions are available prior to termination. EAP providers, trainings, remediation, second chances, workshops, college classes, consultations, and external counseling can be offered or provided. If none of these helps, then termination may be more cost-effective and emotionally effective for the individual and the whole organization.

b. If the emotional terrorist creates a toxic environment, call in a consultant with experience in emotional continuity in the workplace.

Whenever I begin talking about "snakes," or "toxic employees," much less the very charged term "emotional terrorist," nice people get twitchy. People who do not want to move out of their comfort zone suggest I'm overly dramatic. Those who have never confronted emotional terrorism question my motives. Others who have witnessed, been hurt, or challenged by an emotional terrorist thank me. They whisper their story about someone who has caused untold grief to themselves or others.

Whenever I begin talking about emotional terrorism, the emotional terrorists themselves get twitchy. They want to know what I know. They usually heckle me and try to discredit me for a while. I find it amusing. The only thing they truly fear is recognition and exposure.

I have seen too many harsh consequences of emotional terrorism not to be a siren. It was never the role I wanted in life, but I don't mind. I have met enough emotional terrorists in my work to want to help the good guys. And I have met enough good guys who are ready to set up early warning systems at their worksites rather than being taken by surprise ever again.

5.5.3 Tips For Dealing With Bullies And Emotional Terrorists

Don't second-guess yourself. If you look at the attributes of an emotional terrorist, you will know if you are dealing with one or not. If you have become aware that you are dealing with an emotional terrorist, you may need to take a breath and decide if you want to stay in the job or move out of the company. If you decide to keep your job, you may need to keep your own council about what you know. This is the marathon of dealing with a bully at work. All you can do is do the best you can. Find support outside the job site. Take good care of yourself. If you don't feel safe, get help immediately.

- Trust your intuition; don't worry if no one else is noticing.

- Don't: depend on feedback from staff. Trust your intuition.

- Watch, wait, and listen. Things might change.

- Easy does it; time will reveal more.

- Don't take the bully behaviors personally. Try to not be a target.

- Be confident and also seek support.

- Document everything you see, think, and feel.

- Don't confront a bully. Sometimes it is more important to survival to just walk away as if nothing was going on. Think of it like not looking a wild animal directly in the eye. That just tends to make them more dangerous. Go neutral and make an exit to get away from the risk.

- If you think something is going on, you might be right – so stay alert.

- Rest when you are able and practice good self-care for surviving the long haul.

- Re-decide if you want to stay in this job and if so, regroup your energies and resources.

- Do not try to "fix" or save an emotional terrorist unless you are a professional. You can wish them well, pray for them, work with them, go to their birthday luncheon, and look at photos of their dog... in other words, you can be courteous and pleasant when opportunity allows – but do not let your guard down, because these specific individuals are predators.

- Continue with other projects and stay awake. Have your life.

Remember: An emotional terrorist isn't like you. They have a very different agenda than you do. And trust me, they are not interested in your well-being!

You will also encounter times that you will have to be in direct contact with a known emotional terrorist in your office. Stay alert and take good care of you!

5.5.4 Conducting a Meeting Or Interview With a Bully Or an Emotional Terrorist

Although a certain amount of interaction with emotional terrorists has a hidden or covert nature, you will also encounter times that you will have to be in direct contact with a known emotional terrorist in your office. Stay alert and take good care of you! If you have determined that an employee is an emotional terrorist, you can proceed to manage him or her by paying attention to a few careful steps to avoid falling into his or her control:

- Set up a meeting with nonnegotiable times in your power place.
- Stay neutral.
- Be clear and firm; do not let the emotional terrorist call the shots.
- Have a witness, or note-taker present.
- Demand clear boundaries. If the employee is more than five minutes late for any reason, courteously cancel that meeting and reschedule a new one at your convenience.
- If the employee has an emotional reaction to your boundary, stay firm and courteous, and make a notation of their reaction if it is verbal or nonverbal.
- Be courteous and business-like throughout the meeting.
- Make certain the environment is businesslike, and seating is hierarchical.
- No food or snacks; this is not "friendly," this is business.
- Begin with the issues at hand.
- Do not allow discussion until you are done with the meeting agenda.
- Listen and take notes, but do not engage in a discussion.
- Remain neutral. Make notes on your emotions and deal with them at a later time and well removed from the emotional terrorist.
- Avoid questions. Approach all questions as if they were hand-grenades with the pins already removed.
- Do not defend, attack, or make personal comments.
- Do not share your personal opinions.
- Do not praise or support.
- Keep it neutral and business only.

If the tension rises, or the meeting becomes emotional, or the emotional terrorist gains any ground, take a five-minute break, and start over or cancel the meeting and reschedule on your terms.

Close the meeting with a "thank you" by standing up and formally eliminating any opportunity to continue with emotionally loaded comments. If there are lingering statements, comments, attacks, defenses, or trailing comments, repeat the thank you as a punctuation mark at the end of a sentence. Repeat as often as needed to close the meeting courteously. If absolutely necessary, repeat the words "thank you" in a neutral tone as you are opening the office door and indicating that it is over, and time to leave.

> You get to decide where you invest your energy
> in life... You are not married to your job
> – you are just dating it.

5.6 Become an Excellent Manager in a World of Challenges

Commit to Excellence: The Ultimate Tool

You get to decide where you invest your energy in life. I encourage people to take time to decide, and even redecide, on a regular basis, asking: Do I want to do this? Do I want to commit to a path of excellence, even in the face of a bully? Think for yourself: Is this my path? If the answer is "Yes," decide to go for it. Be better than even you think you can be. And give it time. *You are not married to your job – you are just dating it.* If the effort required is too much, move on. If you decide you need to stay, then do it with all the tools you can get.

The first step is to really decide. To master anything takes time, energy, devotion, mentorship, practice, drills, and errors. If you were going to take up a new musical instrument, you would not be playing in a symphony the first year. Even prodigy musicians need experience and training. You may need to settle into the time it takes to learn, expect to make errors, and learn from those errors. Then you must decide if you want to become a master. Just an accumulation of years doing something does not create a master. The idea of "practice makes perfect" is not true unless the practicing is correct. Doing something wrong over time does not automatically turn into good just because time has passed. Masters of anything are very comfortable in their roles of life-long student. True experts want to learn more. Excellence is a journey and process, not a destination.

Steps to Excellence

Let's say you want to be an excellent manager. You are determined to be an excellent manager, unscathed and effective in the face of whatever comes at you in the way of bullies, emotional terrorists, stress, unexpected chaos. For you to be that kind of manager, what would the process look like?

1. **Decide:** What do you really want?

2. **Prepare yourself:** Before lifesavers jump into shark infested waters, they check their gear carefully.

3. **Establish your own support system:** Create your own buddy-system or external cheerleaders.

4. **Prepare your system:** Confirm buy-in that you will not be alone and will be well supported by your administration as well as your support people.

5. **Go for it:** Jump in and give it your best. Pay attention to successes and errors.

6. **Design your style and program:** Look at all the options you know and create a process, style, and program that fit you and your company.

7. **Retreat and recreation:** Treat yourself to a celebration, because there is a good chance no one else will know how hard you have been working!

8. **Recommit:** Restart the process from Step 1 on a regular basis.

These steps are explained in detail in the rest of this chapter.

5.6.1 Step 1: Decide

If you decide, you are not a victim; you have made a choice. Once you have decided to manage, use the following tools to maintain your decision:

A. Avoid management insomnia

Obviously, you are looking through this text because you are awake to the emotional problems in your company. Perhaps you have always been awake and are on top of your game, or you have been suddenly jolted into alertness because of a crisis in the workplace. Perhaps you have cleverly skipped ahead to this chapter because you already know first-hand the chaos and destruction of workplace emotional spinning. Or you are deciding whether or not to purchase this book. Indeed, many books on the market make grand promises and then leave you once again alone in the middle of your chaos, as if struggling in the chaos was part of the fun of being a manager. Yes, it is your job to stay awake in the middle of everyone else's nightmare and remain vigilant to the details of the situation. Like it or not, you are a leader and facilitator and the potential icon for safety. You do not want to be the manager who adds another dimension of disaster inside a catastrophe. Staying awake is difficult when everyone around you appears to be sleepwalking. The only way a manager can survive for the long term is to develop a clear process of self-managed care and staying awake to what is actually going on.

B. Review your job title

Your job title may give you an indication about what you are supposed to accomplish. Most managers say that figuring out what is wrong with people is not their job. If that is what you are saying, you are right that probably is not your job. Your job is to pay attention, witness, evaluate, predict, and document your observations and do everything you can to keep people working and productive. You then pass that information on to your bosses or experts and refer to policies, make referrals, and create mountains of documentation.

Excellent managers are in the unique position to "see" more than anyone else in the company if they are awake. Some managers try to maintain a comatose state to avoid accountability, pass over the tough stuff to HR, blame, pass the buck, reorganize, manipulate, and generally do whatever they can to avoid actually managing. Managing is hard work, underappreciated, and overwhelming at times. It can also be fascinating and entertaining if one stays awake and learns to absorb and endure forces of human emotions. It is not a job for wimps – it is a job for warriors. That might not be in your job description, but you know it is true.

C. If everyone is out to get you, paranoia might be good thinking

The next obstacle to excellence is the point at which managers suggest that all this emotional stuff is "paranoia," saying, "If we spend time in fear, we won't accomplish anything." This may be true, yet the next question needs to be, "How much time do you spend dealing with employee emotions?" Do you think that time could be spent doing something more fiscally productive? If managers are very, very far from being competent, they state something like, "Well, nothing can happen to us; so we aren't going to spend training dollars in paranoia."

Mental health professionals will let you know that clinical paranoia is described in terms of an unnatural or out-of-proportion fear over time. For example, while it is healthy to fear bee stings, fires, and tornadoes, it suggests paranoia if you are compelled to spend all your time in the basement wearing mesh netting and holding a hose. If, on the other hand, you have lost a house in a tornado or have a severe allergy to bees, or been in a fire, a little dose of paranoia is just good thinking and quite reasonable. Paying attention to emotions and extreme emotions is not overreacting. Spending no time on preparation is a dangerous overreaction. Minimization can be more dangerous than paranoia. Balance is the key: Reason and Balance. *Most industries have fire extinguishers, evacuation plans, and other safety processes. This is just one more.*

Managers say "I don't want to think about people in bad ways. I want to keep good thoughts about people." A good thought is a good thing. However, professional development and maturity demands that you come to understand that not everyone is a saint. There is a difference between judging a person as "bad" and making a good discernment, or a good business observation. Managers can remain professionally neutral, personally positive, and observe and document emotional behavior that is less than conducive to productivity within that particular marketplace.

It is necessary for a manager to discern whether someone's emotional behavior is positive and productive or negative and nonproductive. When it is negative, then you must determine if the behavior is due to ignorance, chronic problems, temporary circumstances, or malevolence. Such a determination leads to decisions about remediation, recovery, referral, or removal of an employee.

5.6.2 Step 2: Prepare Yourself

A. Olympic athletes go for the gold

Endurance for the long run takes preparation and maintenance. Imagine that you are a world-class athlete getting ready for Olympic competition. You do not just run onto the field. You do a lot of work prior to the big show. Your preparations should include physical, emotional, spiritual, and mental self-care procedures designed by you, for you. You need to warm up, suit up, and show up. And if it makes you feel more confident to have a rabbit's foot in your pocket, then do so! This is your game, and you are going to have to provide yourself with the stamina and spirit to run a marathon, not a sprint.

B. Remain neutral

The manager must remain neutral, or the manager's emotions will add spin to the problem. Learning to act from a neutral position is a very powerful way to manage. The mechanisms of neutrality are based on the capacity to know your own biases, feelings, opinions, and positions, and then putting them aside temporarily in order to act as a mediator. A mediator does not engage in the problem or the solution. A neutral mediator acts as a facilitator of communication flow. In other words, the manager must understand the flow of the energy and not get in the way of progress by diverting it toward a personal agenda.

When a military advisor was asked what advice he would pass on to managers, he responded: "We had managers that turned out to cause more trouble than they solved and had to be let go. These managers did affect morale and productivity. My advice to managers is that I've discovered that people need an outlet for their emotions. If you have to talk to an employee who has been causing problems, approach it non-emotionally. Stay neutral, keep it professional and do not get emotional when they do. Sometimes just letting them talk with someone gets it out and gone."

C. Determine if you have a problem or an issue

Managers must first assess if the concern on the table is a quick-fix problem or a long-term issue. The tools for one situation will be quite different from the tools necessary to approach another situation.

Management challenges come in two forms: problems and issues.

Problems: Acute, short-lived, addressable, fixable, solvable, tribulations and challenges.

> Examples: A flat tire, the sudden unexpected exit of an employee.

Issues: Chronic, long-term, addressable, less solvable, sometimes impossible-to-fix concerns and challenges.

> Examples: The poverty associated with having a bad car with bad tires and no spare, the long-term systemic disenfranchisement because messages from administration are contradictory and duplicitous in an industry that has a history of layoffs.

D. Consider the dimensions of your situation

Are you facing a dust devil or an F-5? Is it just starting or is it long-standing? Big or little? Limited to one department, or systemic? Managers must take into consideration the full potential range of losses and gains of any business change, whether minor or major. They must also be on the lookout for exploitation and opportunists who will use the loss part of a change as a venue for escalating conflict and risk. An effective manager looks at potential losses and gains that may be incurred on any level of emotional, mental, physical, and even spiritual realms. Change will have effect. No two people perceive a change in the same way. What is minor to one person may trigger overwhelming emotional spinning in another person.

E. Before you ever begin, step away from the spinning

Managers must factor in considerations from the micro to the macro, and then move carefully, quietly, and thoughtfully onto an observation deck, remain professionally neutral, and look around to see what is going on everywhere with everyone. Everywhere! With everyone! This is the key to a good emotional continuity management intervention. The manager often is overwhelmed with the specific nature of the challenge and does not step back to view the entire big picture. Such limited vision is often how a major spin is enhanced as the manager engages in the problem and adds to the mix. Thank everyone for their input, make notes, document, discuss, and determine – then leave the area and be alone for a while. Go out for a coffee. Take a lunch break. Sleep on it! If it is not life-threatening, it can usually wait until you are calm, centered, and ready to make a good management decision. Sometimes a physical break of five minutes can assist you in seeing the big picture so you do not contribute to the chaos.

F. Do your own emotional homework

Managers are often in the middle of the chaos – that is your job. If you do not love that feeling, then you may not be management material. You might be a fabulous administrator or worker-bee instead. Decide if you want to be in the middle. Does it stir up your own problems and issues? Step back and evaluate the situation while also reviewing your position in the mix. How are you doing? How are you managing your own emotions? What do you think your capacity is for grief, anger, fear, and other big feelings? All feelings are natural. Managers must be better at knowing their own feelings than others must be. You do not have to control your feelings; you just need to know them so you can manage them well.

G. Don't fear conflict; use it

Conflict is not meant to be avoided, it is meant to be useful. When tension rises, it can lead to conflict. Conflict is normal. Conflict is not necessarily a problem or an issue. Conflict can lead to war, or it can lead to creativity and invention. Gary Simmons (2001) describes his method of finding peaceful solutions to conflict, and the forces that lead to a conflict storm of "competing needs, wants, and values, combined with misperception, defensiveness, and the need to be right, that create an energetic field of influence that is that storm inherent in interpersonal conflict."

Whatever analogy you use, conflict is the presence of energy that bombards or bumps into other energy. This bumping creates friction. Friction makes heat. Thus, managers feel as though they are always taking the heat from the higher-ups and putting out fires of the line workers. This is because they are taking the heat. However, the energy, in its original state, is neutral and potentially useful. The task is to take the heat or energy and either use it for creative solutions, or return it to a neutral state so it can self-extinguish. A successful conflict resolution does not eliminate the energy but reforms or neutralizes the reactive energy.

> Managers define conflict zones as their biggest
> challenge. However, this is context in which
> everything important is happening.

Management turns conflict energy positive or negative. A conflict is usually about something perceived as sacred that has been threatened. This situation is someone's holy ground. Holy ground is where human beings can become their best selves or their worst selves. It is in conflict that you find out who you are and exactly with whom you are dealing. Conflict is a perfect means to find out what is important. Think of conflict as an excellent location for a potentially important discovery. Conflict provides a mirror so you can see where you are. Do you like how you respond to conflict? Look at your own self to see if you are missing a skill of communication. It is easy to point at the other person. Warriors and excellent managers use conflict for self-discovery.

Managers define conflict zones as their biggest challenge. However, this is context in which everything important is happening. The simple trick to using conflict well is to first see it as a holy spot where something good can be born. That may never happen, but it is where you begin. How you approach conflict is dependent on your opinion about conflict. If you fear it, or have had bad, violent, or terrifying experiences with conflict, do your own homework first, then move into the energy zone. A conflict does not necessarily mean a war.

When conflicting energies start spinning around, they create a sort of chaos. Chaos is the stuff of life, but you need to move slowly at this point, so you do not fall into the chaos energy. Step back, observe, check your emotional homework and then grab the skills that turn chaos into creativity. This is where a manager can shine like a beacon or go into the shadows. Managers can panic and run, join in the fight, or stand their ground neutrally and make something amazing happen.

After you have done your preparation, move forward with caution. Follow the company policy line-by-line to protect yourself and your workplace.

Observe the situation at the location of conflict to see the bigger picture. Step back again if you need to take more time. Always serve the whole system. Do not try to control or block the conflict. Do not get in its way. It will have a life of its own. Take a bit more time to evaluate it within the big scope of the larger mission, and see if can be used for creative value or if it is headed to create a negative effect. Use your tools, and do what you can to establish the conflict as an added value. If it grows out of control, then use the bigger tools. The traditional view is that conflict means bigger weapons. Weapons do not quiet conflicts; they escalate them. Tools are useful. Weapons of mass destruction can certainly appear to end a conflict, as the conflict burns underground until the next incident.

> **You need to be balanced when standing
> in the presence of change.**

5.6.3 Step 3: Establish Your Own Support System

A. Support yourself

Start your support system by learning how to take excellent care of yourself. This means an entire personal program and toolkit of caretaking that will support you from within.

You are a whole person! In an ideal world with ideal people, the whole person should have a repertoire and set of recipes for creating a wonderful life – at home and at work. Everyone else on the rest of the planet must strive for such balance on a daily basis. Healthy people have a plan and a process to care for their physical, emotional, mental, and spiritual well-being. This book would be remiss if it avoided the whole person in favor of one of these four foundations of well-being.

Take ample time to review your foundations for health as you define them. Favoring one of the four cornerstones while ignoring the others leads to operating in an unbalanced state. Doing a daily practice, discipline, or treatment of some kind in each category will keep you balanced no matter what comes your way. You need to be balanced when standing in the presence of change. Balance does not mean fixed; it can mean staying in one position for a long time, or it can mean being alert and ready to spring into action. All athletes have ways to strengthen their balance because they know how important it is to motion. Are your foundations balanced, or do you put all your energies into one category at the expense of the other three?

Physical: Exercise, diet, grooming and hygiene, movement, temperature, senses (vision, taste, touch, hearing, smell), observing art, dancing, wearing different colors and textures, hugs or handshakes, good hand washing, breathing deeply in the morning air, music, trying different foods, a day of silence.

Spiritual: Explore the relationship you have with whatever or whomever it is you think is in charge of the universe. Make that relationship a priority. Find a spiritual or religious practice that is yours.

Mental: Challenge yourself in areas of non-expertise. In other words, if you read all the time, take a break. If you never read, pick up a book. If you read nonfiction, take a break with a cheesy novel, and if all you ever read is cheese, pick up a biography. It's okay if you take four years to read a book. It is the willingness that is important. Go to an opera, or stay at home and play a board game. Do crossword puzzles, or start a nonprofit organization and build a board of directors. Do more, or do less, but do it awake.

Emotional: Your feelings matter mostly to you, but they do matter. You are human because you have discernment and feel differently about different things. At the end of life, people generally don't regret having had a full life with emotions. If they regret, it is that they missed feeling something because they were not paying attention in the moment. Therapeutic writing for stress management is an easy skill to learn to self-manage your emotions at work. It isn't about journal writing or creating narratives for posterity. Therapeutic writing can be done by doodling in the margins of your notebook during an important meeting, writing poetry on a napkin at lunch, writing your grocery list, or a number of other non-writers' tricks.

B. Exit strategy

Confucius is said to have taught that "when you enter, choose your exit." A good support process is to think how you will exit if things get too much for you to manage. You do not want to linger in negativity and fear, but it is foolish to not at least make a quick check of how you might get out of a situation if it goes nasty. Most continuity plans for disaster include looking for the nearest exit, and then getting on with your work.

Some decisions appear to be a good idea at the time and under certain circumstances. Then, things change and a decision may appear to have been an error. This is the nature of human experience. It should be expected. What you did not know at the time may change your opinion. This is when it may be useful to implement the Dr. Vali's "It-Seemed-Like-a-Good-Idea-at-the-Time" plan.

Change happens, and perhaps your decision to work for this company seemed-like-a-good-idea-at-the-time. People are often more likely to end a marriage than a job! Where we might dump a distressful marriage in a flash, we cling to our wretched-battering-lowlife-drunken-betraying jobs for better or worse, sickness and health, until someone's death us do part. We stay at horrible jobs stuck with awful human beings who no one in their right mind would marry! Loyalty can be a good thing. Misplaced loyalty can be insane. In our current state of economic affairs, it can be easier to divorce a mate than divorce a difficult work colleague.

> **It may take many jobs inside your career of choice to find the situation where you would be inspired to make a lifetime commitment. Or it may take a change of career.**

Date your job; don't marry it. Do not allow yourself to stay in a work situation that may be more difficult or demeaning than a bad marriage. Most people won't keep a pair of jeans if they do not fit. So, keep the receipt with any job you take on. You can change your mind. You can use the "It-Seemed-Like-a-Good-Idea-at-the-Time" exit plan, and move on. Use this job as a lesson for personal growth, and then go find a job that suits you better. It may take many jobs to discover your true self. It may take many jobs inside your career of choice to find the situation where you would be inspired to make a lifetime commitment. Or it may take a change of career. Unfortunately, in the current economy, some "bad marriages" of work and career are worth maintaining. Abusive relationships in marriage or work are never a good idea for long duration, but in a difficult financial climate it may be worthwhile to not just "jump-ship" before seeking out support and other options, such as using an EAP, finding a counselor or supportive friend, and researching a next position.

Sit in a theater and before you stuff that first handful of popcorn into your mouth, look around for the exit signs. If there is an emergency, you may have saved your life. It does not mean you are leaving before the film is shown. Do the same thing in your job. Before you commit your life savings, buy a house to be close to your new job, or marry the boss' only child, look around and see if there is a healthy way out if you change your mind. It does not mean you are disloyal and it does not mean you are setting up escape. It means this is a job and not a marriage, and the world economy or your company might divorce you suddenly without notice. What would you do? Where would you go? Who are your people? How would you survive? Make a quick note of your plan, stuff it into a favorite hiding place at home, and hope you never need to read it again.

C. Create your own emotional continuity support posse

Visualize yourself giving your speech at the Oscar Awards. You have won the award and now you stand before millions of people thanking the people who helped you get there. Being a success never means doing it alone. Pick your caregivers, cheerleaders, friends, mentors, pals, coaches, sponsors, nurturers, venting locations, buddies, sisters, brothers, and unconditional fan clubs carefully. You will need more than one place to garner support if you are going to be a master of management. Use nonhuman supports also such as journal writing, yoga, 12-Step programs, religious affiliations, exercise, good nutrition, clear water, fresh air, flowers, literature, music, and pets to nurture and care for yourself as you go out into the world of emotional management.

D. Support your supporters

Managers are mothers, fathers, wives, husbands, and relatives to people who will support you and who will need your support from time to time. Use what you learn to pass on to your people so your circle of support strengthens. Children and spouses who are confronted with emotional terrorists at school and other workplaces need tools. Suggest emotional continuity management training for kids to your children's teachers, and encourage your spouse to create a workplace trauma-toolkit with his or her coworkers. Someone in your family may be dealing with aging parents, angry teenagers, ex-spouses, step-parenting, or other potential emotional spin risks, and you can provide them with tools and training opportunities by advocating they take good care of themselves also. This will support them and you because you will have done something proactive for the people you love, and you will worry a bit less about what is going on with your loved ones when you are trying to wrangle a conflict resolution with five employees who are on an emotional spin.

> What is your theory of management? Can you share that with your boss? Does it justify or support your management choices?

5.6.4 Step 4: Prepare the System

To convince someone that you know what you are doing can be a task in itself. To convince your boss, supervisor, CEO, or manager that you know what you are doing will mean the difference between success and non-success of your hard work. Most professionals stand on some theoretical foundation that they have come to believe in. Psychology, medicine, art, and all fields of endeavor have previous masters who have organized systems of thought, called theories, that they believe define the parameters of the field at its highest order. What is your theory of management? Can you share that with your boss? Does it justify or support your management choices? Is it predicated on excellence or mediocrity?

A. Pick a theory

Management texts are replete with management theories. Research management theories until you find the one you like and practice it until it becomes yours.

B. Consider the diagnosis

Before a good intervention can happen, a good diagnosis must happen. Today's manager must be an emotional continuity diagnostician. Managerial training may provide a basic understanding of human behavior in the guise of keeping up motivation, or healthy workplaces, or the difficult employee. Managers in other times in history were never intended to do the work that HR or EAPs were meant to do. Today's marketplace, with the variances of business continuity and disaster planning, demands that the manager move into a deeper understanding of human dynamics under stress.

C. Honor your own hunches

Managers must make some wise hunches about employees, even if it is not appropriate to "diagnose them" from a mental health clinical perspective. Just as you might have a hunch about your car needing a new intake valve, you would take it to a professional for appropriate care. Every good intervention starts with a hunch, or theory. You can go to your medical doctor with signs and symptoms and say, "I think it might be my sinuses." The doctor will check it out and confirm or deny a diagnosis before treatment. You can start with a hunch. If you call in a mental health professional as a resource, most credible consultants will appreciate your hunches.

D. Listen to witnesses

Most people do not want to witness problems. Intentional emotional spinners do not want witnesses. Therefore, silence works well for emotional spinners until a company becomes engaged in a full-force blowout. Spinners are often quite efficient at hiding and distorting reality so that when their behaviors or intentions are eventually witnessed, they scramble to rearrange the perception of the viewer. If they can discredit the witness, their position is strengthened. It is easier for the regular witness to accept a creative cover story and move back to the comfort of denial than to deal with the ramifications of what they may have seen. The wonderful human brain helps with this. Like an extra eyelid on a camel that protects it from the harsh terrorism of blowing winds, our sweet, protective brains help us blink away icky emotional tornadoes.

Emotional spinners count on this. Emotional continuity management works to keep everyone awake, eyes open, with potential witnesses valued, not scorned. If no one has permission to spin, early signs can be addressed with compassion and humor. If no one has permission to see, the blind will no doubt lead the blind right into a tornado.

Other observers:

Learning to really "hear" what other people are telling you is a critical part of the job of being a manager. Other people will "witness" their own experience and you may need to depend on second-hand information to help make an assessment. Be thoughtful.

Types of witnesses:

- **Accidental:** Someone unintentionally observes something out of context, inappropriate, dangerous, or incongruent because he or she just happens to be in the right place at the wrong time or the wrong place at the right time.

- **Good radar:** Some people are gifted with a sense of clear moral index and natural boundaries which make them able to almost smell trouble or incongruities brewing and not doubt their own perceptions and perspectives.

- **Attuned sensitivities:** Some people have well-developed, natural intuition and sensory acuity and feel safe using it. They respond to it as easily as other use a sense of sight, hearing, smell, and touch.

- **Resolving trauma survivors:** Out of necessity, these people have developed or adapted accurate radar for early warning and detection of trouble. They have experienced or witnessed severe critical incidents and observed the outcomes of such events. They know that such difficulties are real and that early warnings might have served them in the past; so they are vigilant. They are great assets to a corporation when given room and support to verbalize what they have witnessed. Sometimes they can come across as complainers, bitter, or arrogant with an "I-know-what-can-happen-and-everyone-who-doesn't-is-an-idiot" style. Sometimes, they are viewed as complainers, but with good support, they are helpful. They terrify emotional terrorists, who often discredit them as "crazy."

▶ **Unresolved trauma survivors:** Quiet, fearful, high-denial, blame themselves, may try to speak up, but may change their story to protect themselves or others. May give good early warnings, but will not be available to back up the claims or observations under pressure. May start strong and then fade to self-protect from imagined or remembered abuse or trauma. Their information is useful to an observant manager.

▶ **Co-dependents:** They have an active radar system based on their childhood survival mechanisms, and they also may have an overactive translator system. They can see an eyebrow twitch from across the room, but they may mistranslate what it means. The asset is in their acute observational skills. The liability is in their translation of it and their fear mechanisms that suggests to them that it is up to them to control the situation. They may try to fill in the gap with their own translation of what their observation means. Sometimes an eyebrow twitch is just an eyebrow twitch, and sometimes it means more. An alert manager will note the witness report of the eyebrow twitch and keep alert.

▶ **Intentional spinner witnessing:** An intentional spinner or an emotional terrorist may point in a direction to distract attention or increase energy into the playing field. They may even point out their participation in the problem to make it seem as though they are self-effacing allies, actively participating in finding a solution to the problem. Such participation enables them to slip around for an "end run" and start a spin elsewhere. They now demand that all pressure on them be removed. "It's over now, because I pointed it out," and "Consequences don't matter because we are all one big happy family, aren't we?" They press for instant "forgiveness" and want to just move on quickly. Any lingering at this point often leads them to create yet another event to re-distract attention.

> **Whistle-blowing has given witnessing a bad name. People now fear speaking up.**

Respecting healthy witnessing takes some practice. Although witnessing is a risk, not seeing is a greater risk. And if everyone is on board, everyone can co-witness, which lowers the individual pressure. Any witness who is not respected for his or her risk to witness may experience a variety of negative feelings, which can set that person up to add to a spin. Whistle-blowing has given witnessing a bad name.

People now fear speaking up. Instead of feeling honored and appreciated, a witness may end up:

▶ Feeling like a troublemaker.

▶ Feeling like he or she did as a child who saw his or her father get silently drunk while the mother cried in the bedroom.

▶ Feeling like he or she did as a molested 5-year-old.

▶ Feeling like he or she did as a battered spouse.

▶ Feeling like a fool.

▶ Feeling like his or her perceptions of reality are valueless and wrong.

▶ Feeling stupid.

▶ Feeling denied.

▶ Feeling anger.

▶ Feeling depression.

▶ Feeling obsolete.

▶ Feeling crazy.

▶ Feeling useless.

▶ Feeling frightened.

▶ Feeling held hostage.

▶ Feeling there is nowhere else to go with this and return to work feeling defeated and confused and ready to abandon loyalty to the firm.

Do this: Explore the critical value of witnessing with a mental health counselor or an emotional continuity management consultant.

Don't: Discredit a witness. Listen first. Evaluate later. It is not a good feeling to realize too late, after the fact that someone "warned you" about something you didn't see.

The Effective Management of Witnessing

1. Listen to the observations without judging, commenting, agreeing or disagreeing. Stay neutral.

2. Make a note of the concerns for possible future reference.

3. Say something like "Thank you, I appreciate your report and I will make a note of this information and keep my eyes open."

4. Repeat #3 if necessary to support the witness.

If the reporter is not satisfied with this, and demands that the manager engage, it may be an Emotional Terrorist Witnessing. Most witnesses simply want to unload the report, be acknowledged, and move on. Some witnesses need more support and gratitude, but they usually do not need engagement.

A manager does not need to join, agree, investigate, act, react, deny, dance, sing, or create any sort of chaos to "take a witnessing under advisement." Usually, one witnessing event does not make a case unless it is criminal or life-threatening. However, a manager cannot have two witnessings if he or she blows off the first one, leaving the second witness standing alone. That is, unless the manager is an emotional terrorist.

E. Make a management toolkit

Minimum requirements of a management toolkit:

- Conflict resolution methods.
- Communication methodologies.
- Systems education.
- Diversity training and cultural norms of emotions.
- Icons, slogans, and banners for quick recognition.
- Team-building strategies.
- Grief work – education and practice.
- Control and management strategies.
- Personal values tools.
- Humor.
- Emotional terrorism information.
- Tools for new employee orientation.
- Normal and abnormal psychology basics.
- How to recognize signs of traumatic stress.
- Emotional self-defense.
- Cultural and social hierarchy norms.
- Ventilation models for debriefing and defusing.
- Adjustment strategies and practices.
- Stress management tools for the life span.
- Physical, mental, emotional and spiritual health practices.

❱ Resistance and creativity training.

❱ Documentation standards for emotions.

❱ Memos of understanding with external vendors.

❱ Bibliographies.

❱ Corporate models for emotional continuity management.

❱ Other resources.

❱ Emotional tools that generalize across occupations.

❱ A full range of tools to manage the entire range of human emotions.

❱ Emotional quick-fix first aid ideas with pre-arranged referrals for more serious emotional requirements.

❱ Tools that generalize to small and large organizations without significant adjustments.

❱ Tools that are not based in fads or trends.

❱ Tools that are sensitive to gender, culture, socio-economic status, education, race, and ethnicity.

❱ Tools that are designed that are cross-cultural.

❱ Tools that will work equally well for the diverse needs of executive, management, and line staff. Other tools may be needed for volunteers, vendors, clients, and others but should remain in step with all other tools.

❱ Tools that are simple, understandable, and practical will be effective for use inside and outside the work setting.

> **Do not let the fears of other people get in the way of believing in yourself. Even if you do not believe in you, do not let others convince you that your lack of belief is right.**

5.6.5 Step 5: Go For It

Set your eyes on your goal, suit up, pull yourself up straight, rub your lucky rabbit's foot, take a breath and jump in to the midst of the fun. Do not be upset by initial stirs of fears and worries; this is just energy moving. As you accommodate to the energy in motion from a position of personal strength, do not take chaos personally. Begin your work and manage with personal persistence striving for excellence. Start your day with a "bring it on" attitude. Reframe your vision to that of yourself as a management warrior seeking excellence.

A. Learn How to Persist

1. *Listen only to people who give you YES messages.*

Do not let the fears of other people get in the way of believing in yourself. Even if you do not believe in you, do not let others convince you that your lack of belief is right. If you want to be an astronaut, give it a shot. If you do not reach the stars, that's okay. But in the process, you might just find that you like working with the nifty computers at Houston Control. Or you might become an armchair astronomer. If you want to be an excellent manager, use the yes's as doorways to success. Even a no can be said with an attached yes of spirit.

2. *Pick a goal, any goal, and do one small thing toward it every day.*

Some days are harder than others. Once you have picked a goal, do something toward it every day. Even if today you can muster only the strength to sharpen your pencils, say aloud, "Sharpening this pencil is helping me reach my goal of _____." One 70-year-old author was asked how long it took him to write his novel. He said, "Seventy years." It was made into a movie after his 73rd birthday. He was in the film. If you want to be a great and beloved manager, pick a small goal to work on each day.

3. *Suit up and show up.*

Begin to see everything as directed toward your goal. If you are watching TV, watch for programs about your goal. If you are going for a walk, consider how walking will make you stronger for your outcome. If you are eating, eat to get healthy for your goal. If you are reading a cheesy novel, use it to learn to read faster. If you are poor and alone, celebrate your freedom – because when you are successful, you will be busy and up to your chin in people who want to be with you.

4. *Take time to notice the butterfly outside the window.*

As you become more involved and engaged with your visions and goals, make certain that you continue to do reality checking with nature. Spend at least five minutes each day (more if you can) looking out the window, counting snowflakes, picking flowers, sitting on the porch in the sunshine, walking barefoot, hugging trees, or weeping over sunsets. At work, this moment with nature can look like a quick breath of fresh air between meetings, a quiet lunch outdoors, a quick peek at the trees outside your window, or drinking a glass of water very slowly and enjoying the sweetness of the liquid going down your throat and saying to yourself, "Thank you, water."

5. *Don't join those who complain about the process.*

In worksites, employees can quickly establish themselves into two separate groups. One group will be made up of workers who complain about everything (and there is always ample material to complain about at work) and those who do not have time or will not take time to complain. Guess which group is more successful over time? Plenty of time is available to complain after tasks are completed. A good manager will allow time for an occasional group complaint-fest – often best handled over pizza.

6. *Make at least two new friends*

Make one friend who is just a bit less motivated and one who is just a bit more motivated than you are. Pick peers, not staff friends. Choose management peers from a different company or industry if you can. Join a management organization to meet people. Let these two different friends balance your pace. As you interact with the less motivated friend, use a little of your energy to push him or her and yourself. As you interact with the more motivated person, use a little of that person's energy to push yourself. Do not try to overcome the more motivated person or to rescue the less motivated person. Just notice your pace, and use it to keep your energy flowing. Enjoy his or her success, energy, and persistence, and use it to create sources and boundaries for your own forward momentum.

Another gift to yourself is to maintain old friendships with supportive people who may not be "on your train" but will act as witnesses to your growth and celebrate with you. These are the people who love to cheer for the mountain climbers but who themselves would rather wait at base-camp. Ask climbers to join you and ask the base-camp folks to fix a cup of cocoa for you when you return with your grand stories. Both kinds of people are treasures to keep and to protect forever.

7. *Pick an appropriate time to relax with peers. Become devoted to it.*

Every Friday afternoon, your staff could meet at a local café to talk, complain, laugh, and regroup. The ritualized connection can be open to anyone who shows, one or all, and can be used to debrief the week so people do not have to take it home. Recreation is absolutely necessary to keep up a consistent level of persistence, create balance, provide fun stories, encourage light moments, provide places to exchange helpful tips, and eliminate isolation. Isolation is very dangerous when you are striving for a goal because in isolation you can lose perspective about why you began this journey in the first place.

8. *Take care of your soulful self.*

Although it is very important to care for your physical and emotional well-being while working for a goal, it is critical to care for the part of you that goes "beyond the self." Write poetry on napkins, pray, meditate, walk on the pier, compose a symphony, go back to church or synagogue, sing, smile at old people at bus stops, sew a quilt for charity, run a marathon, buy an antique, swim, watch old movies, give blood to the Red Cross, write love letters, make cookies on a rainy Sunday, wait patiently for someone, help a friend move, wash your car, paint your living room, make curtains, walk on the beach, be a birth coach, sit by a dying friend, buy a cat, take your dogs to the park, climb a tree, and do whatever it takes to balance the unilateral selfish energy it takes to push toward your goal by offering service to others.

9. *Re-invent yourself as often as needed.*

Take time to find out who you are and who you want to be in 5 years, 10 years, and 20 years. Find a mentor in someone who has succeeded in your goal; ask him or her for advice. Find someone older who will say, "Just do it now, dear, because when you are my age, you will wish you had."

10. *Learn to jump hoops, even little tiny ones or ones with big flames.*

Being a student, or a learner of any kind, means there are people who are the knowers, and they have the power for now. It's okay because someday, you will have the power when you are the master. If you are really a master, you will not forget the days you were a powerless nincompoop, and you will be more mentor than tyrant. Surrendering gets either easier or more difficult as you age. Surrender can feel like freedom or death. But until you really are the "one who knows all things in your given area of expertise," you can still learn. And even the knower must learn how to be a wonderful knower. The surrender of jumping hoops can feel bad or creative. Hoop jumping is usually a temporary event. The hoop is not the entire truth of the universe; it is only a hoop. Don't make it more than it is or less than it is.

Masters are not necessarily any brighter or more intelligent than anyone else is, but they are more persistent than most and willing to jump through pointed flaming hoops to reach their goals and dreams. There is a story about Albert Einstein, who was trying to fix a crooked paper clip. As he searched for a tool to fix it, he found an entire box of paperclips. Even though he did not need to, he completed repairing the bent clip. He was persistent in completing his task. When asked about this, he explained that this was how he approached every problem, until it was solved.

11. *Know when to push the envelope and when to back off.*

The one-minded focus necessary to reach a goal can lead some to a rather addictive process of obsessive behavior. Figure out when you are pushing it. Watch for signs like: leaving your purse in the refrigerator, forgetting to shower for much too long, talking to friends online rather than taking your dogs for a walk, yelling at your wife, screaming at your husband, thinking the world revolves around you, feeding the kids Chinese food on Thanksgiving because you forgot to buy a turkey, and screaming at friends who just "don't understand your vision." If you are hurting yourself or hurting someone else, you are off track. Maybe your goal is good and valid, but your way of getting there is inappropriate. Seek professional help if you lose yourself in your goal. It is okay to change your mind, change your vision, change your goal, and change your style. If you need to make an exit, use this phrase to explain it to friends, "It seemed like a good idea at the time, but I changed my mind." If you have a special, wonderful vision, at least go for it. Success often means you gave it a shot and re-decided.

> **A wonderful benefit of this kind of thinking is that you will be able to celebrate and honor even the smallest achievements of others. What a wonderful manager you will be then!**

12. *Bless yourself for surviving.*

Survival is not always a pretty sight. It takes a lot of grit and persistence to live through this life. You probably have known people who did not make it this far. If you are reading this, it means you are probably still alive. That's a good thing. All your faults, errors, talents, skills, efforts, mistakes, questions, answers, fears, angers, joys, resistances, problems, victories, and failures have led you to now. You are so brave. As you persist in living on Planet Earth, following your dreams, and working toward achieving your personal goals, you must give yourself permission sometimes to persist and to continue persisting.

Sometimes no one else will encourage you. In fact, some may scorn you for pressing on. That's okay. Be noble. Be honorable. Find and create dignity in everything you do. Then, no matter how big or small your goal, when you reach it, bow deeply to yourself and say, "I am so brave!" A wonderful benefit of this kind of thinking is that you will be able to celebrate and honor even the smallest achievements of others. What a wonderful manager you will be then! The victories of others will be neither a threat nor a joke. You will celebrate success authentically, and support errors compassionately. You will know that someone else's goal may seem small to you, but it may be a Mount Everest to that person. When you know what your vision for greatness is, you will be able to persist toward it while cheering loudly for other persistent people. What if there were no finish line?

B. Know when to quit and head for shelter.

Some emotional spins are bigger than you are. Make certain that you have a best pal or resource (not a spouse or parent) outside your company who can support you and your work. The all-alone nature of management is sometimes daunting in the midst of storms. All warriors know when to quit, know where the foxhole is – and all good managers know where and how they can protect themselves legally, ethically, and emotionally. If things get rough, ask yourself, "Am I dating this job or am I married to it?" If you are married to the job and it becomes too much, perhaps a job-divorce will be necessary to maintain your integrity. If you are dating the job, you might just need to break up and give back the ring. No matter the situation or circumstances, it is always appropriate to work in a safe place.

C. Have appropriate, pre-arranged referrals available.

Managers are not supposed to be mental health professionals. So what happens when managers recognize a major problem with one of their people? Traditionally they send them to HR or recommend an EAP session or two. Then what? The employee is still there. You may need more than these two referral resources to get through a major incident. And there is always the concern that your HR or EAP people might be the emotional problems in your company. If your resources were impaired temporarily by a traumatic event, what would you do? Some companies retain mental health professionals experienced in managing emotional continuity in the workforce, while other businesses create partnerships and memos of understanding (MOUs) between agencies.

5.6.6 Step 6: Design Your Management Style and Your Emotional Continuity Program

You should know your company inside and out. Designing a management style and program needs to reflect your own personal style while fitting within the parameters of the company that pays your salary and the industry that drives the company. Try to look at both the big picture and the small picture when you are researching and developing a program for your company.

A. Start your management design plans:

- ▶ Assess your unique and specific situation.
- ▶ Make a rough-draft plan.

- ◗ Check out the plan with others.

- ◗ Confirm a final, but adjustable plan.

- ◗ Implement the plan.

- ◗ Assess the plan in action.

- ◗ Reorganize the plan as necessary to adjust to changes.

- ◗ Make reports and recommendations.

- ◗ Prepare written documentation of outcomes.

- ◗ Encourage evaluation and ongoing research.

B. Obtain buy-in.

Unless you own the company, you need administrative support or buy-in to move forward. Your administrative buy-in process is perhaps the most critical of the steps in establishing an emotional continuity management plan. Nothing will sabotage hard work more than an upper-echelon authority dispatching your program.

Control, Force, Power, and Management

Control is an attempt to limit, restrict, stop, or remove the expression of something. The desire or motivation for control is to keep something from happening or to regulate it to prevent it from spreading. Emotions cannot be controlled, nor should they be. However, emotions can be managed.

Force is a movement that projects a certain amount of power in one place in relationship to another place. Force creates counter-force that weakens some other area where the power has been removed to contribute to a force. Force is oppositional in that it is moving against something. Hitler was a force, Germany was a power. Gandhi was a force, non-violence is a power.

Power arises from a position that carries a motive. Power is a neutral state that implies influence based on mass or volume. Power is a descriptor for determining the amount of something. In his book *Power vs. Force* (Hay House, 2001), David Hawkins explains that power arises from meaning. His research demonstrates how power always wins over force because it appeals to what uplifts, dignifies, and ennobles human beings.

Management is more about organizing, handling, using, or creating a process for something. If emotions are considered to be simply differing forms of energy, then management is about employing that energy skillfully into the system so that it doesn't become blocked, short-circuited, explosive, or diminished.

> **There are times when a manager must act as a force to oppose the winds of emotional chaos. At other times, a manager must expose his or her own personal power by simply moving out of the way and letting the wind blow.**

Managers need to know the differences between these concepts in order to use the ones that are most appropriate in a given situation. Historically, if you consider the differences between control, management, power, and force, you will discover readily the root causes of fights, conflicts, struggles, and wars. Managers need to manage. They will need to manage powers and forces without being controlling because, in reality, they will have no control over these factors. Managers do not have control. Often, when managers feel this reality, they begin to feel fear. Fear is a force. Faith is a power.

There are times when a manager must act as a force to oppose the winds of emotional chaos. At other times, a manager must expose his or her own personal power by simply moving out of the way and letting the wind blow. This construct is something that tornado chasers understand clearly or they risk their lives. Most tornado chasers do not want to die. They simply want to understand the powers and the forces of these behemoth energies. They respect the powers and meanings of nature. They respect the forces of twisters and comprehend the comparisons between their own human energy levels and the levels associated with the storm. They do not even begin to consider controlling the tornado. They do manage themselves in the presence of these powers and forces. Emotional continuity management is a lot like being a tornado chaser. It is important to stand by while not being sucked into the vortex of the spin.

A Long-Term Tool

So you find that you work with or for a bully. Bummer. You can't quit or change the situation. Instead of feeling like a victim you can do something really bold, such as going to Alanon meetings. I know officially that Alanon is a system designed to manage people who are dealing with the effects of having an alcoholic in their family. But really, isn't having a bully in your life like having a wild drunk in the living room? You never know when he/she is going to be on an emotional bender and make you the target, right? Bullies will blame you for your emotions rather than being responsible for their own mean spirit, right? They will turn you into writhing codependents because of your fear and anxiety of trying not to provoke them, right? You will readjust your behavior rather than seeing them change theirs, right? You feel trapped while they complain about all the power you have, right?

Therefore, I give you unofficial permission to go sit in an Alanon meeting, substituting the word "alcohol" with the word "bully."

Outside Intervention: Alternative support could be gained from Codependents Anonymous (CODA) or other 12-step programs. However, having seen the long term patient/client results of participation in Alanon and CODA, the clear choice for one practice for me would be Alanon. That is my professional position.   Having an emotional terrorist in your midst is quite like having a raging drunk in your living room – you'll never know when he/she will go "off." And for that process Alanon is the better choice for acute acting out of anyone or anything in your circle. CODA isn't immediate enough and provides ample opportunity for extreme levels of denial of your own accountability in the Karpman Triangle set up. It often leads to long-term victimhood behaviors rather than kick-ass accountable recovery when you are in the proximity of crazy people being crazy, drunks being drunk, or terrorists being terrorizing. Someone drunk on power and control still acts like a drunk whether he or she imbibes or not. Thus a "dry drunk" is still a problem for the co-dependent. In my opinion, Alanon is the preferred intervention.

5.7 Emotional Continuity for Employees Transitioning from Armed Services

5.7.1 Transition to Civilian Life – A Career Change, Not a Crisis

Transition from military to civilian life is not a crisis. It is a process, similar to other major changes in career or lifestyle. Again, a healthy person can get through a process, where a dysfunctional one may struggle a bit, and a pathological one will have more of a challenge. The stages of grief apply to transition. Don't assume someone who is recently discharged from active duty is suffering post-traumatic stress disorder (PTSD) or other service-related disability just because he or she is having a bad day or week. Maybe the dog died. Maybe the person has a cold. Maybe the person just moved back home after being far away for a long long time and is adjusting to being near the family for the first time in years. On the other hand, maybe the person is away from home for the first time. Lots of emotions have absolutely nothing to do with being active or retired military personnel.

On the other hand, don't assume the opposite. PTSD is a real thing, and so are suicide and homicide and divorce and other rotten things that happen to military personnel after they have served their country. There are excellent support services for military personnel who are in the process or recently separated from the service. There are amazing support systems for veterans. Of course the system has weak spots, but there are also countless people doing hard work to serve those who serve. Encourage your military veterans to reach out to their specific branch and find out what is available. Or have that available for them. Go to www.militaryonesource.com and find out what is available. Each branch of the military has specialists ready to help smooth the transition from military to civilian.

> Transition includes three phases: The Beginning of a Change, the Middle of the Change, and the End of the Change. Emotions for each phase will include each one of the grief stages.

Leaving the military may mean significant financial challenges, and the job these personnel have now may be critical to their survival and self-esteem. As they learn the new language, culture, and lifestyle changes of returning to civilian life, they may feel more unstable than they were previously. This does not necessarily mean they are "unstable." It just may mean they are in transition. Transition includes three phases: The Beginning of a Change, the Middle of the Change, and the End of the Change. Emotions for each phase will include each one of the grief stages: denial, bargaining, anger, depression, and acceptance. A healthy person will go through these stages in good order and not get stuck in any stage. A dysfunctional person may take longer and be a bit more uncertain. Someone with severe issues may end up getting stuck in a transition stage. This latter is something to be aware of so that you can offer help from EAP or other services in your company, or direct such people to their post-military resources. It makes good sense to have partnerships with local military providers or those familiar with the special and regular needs of transitioning military personnel.

5.7.2 Understanding the Background of Military Personnel

Just like all human beings, military personnel come in all shapes, sizes, genders, cultures, perceptions, choices, religions, sexual preferences, boot sizes, and preferences over Coca Cola or Pepsi. The number one rule for those who have reason to consider the emotional continuity for military, whether active or retired, is do not make any assumptions!

▶ Not all military personnel have had combat duty.

▶ Some military personnel are typists, engineers, nurses, supply chain workers, and truck drivers – and more!

▶ Not all military personnel have PTSD. Some do. Many do not.

▶ Military personnel may have worked all over the world, or in just one location.

- Military personnel have the same life issues as everyone else.

- Military personnel can fit into each category 1) healthy,
  2) dysfunctional, 3) pathological, or 4) emotional terrorist.

- Military personnel have had different duties and levels of accountability, depending on the branch in which they served, their rank,
  their duties, and their experiences.

- Military personnel do not speak a different language than civilians
  any more than a musician who can read music speaks a different
  language. They have had opportunity and experience to focus
  their language on one topic, the military life, and most are more
  than capable of learning something new. Many are already
  bilingual or multilingual.

- Military personnel often have to cross-train, so they are used to
  learning new things.

- Military personnel might call you "sir" or "ma'am" for a while,
  which does not mean they are from the South – it means they have
  learned to respect others in their space.

- Veterans and recently exited military personnel may have different
  needs, just like any other person on your team.

- Some military personnel have had heinous experiences, but will
  recover quickly when they get on with their civilian lives. Some
  will not recover quickly but will do so. Some will take a long,
  long, long time – and a few won't ever recover. It is a continuum.
  Be aware of what that looks like in your work environment, and
  don't assume someone taking a while to recover is a "lost cause."

- When military personnel are transitioning into civilian life, they go
  through the normal stages of transition that anyone else would.
  Do not assume it is harder or easier for them simply because they
  have been military personnel.

Collective Emotional Terrorism

Todd (names have been changed for privacy) returned from a tour of duty in the Middle East to be hired by a large, well-known company that hires many recently separated military personnel as well as other young people, often for their first jobs. Todd was young and healthy and had not been identified as suffering from PTSD or other service-related problems. However, when his managers noted his performance was not up to the standards they had anticipated, they became concerned, calling him in to the HR office to see if he was encountering any problems in his new job. Accustomed to dealing with military protocol and chain of command, Todd was nervous but appropriate during the meeting, describing his situation as "good," and promising to work harder to meet the goals. Unfortunately, his work did not improve and he was fired. Several weeks after his release, Amy, who had been one of Todd's co-workers, requested a meeting with HR. She disclosed that she was upset at the firing because she knew the reason why. Apparently, the company's young (or we might say "juvenile") culture created an atmosphere that was, as Amy put it, "like high school." It seemed, she reported, that – because Todd had been a soldier in a war zone – a number of the employees made it their daily "mission" to try to "freak out the soldier to see if he snapped." They would jump out at Todd to try to startle him, move things in ways that made his work difficult, mess with his belongings, shove and bump him when they could, and generally found great sport in trying to "get the PTSD freak-out" they hoped to witness at some point. Todd did not have PTSD. What he did have, because of his military training, was "loyalty" to his "unit" – so he didn't complain.

Transition Hell

Cal had served his country with great honor and bravery. His combat record was remarkable, and he had done work that was technical, complex, and important. He was a leader, a mentor for others, a shining star. Loved by his comrades and his family, Cal was young and successful in the military and felt good about ending his time in the service well. He received a commendation and he was "good to go." Then Cal got his first civilian job interview and was so terrified that he threw up all morning and failed to arrive on time. His interview was a total disaster. Faced with the prospect of having been a leader in one area only to find himself a complete mess in another, Cal was in shock. Fortunately, the company HR person, who was former military and recognized the situation for what it was, gave Cal a second chance to interview. He did better. His new mentor encouraged him to get some help, and eventually his leadership and talents were once again available, and he was on the road to civilian success.

Transition Translation

In the military, Rita had been an intelligence genius. Because of her security clearances, she could never reveal the details of her job; however, it was clear she was brilliant and had done amazing things. She nailed the interview with a civilian company, but after she got the job, the company didn't quite know how to translate what she knew and had done into the work they hired her for. For the longest time no one asked Rita's opinion. One day, someone finally asked. She was able to tell them how she could take their current operations forward dramatically with only a few minor, inexpensive, purchases of operating hardware and software. The changes were within budget, and fortunately for the company, they listened. While Rita couldn't tell them what she had done in the military, she could show them – by taking a failing company and turning it around into a competitive business. The company discovered that Rita was a professional strategist. Lucky company!

5.7.3 Know the Resources Available to Returning Military

During active duty, all branches have some program and support for almost anything that can come up, including substance abuse, behavioral health, alcohol treatment, child and family assistance centers, families under stress, family advocacy, chaplains, military and family life consultants, victim advocates/sexual assault support, medical support, and much more. What do your company and your community partners have to offer them?

Military personnel are familiar with using services to get support for themselves and their families, more so than civilians in most cases. To support military personnel employees, you need to be aware of the resources in your area that you can direct them towards as needed. A recently or long-separated former member of the armed forces should have available the exact same resources as anyone in your company for exactly the same reasons as everyone one else in your company. In addition to those available employee resources, you can provide an ample collection of services specifically available for transitioning military personnel.

Countless research resources are available to help you hire and mentor great employees who used to be in the military. For example:

▶ *Military to Civilian Skills Translators*

Lists a number of sites to help companies and service members match military skills and experience to civilian occupations and translate the language of military to civilian.
https://www.nationalresourcedirectory.gov/employment/transitioning_from_the_military_to_a_civilian_career/military_to_civilian_skills_translators

▶ Transition Fears

http://usmilitary.about.com/cs/jobopportunities/a/transition.htm

▶ Military Employment Sources

http://usmilitary.about.com/od/jobopportunities/Military_Employment_Opportunities.htm

> **It may be necessary to slightly redesign your interview process a bit in order to facilitate a good hiring process for former military personnel.**

5.7.4 Avoid Damaging Assumptions

Some wonderful military personnel will not disclose their service experiences because they think people will assume they either have PTSD or have killed many people and are just one snap away from being suicidal or homicidal. Or, they have had heinous experiences, and out of courtesy or confidentiality or security clearances, they keep it private. Some military personnel may feel they have to hide their service experience in order to get jobs. The catch in this is they may also feel like they can't compete with civilians who can be more "open" about their job experience. The "job translator" services mentioned above can help employers and employees translate military experience into civilian job descriptions. This alone can be a great service to your entire company.

It may also be necessary to slightly redesign your interview process a bit in order to facilitate a good hiring process for former military personnel. Discuss it with all stakeholders, legal, HR, and your ECM team, and determine how your company would like to support, hire, and manage the human emotions of those who have served our country, particularly during the last ten years of war in the Middle East. Trust me, in a very short period of time many, many, many of the young people who are looking for jobs will have served. They have families and children and dreams. They took time to serve in the military and now they deserve companies who will take a bit of time to help with their emotional continuity as they transition from military to civilian work.

Heroes and Not

In my humble opinion, most military personnel are heroes. That being said, some, of course, are not. And I have met them also. That being said, the spouses and children of military personnel, in many cases, rank as heroic also. And they, too, have jobs in your company. Depending on the service, rank, experience, age and countless other factors, the service member, the spouse, and the children have had a different experience than someone who has not had a military career, but that may be the only difference. Some military personnel, spouses, and young people who have had military parents, have been to the most interesting or most horrid places on the planet, done the most absolutely amazing or most tedious work in the known universe, and may find that the transition to your company is either a big step up, or that boredom is their new enemy. Ask them what they did and find ways to translate it into new tasks for your company.

Some, But Not All - A Heads Up List

As a company decision-maker, ECM member, or professional in HR, EAP, or other area, it will probably serve you well to consider these last thoughts as you plan policies that include military and former military employees:

▶ Some, but not all, members of the military have seen or done the most heinous things that you can imagine, or worse. It was their job description. They have moved on to a new job, with your company. Help them be successful.

▶ Some, but not all, employees in your company are 100% anti-military, against all things associated with the current war, politically on the rampage against all things having to do with military service. They get to have their opinions, but in a work setting they need to keep those opinions to themselves or be considered spinners and potential emotional terrorists.

▶ Some, but not all, women in the military have experienced sexual assault. So have approximately 20% of the rest of your staff, male and female.

▶ Some, but not all, of your employees will assume that anyone who has military training is a killer. Generally this will be your dysfunctional, pathological employees. Emotional terrorists may exploit this fear to gain their own agenda.

▶ Some, but not all, of your employees will have someone they love in the military. They may have mixed feelings about it.

▶ Some, but not all, military personnel have had combat-related injuries, physical and mental, and they have and will receive military support services for that. Your other employees have the same risks and potential issues. All they are missing is a direct reason for their diabetes, high blood pressure, bipolar disorder, paranoia, obsessive compulsive disorder, or addiction. Take care not to assume that a military person is at a risk that is different than civilians. Military personnel are easy to make statistics about because they are in a fishbowl environment and can be easily counted and turned into a media frenzy discussion.

▶ Some, but not all, military veterans may want to talk and share their stories. Some of them won't even tell their spouses; so why would they share with you? Be respectful or risk a harassment violation. In a work setting, it is no one's business unless it has some influence on job performance or emotional continuity.

▶ Some, but not all, people who have true emotional damages as a direct result of participating in combat or war, can become unpredictable, dangerous, and violent. Such behavior can include, but is not limited to, PTSD and other issues that are often redefined during a war. Similar violence can occur in other people under other circumstances. Don't link the behavior necessarily to military service.

▶ Some, but not all, people who have given military service, are heroes. I'm one of the people on the planet who are grateful and proud to serve those who serve – and their families.

Questions for Further Thought and Discussion

1. What is your emotional range? Can you describe the markers on your emotional thermometer?

2. If you recognized you were working with an emotional terrorist, what strategies would you use to stay out of the line of fire to avoid becoming a target?

3. How do you think employees should manage their small and large emotions?

4. What are your rules about "feelings"? Did you learn those rules in your family of origin or elsewhere? How does that affect your relationship to other people having emotions?

5. Discuss the topic of "personal power" and "vulnerability." How does this fit into any consideration of emotional continuity management for the protection of the bottom line of your organization?

6. Consider Todd's story. The ringleaders who led their immature co-workers in the cruel campaign of tormenting Todd probably excused it as "teasing" or humor, part of a lighthearted departmental culture. From what you have read so far, you can now identify this behavior as bullying or emotional terrorism. This same type of destructive "kidding around" can also take place when the new employee has gray hair, has different religious practices, has a different ethnic background, has physical or mental challenges, is sexually attractive, or is considered odd or "geeky." After reading this far, what steps can you take, starting Monday morning, to make sure that no newcomer to your company or department has to undergo this treatment?

6

Tools for Companies Dealing with Bullies and Emotional Terrorists

In this chapter, I'm going to walk you through the range of tools, from a simple *bully policy* to a full range system-wide *emotional continuity plan* (*ECP*). Are you ready right now for *emotional continuity management* (ECM)? No? Just want to take care of the problem and not the issue? Okay. We'll start small. How about starting with a simple bully policy, and then I'll walk you through the basics of the "full-meal deal" if you want a company that is on the cutting edge and willing to go to any length to protect people and business at the same time.

6.1 Starting the System-Wide Approach

In order to acknowledge and balance emotions in the workplace, a system-wide approach to ECM first begins with a buy-in process from the top down. Without complete buy-in from the top, there will not be sufficient support to back up a manager who is confronted with the natural, subsequent challenges and resistances. If an emotional terrorist is in the midst of the employee pool, the manager absolutely must have support and backup from superiors.

6.1.1 Getting Buy-in From the Top Down

Once the top officials, CEOs, owners, and administrators buy on to the concept of managing emotions in the workplace, the process can begin by providing managers with training in the sets of tools necessary. A regular employee transitional process or any significant change can stir up emotions from small to large. Whether the changes are internal or external, natural or man-made, change is easy for some and difficult for others. Thus, the exact same training program is introduced into the entire working population. Standardized trainings, follow-ups, individual recommendations, adjustments, and fine-tunings comprise the introduction of any solid new procedure into a system.

When the systematic introduction of new, consistent information starts moving through the organization, response to it always moves toward the top. The top administrator must become the containment lid for the bubbling and stirring process of system-wide change. If the administrator is committed to the theory, plan, and process, the organization quickly stabilizes. If the administrator is ambiguous or oppositional, the emotional backlash will move back down toward the bottom of the system. All emotional fluctuations, grievances and anomalies are instantly reflected back into the system for integration and absorption. Or, they become more emotional substance that creates more spinning and disruption. Management is left to control all adjustments.

If managers have been trained to respond appropriately to these fluctuations, the emotional content can be absorbed by a healthy system. If managers have been trained to recognize what is normal and what is a threat to containment and adjustment, they can implement a variety of new tools and options to increase their effectiveness. Clear directions with consistent information stabilize the flow of emotional energy in the system as it moves toward anticipated outcomes rather than toward escalated emotional spinning.

The top-down process validates and legitimizes that everyone is on board. This significantly increases loyalty for all stakeholders. The bottom line is encouraged as outcome. At the same time, all the people involved see that their emotions matter, when well managed within workplace-appropriate boundaries. If people are not on board with the process, they are quickly identified as anomalies in the system. Managers can offer such persons increased training, education, readjustment, reorientation, encouragement, or appropriate transition out of the system. New system standards are established with a set of expectations that are defined internally and managed internally. This internal activity increases stakeholder buy-in for management and line staff. Rather than escalating to an us-versus-them dynamic, it can become us-for-us.

6.1.2 Advantages of the Process

A well-conceived emotional continuity management process provides clear definitions, reinforces company-wide expectations, and provides the entire system with easily accessible, practical, industry appropriate tools. If there is any kind of simple leak, tear, break, or rupture in the system, it can be repaired or managed quickly if it is an expectation of the dynamic of change. Management will have a tool available and ready to go. If the rupture is catastrophic, management will have a cadre of resources beyond peers. It is useful to pre-train systems before incidents occur and introduce managers to the resources available. During a catastrophic event, external providers can be seen as "outsiders" or "heroes." Law enforcement and fire services have discovered that when systems are in place before incidents, counseling and debriefing by external providers is seen as an internal policy decision that does not become an additional external threat in times of disaster or catastrophic challenge.

6.2 Making a Bullying Policy

As awareness of workplace abuse issues increase, organizations will be compelled to create policies to discourage this abusive behavior. Some organizations choose to create a wide-range policy that provides a system-wide organizational management for the full range of behaviors – emotional continuity management.

Other companies start by successfully designing a bully policy first.

If you have been tasked with writing a policy that focuses on bullying alone, here are a couple of ideas to begin with so you can have a place to launch a larger and more comprehensive positive workplace program:

6.2.1 Examples of Policies about Workplace Bullying

Example 1:

Company XYZ considers workplace bullying unacceptable and will not tolerate it under any circumstances.

Workplace bullying is behavior that harms, intimidates, offends, degrades, or humiliates an employee, possibly in front of other employees, clients, or customers. Workplace bullying may cause the loss of trained and talented employees, reduce productivity and morale, and create legal risks.

Company XYZ believes all employees should be able to work in an environment free of bullying. Managers and supervisors must ensure employees are not bullied.

Company XYZ has grievance and investigation procedures to deal with workplace bullying. Any reports of workplace bullying will be treated seriously and investigated promptly, confidentially, and impartially.

Company XYZ encourages all employees to report workplace bullying. Managers and supervisors must ensure employees who make complaints, or witnesses, are not victimized.

Disciplinary action will be taken against anyone who bullies a co-employee. Discipline may involve a warning, transfer, counseling, demotion, or dismissal, depending on the circumstances.

The contact person for bullying at this workplace is:

Name: _____

Example 2

Company XYZ is committed to providing a positive working environment free from intimidation, ridicule, and harassment. Company XYZ will not tolerate threatening behavior, including bullying, harassment, intimidation, threats, and physical violence in the workplace.

Company XYZ considers workplace bullying unacceptable.

Workplace bullying is unreasonable behavior, generally persistent, that demeans, intimidates, and humiliates employees, either as individuals or as a group.

Workplace bullying may cause the loss of trained and talented employees, reduce productivity and morale, and create legal risk.

Company XYZ believes that all employees should be able to work in an environment free of bullying. Managers and supervisors must ensure employees are not bullied.

Company XYZ has procedures for issue resolution and investigation to deal with workplace bullying. Any reports of workplace bullying will be treated seriously and investigated promptly, confidentially, and impartially.

Company XYZ encourages all employees to report workplace bullying. Managers and supervisors must ensure that employees or witnesses who make complaints are not victimized.

Disciplinary action will be taken against anyone against whom a valid complaint of bullying is made. Disciplinary action may involve a formal warning, counseling, or dismissal.

Example 3

An effective policy will describe the process from the complaint stage to the consequence stage (Whitney, 2009).

Duffy suggests 12 elements to be included in a workplace abuse policy. The 12 elements are broken down into 4 sections as follows (Duffy, 2009):

Anti-bullying Policy Section 1: Purpose, Statement, & Examples

Purpose of policy. The purpose of the policy should clearly reflect the values of the organization.

Statement. Describe the definition of workplace bullying. Also include the organization's position and how the behavior hinders company goals and negatively affects employee health.

Examples. Indicate examples, such as humiliation, character attacks, isolating an employee, name calling, etc., but be sure to acknowledge that this type of workplace abuse is not limited to the behaviors listed.

Anti-bullying Policy Section 2: Complaint and Resolution Process

Identify appropriate contact people. Identify the people to contact if there is a problem. The contact list should be across all levels of the organization.

Informal resolution. Such an approach should be an option as long as all parties involved agree to it. It can be an open dialogue between parties to work through the problem. This option would require the person charged be receptive to information about the effects of his or her abusive behavior.

Examples. Mediation, negotiated agreements, restorative justice, or other resolutions agreed to by all parties.

Anti-bullying Policy Section 3: Action

Formal charge. Clarify the procedures by which workplace abuse complaints are handled by the organization from beginning to end.

Privacy. Distribute a statement of confidentiality to all parties involved.

Timing. Indicate that the investigation will be conducted in the shortest time possible.

Results Reporting. Distribute the results of the investigation to both parties separately.

Anti-bullying Policy Section 4: Consequences

Accountability. Discuss the personal and organizational consequences when an investigation has uncovered workplace abuse.

Appeal. Communicate the appeals process to all employees. Both parties should have the ability to submit an appeal.

For more guidance on creating an anti-bullying policy, see the list of resources in the References list at the end of this book.

http://www.fredlaw.com/articles/employment/empl_0604_mmk.html

6.3 Creating System-Wide Emotional Continuity Management

Why should companies do this instead of just a quickie bully policy? Like the old saying goes, "Give a man a fish and he eats for one day; teach him to fish and he eats for life." A problem (like a flat tire) can be solved quickly. An issue (like poverty or emotional terrorism) doesn't go away just with a quick fix. Many companies do a quick fix, only to find an unexpected new problem crops up later because they never addressed the greater issue. Wise companies deal with the big picture and plan for both the "thinkable" and the "unthinkable." There are lots of ways companies can approach the problems and the issues. If everyone is on board, there is a much stronger probability that your company won't be caught off guard by anything or anyone. And if you do encounter the unexpected, you will already be prepared for recovery.

6.3.1 How Some Companies Have Approached Creating System-Wide Emotional Continuity Management

▶ Hired specialized professionals for training, put them on retainers for disasters, have their people get to know them in advance so they don't appear as outsiders when the chips are down.

▶ Hired a field-tested disaster emotional continuity management coach to support and train managers to deal directly with the bridge between business and emotion.

▶ Hosted a consultation session using combinations of resources from inside and outside the company and making links with top-end, credentialed professionals in the appropriate areas.

▶ Assigned a person or team to provide ongoing training for staff, orient new employees, write policy, create education, and establish standardized expectations while learning how to recognize the early warning signs of emotional dysfunction and to track developing emotional tornadoes on the horizon.

▶ Provided high-end, quality traumatology or critical incident management training for all department managers.

A proactive position for emotional continuity management begins with data that supports your position. Start your buy-in discussion with hard data, facts, statistics, fiscal risk projections, and historical relevance. Follow with human-compassion-centered data that is translated into value-added benefit for your company. Show how taking care of human emotions is a decision that is fiscally advantageous, valuable to the bottom line, adds value to customers, and increases stakeholder loyalty. Use the following questions to create a presentation document before you approach your administration to establish buy-in.

6.3.2 What a System-Wide Emotional Continuity Plan Should Start to Address

▶ What are the predictable fiscal consequences of an emotional spin?

▶ Can your emotional continuity management team manage small and large emotions?

▶ Is everyone ready to manage the emotions of a disaster?

▶ If a small spin begins, who will stop it?

▶ Are employees able to help themselves enough to help others?

▶ Do you have enough tools to manage emotional situations?

- Have you drilled and rehearsed for emotional incidents, small to large?

- Does your company have special needs employees?

- Does your company have special equipment?

- Do your employees know what to expect in case of a disaster?

- Has your entire company developed system-wide intervention strategies?

- Does anyone on your team have any specialized emotional continuity management training?

- If all top managers are gone, can your line staff take over the peer responsibilities?

- How will your employees know when external help is required?

- Are your people willing to call in outsiders for emotional support?

- What resources are available to all employees?

- Do you have external consultants, including teams of debriefers and trauma experts who are familiar with your business? Will they come immediately when called?

- Are your managers, employees, or consultants field-trained in real-time disasters?

- What are the predictable emotional outcomes from a disaster?

- What emotional continuity management tools have employees rehearsed?

- Who is familiar with the emotional continuity management tools and can use them under stressful conditions?

- Does your company have unique emotional needs?

- Are there emotional continuity management tools in place that increase employee understanding about what humans are likely to do under a wide range of circumstances?

- Has your entire company been trained in system-wide intervention strategies and tools?

- Who in your company has extensive and advanced psychological trauma management training?

- What emotional continuity management tools would serve a simple problem, a complicated issue, or a complex emergency?

- If managers are gone, who assumes the responsibility for emotional continuity management?

▶ How do you know when external help is required?

▶ Are your people willing to call in outsiders?

▶ Are supportive resources ready and in place if something happened today?

▶ Are your external consultants field-trained experts?

▶ Have you prepared a way to manage voluntary "helpers" who will show up to disasters?

▶ How will you protect yourself and your company from opportunists who show up without appropriate training and credentials when you are the most vulnerable?

6.3.3 Ask These Questions for the System-Wide Buy-In Process

▶ How well does administration support the emotional continuity management plan?

▶ How completely has the emotional continuity management plan been incorporated into the emergency management plan of the company?

▶ How well have other departments in the company been informed or notified about administrative buy-in?

▶ How well have other departments supported the emotional continuity management plan?

▶ How well supported is the need to practice and drill for emotional emergencies?

▶ How extensive are the opportunities to drill for emotional emergencies?

▶ How financially supported is the emotional continuity management plan?

▶ How supportive is the administration to providing opportunities for training employees in emotional management?

▶ How supportive is the administration to providing opportunities for training management?

▶ How supportive is the administration to creating cooperative partnerships with other emergency response agencies prior to a disaster or emotional event?

▶ How supportive is the administration to providing pamphlets, books, literature, posters, media education, and other hard-copy information on emotional continuity management planning?

▶ How well do personnel know what they should do in an emergency to care-take their emotions?

▶ How well prepared are you to manage extreme emotions in the workplace?

▶ How well prepared are you to manage emotions resulting from a catastrophic disaster?

6.3.4 Steps for Writing an Emotional Continuity Management Plan

1. Research.

▶ Find your highest order of management style.

▶ Explore a variety of possible forms.

▶ Call someone in your position in another company for an idea meeting.

▶ Read magazines and books.

▶ Go to workshops or classes.

2. Create a Blueprint.

▶ Visualize your perfect style.

▶ Take time to sketch or write your plan.

▶ Create a notebook or journal of ideas.

▶ Draw pictures and doodles of your ideal work process.

3. Decide and Commit.

▶ Remove barriers.

▶ Prepare the space.

▶ Gather resources.

▶ Survive first challenges.

▶ Continue to commit.

▶ Work for buy-in.

▶ See the big picture so there is no emergency in the planning stage.

▶ Continue your research and creative stages.

▶ Use challenges and obstacles as learning/teaching moments.

▶ Write and rewrite your plan as it continues to evolve into a final draft.

4. Begin.

- ❱ Take actions.
- ❱ Safeguard resources.
- ❱ Survive ongoing challenges.
- ❱ Recommit.
- ❱ Talk with others inside and outside your work: create networks.
- ❱ Review and strengthen your database.
- ❱ Create professional documents and forms.
- ❱ Accept and review feedback with your ideals in mind.
- ❱ Review persistence materials.
- ❱ Begin implementation stages.
- ❱ Review highest order ideals.
- ❱ Review original visions.
- ❱ Reconsider if appropriate.
- ❱ Recommit and continue.
- ❱ Review previous stages with ideals in mind.
- ❱ Continue to face challenges with open mind and commitment.

6.3.5 Emotional Continuity Management Checklist

As you are creating your Emotional Continuity Training for teams and employees use the following checklist to track your consistency:

- ❱ Does each module of training follow the same "scripted" procedure so that the information is uniform and repeatable?
- ❱ Is attending mandatory? Mandating attendance creates a sense of unity among participants and immediately limits options for spinning.
- ❱ Do follow-up meetings provide creative input and collaboration from all members?
- ❱ Has there been buy-in from the top? The top-down process allows the administration/management to discover which employees are on board, which are potential emotional saboteurs, and which are simply trainable "problem children."
- ❱ Does each module include practice time and drills for new tools, language, and concept acquisition? Adjustment and absorption of new ideas takes time and familiarity.

▶ Do units of education or modules exceed teachable timeframes? Two hours for group education is appropriate, with shorter individual consultations when required. This process should add minimum emotional impact to the organization's functioning. Do not let lengthy trainings become fodder for emotional spinning.

▶ Do emotional continuity management trainings have written policy and clearly defined statements for:

❒ Trainer qualifications.

❒ Company mission and team visions.

❒ Top organizational buy-in defined/clarified.

❒ Rules for mandated participation and non-negotiable consequences for non-participation.

❒ Expectations and timetables for skills practice and drills.

❒ Value-added incentives for participation.

❒ Are reproducible documents prepared for:

❖ Personnel interview charts.

❖ Models for explaining human emotions.

❖ Models for explaining human responses.

❖ Models for conflict resolution.

❖ Models for grief work and trauma management.

❖ Self-care tools ranging from simple to complex.

❖ Grading assessments.

❖ Models for managing individual differences.

❖ System-wide backup plans.

❖ System-wide backup plans for the backup plan.

6.4 A Five-Step Spin-Free Workplace Training Model for System-Wide Emotional Continuity Management

The five steps are:

1. Preparation.

2. The wake-up call.

3. Invitation.

4. Clarity and recommitment.

5. Remediation.

6.4.1 Preparation

Managers begin the process by deciding: exactly what they want; their expectations; how the readjustment process will lay out; and who will be involved in research and development, individual committees, task forces, brainstorming sessions, and system-wide implementation. It is the blueprint of the new infrastructure. It is not necessary to tear down the old one while building a new framework. It is necessary, however, to have a plan of action along with specialists to back up the plan. The rough draft of the policy is created here.

Some Potential Preparation Components:

- The original mission/vision statements.
- All documents/policies/procedures that may be affected or changed.
- Legal counsel.
- HR (managers and above).
- Internal auditors (managers and above).
- Security (managers and above).
- External mental health consultant.
- External anti-terrorist specialist.
- Trainers/educators.
- Support staff to schedule meetings and trainings.
- General timeline/deadline.
- Meetings with all department heads and managers to dispel potential rumors.

It is important in this first step to have very rigid boundaries in order to prevent leaks, fragmentation, half-truths/half-lies, and rumors. If there is an emotional terrorist within this first unit, it will be evident via leaks.

6.4.2 The Wake-Up Call

After preparation, it will be time to inform all employees, system-wide, that a new policy is on its way to the organization; that it is positive; that it has nothing to do with layoffs; and, that it will be announced at a specific meeting (or meetings). Location and time are included in the memo or will follow within 24-48 hours.

The meeting should then be held for everyone. Everyone must be mandated to get this initial information. This meeting should not be a long, drawn-out process and, in fact, should only take a small period of time, preferably less than an hour. Everyone should be informed in person, in group meetings (not individual meetings), as well as in writing within a 48-hour period. Make provisions for a make-up meeting for absent employees. Emotional terrorists will avoid the meeting unless it is mandated, which includes a mandated make-up meeting. Terrorists will do anything to avoid this meeting.

The information given should be scripted to limit misinterpretation as well as to protect the messengers. The meeting script will announce the introduction of a new "anti-spin workplace policy" and present the expectation that all employees are expected to raise their consciousness about the possible effects and consequences for business and human beings in the presence of emotional spinning.

This meeting should be presented in an active, upbeat, celebratory "you-are-part-of-the-solution-or-part-of-the-problem" format strategy. Such an atmosphere engages the collective energy, and if there are emotional terrorists aboard, they will see that there is no turning back. It is the first statement of commitment, the line drawn in the sand, the "just say no" to the dealer. This new standard must absolutely be driven by the policy of zero tolerance for emotional spinning or emotional terrorism agenda that has been presented by the administrative body of the organization to everyone. Emotional players will immediately try to manipulate it into something more comfortable. With a lot of built-in flexibility for readjustments and realignments, trainings and support, understanding and compassion for all, the one thing that cannot be flexible is the zero tolerance position.

Stage 1:

The management teams are instructed on the topic of emotions at the workplace and educated in recognition skills. They are informed of the expectations of administration and given ways to support its implementation. At these meetings, there will be a period of time during which managers may contribute their ideas for developing policy.

Some Potential Talking Points for Discussion:

- ▶ Recognition of normal and abnormal emotions.
- ▶ Statistics.
- ▶ What/so what/now what.
- ▶ Denial, minimization, fears.

- Wherever you work is sacred ground.
- Predators versus prey.
- Tricks of terrorism.
- Anti-spin strategies.
- What to expect from whom and why.
- Specifics of your industry.
- Administration's buy-in support.

Stage 2:

All employees are brought on board with the same scripted program given to management with a series of group meetings to accommodate all staff. All meetings must be mandatory or made up with a short turnaround, non-avoidable deadline. Period.

6.4.3 The Invitation

At the end of the wake-up scripted sessions, all staff, management, and employees are given an invitation (either written or verbal) to become part of an anti-spin action team. After providing clear and specific information about the physical, mental, emotional, spiritual and financial danger of allowing emotional terrorists to run their organization, they are given an opportunity or invited to become emotional stakeholders. All are allowed and encouraged to describe their own view of possible emotional spinning effects in this environment (i.e., the organization's unique mission; payoffs for work ethic; personal integrity; service; care for self and others; and concerns for their own family, community, and individual success) as well as individual stories and experiences which may be useful to the group well-being.

> **Many good employees have not "ratted" on their co-workers out of either fear of reprisals or a commitment to professionalism. They have been silent and miserable trying to stay out of the path of the emotional tornado.**

When healthy and dysfunctional employees begin to see that it is in their best personal and collective interest to be part of the solution, they generally get on board quickly and with great vigor. In fact, they are often relieved that the threat of emotional spinning or terrorism, present or future, may be identified and addressed. Many good employees have not "ratted" on their co-workers out of either fear of reprisals or a commitment to professionalism. They have been silent and miserable trying to stay out of the path of the emotional tornado. Their faith in management begins to be restored. Immediately, terrorists will question the bottom line to see if it is real or going to disappear. Reinforcement of the policy for zero tolerance for emotional spinning or terrorism will need to be repeated.

Once management issues the invitation to join in a system-wide team-building process, it becomes evident immediately, usually within a few hours, which employees are going to support the agenda and which are going to try to sabotage it. Track all fear rumors directly back to the source and extinguish them immediately. Whining is okay, but any rumors must be stopped, assessed for spinning and intentional terrorism, and completely quelled. After a very brief initial discomfort and rattling of the cages, healthy people get on with the job of recovery and cleanup, while emotional spinners and terrorists begin to reveal themselves. Feedback will be clear, documentable, and immediate.

Everyone gets the benefit of the doubt to start with, even terrorists. All are given a small window to adjust. They must be given time to adjust, change their minds, get on board, exit, shake, shudder, and join in the new standard. Everyone adjusts at a different pace; 72 hours should be the amount of time to expect reasonable adjustment for new information. Adjustment does not mean competency, but it does mean compliance and a willingness to take the next step. Emotional terrorists will get very creative in their efforts to protract and expand the time between announcement and compliance.

Those who are dragging their feet can be evaluated by their history. Through review of work history, personal observations, and appropriate grievance procedures, management can identify those who are the regular "slow-pokes" and those who are emotional terrorists engaged in instigating resistance and sabotage. Be suspicious of everything from absenteeism to escalating stories of personal victimhood. Listen with compassion, repeat the zero tolerance agenda, and move on.

Some Potential Talking Points for Discussion

▶ Following an appropriate grievance process to effect change, what is the critical difference in behavior between healthy venting and complaining and emotional terrorism tactics?

▶ Why do some people take higher ground when others take the low road?

▶ What is the difference between a workplace soldier and a workplace warrior (hint: the warrior is actively seeking excellence)?

- ▶ What are the payoffs for becoming a workplace warrior?

- ▶ What are the ranges and levels of spinning from small to large?

- ▶ What are the differences between physical, emotional, mental, and spiritual spinning?

- ▶ How can we support those who struggle with change?

- ▶ What are the differences between sharing our emotions and spinning?

- ▶ What are your experiences with emotional terrorists?

- ▶ What place do emotions fit in the workplace? Do they?

- ▶ What does it mean to be held in an "emotional hostage" situation in the workplace?

6.4.4 Clarity and Re-Commitment

The bottom line must remain in place, even when challenged. Countless people stand up and decide to change their lives. They make great progress, overcome significant and daunting obstacles, and are within five minutes of reaching their personal miracle when offered an "out," an easier path, a less-than-miraculous option that gets them to the land of "almost right." After grand struggles and victories, they are tired, vulnerable and ready to taste success. Cue the opportunist or emotional terrorist who arrives and offers them a bargain for half the price. The opportunist has radar for these moments of potential emotional cave-ins or collapse. They can almost smell the moment of critical mass and swoop in with the brightly wrapped, sparkly rescue package. If the invitation is accepted, the process can slide back to the beginning or even farther back.

Here's a sample of what this dynamic looks like:

Example

1. The mission has been announced that everyone must upgrade his or her computers from level 3.0 to level 5.0 by January 1.

2. The consultant, trainer, CEO, and management begin the work of training and helping the staff adjust.

3. Person #1 upgrades to 5.0 instantly. He or she has been prepared.

4. Person #2 upgrades to 5.0.

5. The system wiggles and feels a bit disrupted.

6. Person #3 upgrades to 5.0, and several others upgrade to 3.5 and 4.0. Progress is happening.

7. Several persons resist, one employee quits, others begin to whine, one starts a rumor about layoffs.

8. Person #4 upgrades to 5.0 and several others are prepared to upgrade, but want to see what administration is going to do, if the administration and management are serious.

9. Enough people are now at 4.5 or better, and the old system begins to collapse in on itself.

10. There is stress and anxiety as some are catching up, others are failing and seeking help, others are waiting to see if the rumors are true so they can avoid the change, and some are getting their resumes in order. Resistance increases.

11. Person #5 upgrades to 5.0, and the old system is vulnerable to total collapse. Anxiety is high.

12. December 30, the system is extremely fragile before the deadline as people upgrade, adjust, struggle, or resist. A few "slowpokes" are working hard to make the shift.

13. The expectation is that on December 31, the system will shift to the new level. Tension is elevated, some people panic, others are excited, some are concerned and fearful.

14. Two more employees bail out and jump ship, someone retires early to avoid the change, a pregnant mom exits earlier than planned. Another slowpoke upgrades unexpectedly to 5.0.

15. **Critical mass happens**, and all eyes look to the CEO and management for clarity, support, recommitment, and consistency.

Therefore: On January 1, the CEO and management either stand by this original mission, with allowable room for minor or simple procedural and technical adjustments and reasonable catching-up behaviors, or:

1. The project will be seen as a test, a hoax, a manipulation, a trick, and a scheme.

2. Faith collapses. Confusion ensues. The system collapses.

3. There is a relapse back to a level below the 3.0 standard.

4. The program must be started all over at square one; faith has been lost, confidence has been shattered. All the work, tension, changes, and challenges are now seen as vaporous in relationship to the CEO's expectation. People are confused, disappointed, lost.

5. Those workers who have already completed the shift to 5.0 will now accept positions elsewhere readily, usually offered them without their solicitation. These new positions offer a setting that permits these workers to use their 5.0 skills (that your organization has paid for) in a 4.0 setting to become leaders, or the positions offer them a setting that has a 6.0 expectation that will enable them to grow.

6. At this point, you might find that the business has lost the 3.0 people and the 5.0 people, and your company is left with the less-than-cream-of-the-crop to maintain a very challenged and confused organization. *The brightest and best will leave when they lose confidence in the leadership.*

6.4.5 Remediation

Remediation is an educational process that fine-tunes the team into the level it wants to achieve. It leaves room for missed bits of information and the natural errors associated with human beings. Any current emotional terrorism flurries should be peer-managed by the policy, and anti-terrorism efforts should quickly be in the hands of managers, regular staff, and on-site managers. The worker who is still working at achieving the 5.0 system but is still stuck at a 3.0 system needs more assistance. If reasonable, visible progress is being made at a reasonable pace, then there should be room for support and encouragement.

▶ *Healthy employees* generally transition with no difficulty if they are provided clear guidelines, training, opportunities for success and mistakes, management support, and a direct indication of personal payoffs.

▶ *Dysfunctional* employees take a bit more time and attention. If they are progressing, they should be supported and encouraged. If they are valuable employees and have simply gotten on the wrong track, this is time well spent and usually is value-added and cost-effective.

▶ *Pathological* employees and emotional terrorists are generally found to be more expensive to teach than replace. Terrorists who continue resistance, sabotage progress, and fail to support the policy – while adding fuel to tension – are now reprimanded for potential policy infractions of emotional terrorism. Ongoing breaking of policies or persistence in terrorist activities need to be addressed directly and removed from a healthy system before it causes irreparable, irreversible, terminal harm.

6.5 Review Resistance to Training Programs

6.5.1 Responses from Different Types of Employees

Healthy Employees

These can be defined as: Salt-of-the-earth, fun, pleasant, groomed, inclusive, engaged with life, open, thoughtful, manage their emotions well, open with positive and negative feelings, compassionate, reasonable, fairly consistent over time, have a life.

Response to an anti-spin policy: Look forward to growth and development. May have some concerns about time involved or group commitment, but eager to see the results of more clarity and definitions of policies. No resistance.

Dysfunctional Employees

These can be defined as: Open to growth with some minor to larger fears, naive, young or old, have not been given the correct information, may be in a weakened state, vulnerable to suggestions and influences, subject to emotional swings, able to be coerced by stronger positive or negative influences, emotions are more central, may be hard workers with limited skills and options, differing levels of willingness to be taught.

Response to an anti-spin policy: Potential to be remediated, trained, informed, and educated. May either value or fear growth and development. Minor resistance.

Pathological Employees

These can be defined as: Having an agenda and a mission, willing to destroy people, places and things to protect themselves or their personal beliefs and agendas, even when masked as the "greater good." They may be using individuals or the entire system for their agenda or as a legitimate cover, may target others who appear to threaten their agenda. Emotions may be central or invisible.

Response to an anti-spin policy: May resist remediation. May escalate their efforts, go underground, or leave. Emotional escalation is traceable to them and therefore easy to remedy, more difficult if they go underground or become covert. Once underground, they may be at risk for participating in sabotage, selling proprietary information, or other ethical violations. Early identification of these employees protects all concerned. Major resistance, which can be passive or aggressive.

Emotional Terrorists/Bullies

Entitlement: "I don't have to attend, I'm too busy/important, etc."

Bulletproof: "I don't need this stuff. I've been here 27 years!"

Antagonistic: "No one else wants to come either!"

Entrenched: "We've never needed this before. This is over-reacting."

Multi-talented: "I've got other ideas that will help."

Able to attract innocent supporters: "Let's not go. I'll back you up!"

Charismatic or tragic: "I think the company is out to get us."

Hostage takers: "I have a number of questions before (and while) we start."

6.5.2 Track the Contagion

Like a virus, emotional terrorism can spread between departments if the environment within the department has vulnerable units. For example, a harmless rumor that might be laughed off by two healthy employees may be taken seriously by a dysfunctional member of the team. That same rumor, used by someone with pathology, could be the last straw for the vulnerable employee. It helps to know who the players are, so that an unexpected invasion, such as a rumor or disruption, can be anticipated and stopped in its tracks. Knowing or defining the players does not mean anything must be done other than determining the risk factors involved in developing situations.

Keep Trainings Consistent

Does each module of training follow the same "scripted" procedure so that the information is uniform and repeatable?

Is attending mandatory? Mandating attendance is important to create a sense of unity among participants and immediately limits options for spinning.

Do follow-up meetings provide creative input and collaboration from all members?

Has there been buy-in from the top? The top-down process allows the administration/management to discover which employees are on board, which are potential company emotional saboteurs, and which are simply trainable "problem children."

Does each module include practice time and drill for new tools, language, and concept acquisition? Adjustment and absorption of new ideas takes time and familiarity.

Is the time required for units or modules of education within teachable timeframes? Two hours for group education is appropriate, with shorter individual consultations when required. This process should add minimum emotional impact to the organization's functioning. Do not let lengthy trainings become fodder for emotional spinning.

Do emotional continuity management trainings have written policy and clearly defined statements for:

▶ Trainer qualifications.

▶ Company mission and team visions.

▶ Defining and clarifying top organizational buy-in.

▶ Rules for mandated participation and non-negotiable consequences for non-participation.

▶ Expectations and timetables for skills practice and drills.

▶ Value-added incentives for participation.

Are reproducible documents prepared for:

▶ Personnel interview charts.

▶ Models for explaining human emotions.

▶ Models for explaining human responses.

▶ Models for conflict resolution.

▶ Models for grief work and trauma management.

▶ Self-care tools ranging from simple to complex.

▶ Grading assessments.

▶ Models for managing individual differences.

▶ System-wide backup plans.

▶ System-wide backup plans for the backup plan.

6.5.3 Rehearse

Follow the steps to create an emergency drill that includes emotional continuity management as part of the scenario. Find ways to implement your emotional management skills and tools into the practice and exercise activities.

Retreat and Recreation

Everyone requires rest and time to play. Find ways to rest and play that work for yourself and your team. Provide a retreat, a play day, a luncheon, a surprise ice-cream party, movie tickets, a jazz band in the employee lounge, or whatever sounds wonderful and easy that will give respite before, during, and after problems and issues – and always after rehearsal drills.

Recommit

Take a deep breath and start again from Step 1, and move forward because emergencies and the emotions that go with them are not going away! The daily annoyances of humans working along side humans are an expectable part of life and working environments.

6.6 Starting an Emotional Continuity Management Team

6.6.1 Constructing Your Team

- Who is on your emotional continuity management team?
- Will they be trained and ready to get your company up and running during or after an incident?
- How do others respond to this team emotionally?
- Are they well thought of in the organization? Trusted? Safe?
- Who will show up?
- Have all members been trained in leadership to take over in case of loss of life?
- What does your company need to get back to 100% services?
- Can your company operate at 10%? 35%?
- What qualifications are acceptable to be on the emotional continuity management team?
- Have they been pre-screened for PTSD from any prior catastrophic incident?
- Are they emotionally stable, mature, trained, and willing?
- Have they had sufficient training?
- What levels of training are sufficient for your team members and leaders?
- Are your emergency and disaster plans specific or generalized?
- What is vague and what is specific?
- Have you tested your plan?

▶ Has the testing consisted of table talk or real-time drills and exercises?

▶ Have your team members discussed and planned for emotional shock, loss, and terror?

▶ What support does your team have to manage their own feelings while they are supporting others?

▶ Have all team member been trained to understand the variety of emotional reactions to expect in case of a catastrophic incident by a qualified disaster or trauma specialist or qualified licensed mental health professional?

▶ Who will replace you if you are not present? How would your team deal with losing you?

▶ Does everyone know all the parts of the plan?

▶ Qualifications Checklist for Team Members, External Consultants, Emotional Continuity Management Trainer, Services Provider.

▶ Decide what your best practices and standards are for qualifications and then document the following (all licensing and certification credentials should be documented with copies of current status that can be updated on a yearly basis as needed):

   ❏ Formal training.

   ❏ Informal training/experiences.

   ❏ Real time disaster experience.

   ❏ Continuing education.

   ❏ Licensures.

   ❏ License number and date of expiration/photocopy.

   ❏ Malpractice insurance.

   ❏ Specialized training.

   ❏ Experience.

   ❏ References.

   ❏ Special skills.

   ❏ Special population skills.

   ❏ Availability.

   ❏ Locations.

❏ Types of services.

❏ Application forms/process.

❏ Photo ID.

❏ Criminal background check including fingerprints.

❏ Security clearance if needed.

❏ Vehicular background check if needed.

❏ Signed contract for services including clear fee arrangements.

6.6.2 Constructing a "Team Notebook"

Minimum requirements for notebook content should include:

- Team composition.
- Chain of authority.
- Exit strategies.
- Member list and all contact methods.
- Verifications of qualifications of all team members.
- Verification that all team members have been screened for PTSD and prior trauma.
- Plans for changes in circumstances, shifts, time off.
- Complete data about what your company will require to return to 100%, 75%, 50%, 25% services.
- Anticipated obstacles to complete recovery.
- Written plans for the emotional continuity management for specific incidents, even those that appear to be unlikely or even unthinkable:

Tornado	Emotional Terrorist
Earthquake	Winter Storm
Suicide	Hurricane
Cyber-Crime	Chemical Spill
Shooting	Shelter In Place
Fire	

- Extensive lists of local, regional, national and international resources.
- A chronology of how you have tested your plans and lessons learned data.

- Reproducible copies of required or preferred forms or documents.

- Emergency numbers for team members and families.

- Complete written policy and procedures.

- Company/administrative buy-in statement.

- List of insurances and legal support.

- List of all employees under the domain of the emotional continuity management team.

Notebook Tips

If your team members have special notebooks, smart phones, notebook devices, apps, and other gadgets that they can carry with them to a site, they need to be colorful, valued, portable, useable, "awesome," and easily accessible so they can just grab-and-go out the door and not have to search for them under duress. Notebook pages need to be removable and covered with plastic sheet protectors. Be sure to include blank lined paper for jotting notes, an attachable pen, and perhaps even a backpack or carrying case that team members think looks cool. The point of these details is that during duress, your team needs to not have to think about anything but doing their work as calmly as possible. Looking for a bit of paper to write a phone number, or scrambling for a pen, is contraindicated for an emotional continuity manager.

Start collecting data for an ever-evolving team notebook with reproducible documents, forms, logos, policies, plans, procedures, checklists, guidelines, resources, requirements, and anything your team members decide would assist them in emotional continuity management during an emotional incident or disaster.

Everyone comes to the table wanting something different. Counters want numbers, helpers want to be useful, and managers want to manage. Setting your own goals will necessitate your understanding of your position at the table and your own personal sense of style. Extroverts and introverts will approach the process from opposite ends of the same continuum. I tell people that they cannot fail. They can learn or not learn. Successes should be studied for what went right, and failures are studied for what can go better. Spending time on blame is a waste of energy and a potential spin. Finding something to celebrate on a daily basis can keep your motivation going even in the dark nights of the manager's soul. It is the little things that keep hopes alive and spirits moving toward the goal.

Find things to be amazed about in yourself and others. After major disasters there are always pieces circulating on the Internet about the "little things that kept people alive." Take the time to ponder your own philosophical and theoretical basis, because these are the foundations of your daily work. Do not be afraid to ask questions. And do not let the "little things" get in your way. Read this Internet piece to start making your own perspective (*Those annoying little things*, 2003):

> After Sept. 11, one company invited the remaining members of other companies who had been decimated by the attack on the Twin Towers to share their available office space. At a morning meeting, the head of security told stories of why these people were alive. All the stories were just about the "little things."

❑ The head of a company got in late that day because his son started kindergarten.

❑ Another fellow was alive because it was his turn to bring donuts.

❑ One woman was late because her alarm clock did not go off in time.

❑ One was late because of being stuck on the New Jersey Turnpike because of an auto accident.

❑ One of them missed his bus.

❑ One spilled food on her clothes and had to take time to change.

❑ One's car would not start.

❑ One went back to answer the telephone.

❑ One had a child that dawdled and did not get ready as soon as he should have.

❑ One could not get a taxi.

❑ Then there was the man who put on a new pair of shoes that morning, took the various means to get to work but before he got there, he developed a blister on his foot. He stopped at a drugstore to buy a Band-Aid. That is why he is alive today.

So you are observing, thinking, intuiting, hearing stories from witnesses, seeing there is chaos or a problem and start thinking, "Now what do I do?" Start collecting and documenting. It may take a long time. Commit to the process and it works.

6.7 How to Make Hard Technical Data and Soft Technical Data Assessments

6.7.1 Part One: The Hard Technicals

The following is a guideline for anyone trying to develop a hard paper evaluation, auditing criteria, or assessment policy. You can use the following to create policy, set standards of excellence, define best practices, create documentation, or begin appropriate dialogue about your company's requirements for excellence:

▶ Ongoing evaluation of training standards and practices of HR staff/CEUs/credentials.

▶ Training standards and practices of EAP, third-party providers, medical providers, and mental health providers.

▶ Hiring practices: psychological screenings.

▶ Firing practices: risk assessments.

▶ Security professional standards: CEUs, credentials.

▶ How are people taught to catch or react to discovery of fraud?

▶ Criteria standards for disaster preparation/management.

▶ Correlations between sick days and project agendas.

▶ Absenteeism patterns.

▶ Grievance patterns.

▶ Health dollars spent.

▶ Mental health dollars spent.

▶ Employee satisfaction.

▶ Employee perceptions.

▶ Vendor satisfaction.

▶ Vendor perceptions.

▶ Community satisfaction.

▶ Community perceptions.

▶ Competency standards of all interagency support interventions.

▶ Level and credibility of intervention specialists and options with industry standards.

- Industry standards for impairment interventions.

- Participation patterns for interventions/treatments/consultations.

- Emerging patterns of behavior at 30/60/90 and 365 days after hire.

- Post-hiring, post-firing, post-retirement, or post-transition follow-up procedures.

6.7.2 Part Two: The Soft Technicals

The following is a guideline for anyone trying to develop a hard-paper evaluation of soft-sided information. It can be turned into auditing criteria or an assessment policy. This information can also be turned into checklists, discussion points, impressions to share, didactic data points, or action points. You can use the following to create policy, set standards of excellence, define best practices, create documentation, or begin appropriate dialogue about your company's requirements for excellence:

- How does it feel to be in the presence of this person?

- Demonstrations: body language, voice tone, gestures.

- General hygiene.

- Strength or weakness of the general infrastructure.

- Strength or weakness of relationship links.

- Power balances or imbalances.

- Real or perceived power.

- Commitment to the organization.

- Commitment to self, others.

- Loyalty links.

- Rigidity/flexibility.

- Sense of the big picture: mission.

- Sense of the small picture: units.

- On same page as CEO/management/agendas.

- Self-perception.

- Discrepancies between self and other perception.

- Level of satisfaction.

- Communication skills/styles.

- Willingness to learn.
- Willingness to contribute.
- Willingness to mentor.
- Willingness to change.
- Willingness to self-disclose.
- Willingness to self-evaluate.
- Comfort with own humanity.
- Perception of the organizational change: past/present/future.
- Perception of the organizational change's effect on self/others.
- Language of enhancing or demeaning self or others.
- Whining, victimhood, aggression, anger, blame, shame, fear, hostility, rumors, threats, apathy.
- Once again, how did it feel to be in the presence of this person?

Documentation Can Be Your Best Friend

- If you are asked five years from now to defend yourself, will you have documentation to protect yourself and your part of the story?
- What level of documentation will be necessary to underwrite your risk?
- Did you notify all parties with whom you shared information? It doesn't have to be a narrative or long observation notes. It can be code in a daybook that you can recognize if needed.

Simple Documentation, Including Formal or Informal Notes

- When and where did this meeting happen?
- Why was the employee in your office?
- What happened?
- What was the emotional environment?
- Describe the dilemma or concern.
- What was said?
- What plans or recommendations were made?
- What are potential risks to these plans or recommendations?
- Did you discuss any potential risks?

▶ How did you intend to follow through with recommendations?

▶ Did you follow through?

▶ Did the employee follow through?

▶ When?

▶ Who else was involved in this action?

▶ What phone calls or meetings occurred with this action?

▶ Were there any other emotional responses that should be noted?

> **Removal is not always the best strategy because there is always another emotional terrorist with an excellent resume just waiting in the wings to fill the next empty slot.**

If an emotional terrorist is under a contract or has the support of a union, dealing with an emotional terrorist could be a prolonged process. The goal may not be to remove the person from the team. It may work better to micro-manage an emotional terrorist until he or she is either on board, compliant, or exits voluntarily. Removal is not always the best strategy because there is always another emotional terrorist with an excellent resume just waiting in the wings to fill the next empty slot.

When there is clear, unambiguous policy spelling out expectations, management is certainly within its rights to reprimand and remediate. If such a policy is in place, even in its earliest formats and rough drafts, and an employee does not respond or honor it, you will immediately have some excellent information. This information becomes worthwhile criteria for documentations, reprimands, trainings, remediations, or removals. Include your legal staff and HR management as you organize the paper documentation chain to support and maintain the policy. A written policy is mandatory when dealing with an emotional terrorist or the person will turn the problem back on you.

Documentation May Include the Following Attributes

▶ We (the organization, the members of the task force, the department, individuals) set the policy on this date.

▶ This is the policy (full written document/history/mission/ statistics/justification).

▶ The policy was explained to all employees on this date (trainings).

▶ Opportunity for training and advanced information was provided in this format.

- Ongoing and secondary training options were available and recommended to all employees.

- This worker did not respond/or responded in specific manners not within expected levels (document specifics and how it links to policy).

- This worker was individually encouraged to review expectations and given ample opportunity to gather increased information, training, mentorship, or other third party assistance in achieving adequate standards (options offered, dates, training opportunities, private meetings, consultations, EAPs, etc.).

- Policy on adequacy standards repeated (clarify expectations between the A+ and the C- expectations of compliance to policy).

- This worker was encouraged to attend specific trainings or learn specific procedures to assist the worker in getting on board with these opportunities. All impediments to the worker's participation were removed in the following way (time off, transportation, per diem, etc.).

- This worker was again encouraged to attend special trainings or procedures to assist in the worker getting on board with these opportunities. All impediments to the worker's participation were removed in the following way (time off, transportation, per diem, etc).

- The worker did not respond (specific non-compliance reports).

- The worker was given another good faith fair warning, clarification, and opportunity to address expectations. (List next trainings, individual meetings, consultations, educational opportunities offered).

- Compliance successful (date, examples, support evidence).

- Compliance failed (date, examples, support evidence).

- Recommend extended training or dismissal. (The organization must determine the cost variances and value added benefits of ongoing extended training for behavior adaptation over the costs of rehiring or re-training another employee.)

Documentation Example

1. (Company name) established a (policy name) on (date).

2. A copy of the policy is attached.

3. Trainings on this policy were given to all employees on (dates).

4. Ongoing training was offered to all employees and announced through the following communications and in the following formats: (formats), (advertising).

5. (Name) did not respond to the company expectations for this policy within expected levels (document specifics and how it links to policy, including a section on "intangibles, impressions, and intuitions").

6. (Name) was individually encouraged to review expectations and given ample opportunity to gather increased information, training, mentorship, or other third party assistance in achieving adequate standards (options offered, dates, training opportunities, private meetings, consultations, EAPs, etc.).

7. Policy on adequacy standards and expectations was reviewed and repeated on the following dates in the format specified: (dates).

8. (Name) was encouraged to attend special trainings and offered mentored or tutorial procedures to assist compliance by_____.

9. Any reported impediments to their participation were removed in the following way (time off, transportation, per diem, etc.).

10. (Name) was again encouraged to attend special trainings or proce-dures to assist in compliance and impediments to their participation were removed in the following way (time off, transportation, per diem, etc.).

11. (Name) responded with/ did not respond (specific non-compliance reports).

12. (Name) was given another good faith fair warning, clarification and opportunity to address expectations. (List next trainings, individual meetings, consultations, educational opportunities offered.)

13. Compliance successful (date, examples, support evidence).

14. Compliance failed (date, examples, support evidence).

15. Costs associated with non-compliance to policy to date. (The organization must determine the cost variances and value added benefits of ongoing extended training for behavior adaptation over the costs of rehiring or re-training another employee.)

16. Recommendations.

17. Notifications.

18. Signatures, witnesses, additional information.

19. Follow-up.

6.8 How to Write New Policies

Many organizations have infrastructure based on management policies and procedures. The procedures get things done, and the policies are the frameworks or principles to guide the flow. When things break down, policies are reviewed and rewritten. Policies are more than guidelines and less than laws; they can serve to direct system energy, block the flow, or create disruptions.

6.8.1 Policy Writing Guidelines

A policy is a course or management of methods and actions that guide and determine present and future decisions or practices.

There are many other ways to formulate policy, depending upon industry standards and expectations.

- ▶ *Some policy is better than no policy.* Policy can be a safety net or an impediment to movement.
- ▶ Good policy is part science and part art combining data, facts and aesthetics necessary to keep the flow moving forward.
- ▶ Policy is a framework so should be open and fluid.
- ▶ Policy incorporates ethics.
- ▶ An effective policy spells out the rules clearly, avoiding misinterpretation.
- ▶ A policy is written in clear and simple language.

Policy can be general and/or specific. For example,

General	Specific
No-spinning-at-the-workplace policy	No gossip policy
Dress code policy	No slogan T-shirts policy
Anti-harassment policy	No sexual jokes policy

A well-written policy has roots and flexibility. The roots must come from the administrative level of support. These roots are absolutely necessary for any policy to withstand any winds that may come. Without this support, the policy will necessarily fail as it blows away in the dust if challenged.

Flexibility adds the bend and movement to a policy so that it does not become fixed and rigid over time. The sources of flexibility should be gleaned from the specific daily demands at your worksite or in your industry and include any cultural, ethnic, economic, or emotional dynamics that are part of the place the policy is intended to serve. It should offer protection and openness.

There needs to be enough flexibility to serve production as well as the people who perform the production. A policy should serve the bottom line concerns of the company, the community, the global marketplace, and in the best of all worlds, the planet. Policies should be living forms and not rigid statutes set in mental concrete.

6.8.2 How to Write an Anti-Emotional Terrorism Policy

An *anti-terrorism policy* should be strong enough to withstand an F-5 emotional tornado. That means any policy you craft needs amazing roots and an incredible amount of flexibility. When any policy is in place, it becomes exquisitely clear who the players are. Identification of players is even clearer when you are creating a policy to manage an emotional terrorist at the worksite. Emotional terrorists will offer grand and creative resistance. A strong policy clarifies the boundaries, which can set up a reactionary environment until the policy is standardized, tested, and supported by the administration.

Those employees who do not like boundaries, like emotional terrorists, will feel compelled to act, react, respond, go overt, go covert, or create spinning in others. While other employees whine and complain and inevitably either exit or adjust to the situation, emotional terrorists will escalate their agenda in order not to be bound by the rules of others. The creation of a policy often illuminates a hidden terrorist instantly when the person's resistance becomes visible. Knowing and expecting this evidence of resistance is useful if you are grounded in good theories and procedures prior to implementating and announcing new policy.

The following is an introduction to how you might start thinking how you are going to develop components for your "No Emotional Terrorism at the Worksite" policy.

A "No-Spinning-Allowed" Policy

- Develop and define the limitations your organization is able or willing to manage if confronted by emotional disruptions from small to catastrophic.

- Demand zero tolerance for going beyond the level defined as tolerable by your organization.

- Build into the policy enough room to handle the strong human emotions of extenuating circumstances, natural disasters, man-made disasters, and unexpected events.

> Build into the policy a pre- and post-disaster emotional support and management program such as critical incident stress management, defusings, debriefings, training, counseling, EAP, or ongoing intervention strategies.

> Create a close relationship between legal, HR, security, internal auditing and administration to develop procedures to track, evaluate, and measure emotional intangibles and to protect all employees from emotional terrorists. This should be part of any disaster plan.

> Provide ongoing training for all strata of employees in the areas of understanding normal as well as abnormal human emotions, the relationship of these emotions to the business world, and what happens to real people.

> Supply ongoing training in human emotions management to all staff. (Anyone left out becomes a risk.)

> Describe minimum qualifications for external consultant or service provider.

6.9 Drills for Emotional Incidents

6.9.1 Preparing For Drills

"Everyone thought we were crazy for drilling and preparing for terrorism."

Jerry Hauer, former director of the NYC Office of Emergency Management, testifying before the 9-11 Commission, May 19, 2004 (CNN U.S., 2004).

The expression "practice makes perfect" is not necessarily correct! If you are practicing something incorrectly, doing it over and over and over will not correct it. The phrase should be, "practice something perfectly to maintain perfection." The only way to attain anything close to perfection is to practice until you discover your errors, get feedback, and make corrections. Emergency, disaster and readiness drills need to address the physical and the emotional needs of your people. Reading this chapter will get you started in seeing how to include emotions in your regular emergency drill practices.

6.9.2 Create an Emotional Continuity Management Event Hot Sheet

> What is the nature of the event?

> What is the scope of the emotional impact?

- How much geography/territory is involved (i.e., a fire in the break room, a devastated community or a devastated one-block radius, a 48-car pile-up in front of the main entrance to the worksite, death of one colleague, death of many colleagues)?

- Who is in charge, authority/command structure? (Whom do I report to?)

- Has there been property damage?

- Who has authority for restoring the property damaged?

- Have people been displaced, injured, or killed?

- How many victims are involved?

- What are their ages if known?

- Are any children involved?

- Will the needs of the children be treated separately from those of the adults? Elderly? Special needs/disabled?

- Are there any fatalities?

- What is the general nature of any injuries (mild, moderate, severe, catastrophic)?

- Will I have access to medical information?

- How many support staff will be involved?

- Support systems and teams in place now? On the way?

- How long will I be expected to respond?

- Will I be safe? How will that be accomplished?

- Is there a dress code? Or are there any special circumstances in which clothing or footwear should be a factor (i.e. weather, walking through rubble, ethnic or cultural needs, attire for funerals)?

- Is the entire staff trained in full range of disaster protocols from shelter in place to full evacuation?

- Has the entire staff been trained in what emotions to anticipate during this kind of incident?

- Are there cultural, religious, political, or ethnic variables that I should know or understand?

- What languages will be spoken? Will there be translators?

- Am I covered by company liability insurance or my own? Or both?

▶ What duties am I expected to perform or will I be responsible for providing (i.e. debriefings, defusings, counseling, crisis response, medication assessment, diagnosis, mediation, communications, transportation, referrals, hand-holding)?

▶ What paperwork will be required to manage this incident? Do I have all the required forms?

▶ What are the mental health or disaster professional qualifications necessary to deal with this?

▶ Who else will be helping me on this?

▶ Will I be fed, housed, provided for, given chocolate?

▶ Will there be an expectation of continuous service, or will there be opportunity for self-care, support for me if I need it, breaks, days off, etc.?

▶ What are my other resources?

▶ If I find that the situation is beyond my scope, expertise, or personal tolerance, or if I become ill or injured or incapacitated, what is the protocol for a professional exit strategy, and will that be supported?

▶ Who will take over my assignments?

▶ What are the qualifications of the disaster team?

▶ What are the qualifications of the emotional continuity management team?

▶ How do I protect my team and myself first?

▶ What is the emotional environment needed for rapid recovery?

▶ What is the physical environment (locations on-off site, recovery equipment, communications, paper/pencils, water bottles, cell-phones, toilet paper) needed for rapid recovery?

▶ Do we have event-specific planning strategies?

▶ Do we have memos of understanding (MOUs), agreements, contracts with local, national and global resources?

▶ Have we tested this plan?

6.9.3 Drill and Rehearsal Form Checklist

▶ Establish full buy-in administratively.

▶ Pick your team.

▶ Assign roles.

- Determine leadership or authority chains.
- Define the emotional needs of your company.
- Decide on what kind of drill you will have.
- Establish timetable.
- What is the purpose of the drill?
- What are five specific objectives you will seek?
- What documentation will be required?
- Create and write the emergency and emotional scenarios.
- Make participant assignments.
- Consider how you would manage a real emergency or unexpected event if one occurred during the exercise.
- Make a detailed list of all activities, small and large.
- List emotions that you wish to exercise and the interventions you would use.
- Decide on how you will evaluate the exercise after it has been completed.
- Conduct the drill.
- Collect documentation.
- Analyze data.
- Celebrate the closure of the drill formally.
- Debrief participants and planners without critique.
- Planners evaluate the success or failure of goal achievements:
  - ❏ Lessons learned.
  - ❏ Add or subtract necessary components for the next drill.
  - ❏ Decide on what training will be necessary and who will get it.
  - ❏ Schedule the next drill.
  - ❏ Send written thank you notes to all participants. No memos, real letters.

Additional Steps

- "This is a Drill" instructions given.
- Identification tags.
- Focus evaluations on positive points.

- Have fun.
- Add a surprise.
- Associated agencies participation.
- Drill a full range of emotions from small to large, annoyances to catastrophic.
- Participants told to maintain their acting roles until excused from the drill.
- Notifications.
- Exit information.
- Practice mock debriefings.
- Debriefing schedule.
- Formal thank you notes.
- What questions will you need answered to make good decisions?
- What resources will you need in each case?
- What resources will you activate immediately?
- What resources will you put on stand-by?
- How will you approach administration, employees, vendors and ancillary participants?
- What plan will you write?
- What policies for emotions will you want in place?
- What people with what qualifications will serve you best?
- What level of emotional impact will this possibly have?
- What risks will there be for solo or group emotional spinning?
- What tools will you use to manage the emotions of employees?
- How will you take care of yourself as you participated?
- What would be the estimated costs of this for your company?
- Outline the performance tasks that must be accomplished.
- Outline the emotional components for yourself, the staff, and the community that you must accommodate as the process evolves.
- What emotions are likely to be demonstrated?
- What might be a surprise emotion?
- How will you manage the emotions of your employees and clients?

▶ What fears or concerns can you anticipate because they were
exposed to a potential health threat? Exposed to injury? Exposed
to death?

How will you plan for managing these emotions?

Fear	Anger
Rage	Terror
Sadness	Concern
Ambivalence	Hysteria
Boredom	Numbness
Confusion	Shock
Horror	Disgust
Disappointment	Grief
Denial	Horror
Grief	Disgust
Disappointment	Withdrawing
Irritation	Rancor
Pessimism	Impatience
Passivity	Aggression
Nervousness	Embarrassment
Edginess	Sensitivity

6.9.4 Setting Up a Drill

1 Establish full buy-in administratively.

2. Determine leadership.

3. Prepare with paper drills and table-talks prior to simulation drills.

4. Define the goals of the drill.

5. Develop appropriate and safe logistical settings.

6. Develop appropriate scenarios.

7. Create scenario assignments.

8. Consider management of a real emergency or unexpected event
during the simulation.

9. Review plans and gather feedback.

10. Conduct the drill.

11. Collect results.

12. Celebrate the closure of the drill formally.

13. Debrief participants and planners without critique.

14. Planners then can evaluate the success or failure of goal achievements.

15. Add or subtract necessary components and schedule next drill cycle.

16. Send thank you notes to all participants.

17. What questions will you need answered to make good decisions?

18. What resources will you need in each case?

19. What resources will you activate immediately?

20. What resources will you put on stand-by?

21. How will you approach administration, employees, vendors, and ancillary participants?

22. What plan will you write?

23. What policies for emotions will you want in place?

24. What people with what qualifications will serve you best?

25. What level of emotional impact will this possibly have?

26. What risks will there be for solo or group emotional spinning?

27. What tools will you use to manage the emotions of employees?

28. How will you take care of yourself as you participated?

29. What would be the estimated costs of this for your company?

30. *What would be the estimated costs for your company if it were unprepared for a real emergency?*

6.9.5 Tips for Success of Drills

Clear Notifications: Always state *"This is a drill"* when making phone calls or contact calls during the drill. You have probably heard about what happened during an October 30, 1938, radio broadcast, when Orson Welles and his group of actors performed a dramatization of the H.G. Wells science fiction novel, *The War of the Worlds*, complete with very realistic sounding "news bulletins." The performance sounded so real that some people – who tuned in late and didn't hear the message that this was a theatrical performance – began to panic, thinking that aliens were really invading the Earth. People are nervous. Our world is scarier today than it was even a few years ago. It is better to be cautious than to create more emotional impact. It is critical to inform and notify all players and anyone who might be concerned that this is not a drill.

Identification Tags: For the same reasons as above, and for ease in managing the participants, all members should have visible and highly identifiable temporary identification that is collected after the drill.

Time them well: A drill during a layoff phase is dangerous. A drill during an earthquake is pointless and dangerous.

Evaluations should focus on positive points: Negative critiques destroy buy-in. Attempt to phrase weaknesses and losses in positive "can-do-better-next-time" language.

Have fun: Simulations can be fun and exciting when people are motivated to do their best for the sake of everyone else.

Add a surprise: The unexpected is where drills show holes in preparation. Don't add anything extreme, but include a small twist to make it interesting.

Ask other experts to play with you: Go to your local fire department, hospital, or chapter of the American Red Cross and ask someone to help you plan your drill.

Drill a full range of emotions: Include all feelings from small to large, annoyances to catastrophic.

Maintain the illusion: Encourage participants to maintain their acting roles until excused from the drill.

Explain exit strategies and ending calls: Inform your participants how they can exit the drill if it becomes distressful. Also inform everyone when or how the drill will conclude.

Debrief even when it is a drill: Make certain any individuals who exit a drill have a mandatory debriefing to deter people who simply want to exit the process so they can go home early, and to protect participants who may really have difficulty. This also gets people into the good habit of debriefing.

Pleases and thank-yous: Courtesy goes a long way to create closure and future buy-in. Write a formal thank you letter to all participants.

Make Lists: Extensive contact lists are a good thing! Make an **Emergency Assistance Resource** list of phone, email, text, addresses and primary and secondary contact names and numbers. Include as many as you can:

- First responders (Fire, Law)
- Emotional Continuity Management Team (ECMT)
- Business continuity management team (BCP)
- Employee assistance providers (EAP)
- Mental and medical health providers
- Insurance providers/agents
- U.S. Department of Homeland Security (DHS)
- Weather (NOAA)
- U.S. Department of Justice (DOJ)
- Federal Emergency Management (FEMA)
- Department of Energy (DOE)
- Environmental Protection Agency (EPA)
- Department of Health And Human Services (DHHS)
- U.S. Department of Transportation (DOT)
- Department of Defense (DOD)
- National Transportation Safety Board (NTSB)
- American Red Cross
- Emergency medical services
- Public works
- 24-hour crisis hot line
- Volunteer services assistance organizations:
  - ❏ Salvation Army
  - ❏ Critical incident stress management teams
  - ❏ Spiritual support network
  - ❏ D'Mort (death support)
  - ❏ Dive or search and rescue
  - ❏ HAM radio providers
  - ❏ Ski patrol
  - ❏ Canine search and rescue

Emergency contingency experts contend that drilling and exercising for unexpected catastrophes is critical to speedy recovery. As any number of disaster managers can attest, there are times when infrastructure and technology survive or can be replaced, but if your employees are consumed by their emotions, all the trendy technology in the world will not calm those emotions. Machinery cannot lead the recovery of the emotions of human beings. Only other human beings can do that.

Practicing emotional emergency drills is different from drilling for emergency technology or structure disruptions. It is difficult for most people to pretend to have feelings the first few times and can feel somewhat ridiculous. Students who have practiced the techniques of role modeling, drama students, and extroverts may enjoy filling the roles of emotion actors during your first practice drill. Red Cross volunteers would probably be more than happy to show you how to "play disaster." Although everyone will know this is artificially staged, employees and emotional continuity management team members can begin to think through their responses and develop a repertoire.

One of the intriguing parts about creating a drill which includes the emotional component is that once the veneer is gone and everyone is given collective permission to "play," you may be surprised at how real it feels, how introverts become extroverts, and how engaged your participants become in the process. You should have a mental health professional available in case someone becomes unexpectedly authentically distressed.

An Example

The emotional continuity management trainer had prepared the company volunteers on what to expect in case of a real chemical weapons emergency. The drill was going along smoothly until two unexpected events occurred. First, one of the volunteer victim actors had a real psychological panic attack and began screaming uncontrollably. Most of the volunteers assumed it was part of the act of participating in a lifelike emergency drill. When she did not stop in a few minutes, the team realized that the drill had turned into a real event, at which point they followed their guidelines to assist the authentically distressed participant.

The second unexpected surprise was when a planned surprise turned into an emotional disturbance. As in other disaster drills, the planners wanted to throw in a few surprises to see how people would respond. Unbeknownst to the participants in the exercise, the trainers had asked the coroner to send a team of deputies to practice death notification. When the deputies and the coroner arrived, and began asking for assistance from the participants to notify a family member about a "death," the company team slipped from practicing emotions to real emotions. Facing the coroner brought up a ripple of terror in the exercise that was unexpected. Because the scene of the drill had been so well staged, several participants began to question if this was a drill or a real event. One mental health professional became so visibly upset that she was relieved of her duty. Another volunteer stepped forward to address the issues, now uncertain if it was real or drill. The team continued to follow procedures although distressed and managed well by using previously practiced methods. The volunteer took a quiet leadership role and directed others to assist one another with their emotional concerns.

Do this: Factor in the concept of emotional continuity management (which includes post-traumatic stress disorder training, stress management, debriefing, and defusing as well as normal and abnormal and mental health considerations) into your drills.

Don't: Have drills in close proximity to a real event in your community; include people who have had recent trauma; or, involve children in the drills. Don't have a mock drill without a post-drill mock-debriefing by trained individuals.

Actual Drills

Emergency responders drill their technical tasks and their emotional tasks. They learn teamwork techniques to support and enhance performance and emotional stability. The buddy system or check-in process keeps people on track emotionally during distressing incidents. Post-incident training usually requires a debriefing process of some sort that allows participants to ventilate their emotions. First responders have discovered that individuals who take care of their emotional equipment as well as their technical equipment are less likely to be candidates for PTSD and generally have a more durable career. The concept is that toxic emotions enter into the human system during an incident and must find a way to exit. That exit can be healthy or dysfunctional, but the emotions will come out. If they do not exit, they will remain in the system and cause toxic and potentially terminal damage on the system. Debriefing does not "fix" feelings. It only allows them appropriate ventilation so they don't build up to a dangerous and toxic overload that can either explode or go deep underground to cause hidden damage.

A well-conceived drill verifies the emotional continuity management plan, increases goodwill for a job well done, demonstrates weaknesses and strengths, identifies additions or subtractions to the plan, increases buy-in for stakeholders, and protects companies from the liability risk of not being employee-centered. Remember that the old adage of "practice makes perfect" is only applicable if the practice is done correctly. Practicing something incorrectly over and over does not make it perfect, unless your goal is to make it perfectly wrong. In fact, an abbreviated definition of insanity is doing the same wrong thing over and over, expecting different and better results.

All emergency management organizations practice and evaluate their tools and techniques to fine-tune their systems. Critiques and table-talks are arranged to hash over the successes and failures of plans and procedures. These generally cognitive, businesslike, and non-emotional exchanges are arranged to find the weak links, missed ideas, or new data necessary to update emergency responses. New information provides new ideas.

Some organizations have the forethought to include the emotional components into their planning exercises. Some local chapters of the American Red Cross, for example, participate in expansive community emergency exercises that include a number of different agencies and responder components. They often include in the prepared scenario a number of actors who will demonstrate what a real victim may present at the scene. These actors and actresses are often community volunteers who enjoy the opportunity to be made up with a technique called "medical moulage" that realistically simulates blood and gore. Some volunteers allow themselves to be put in body bags and others volunteer to act as grieving relatives. Firefighters, law enforcement professionals, health care teams, security guards, city officials, and coroners act out their roles in these scripted dramas while disaster mental health responders artificially comfort the fake survivors. These drills and exercises have been shown to be priceless opportunities to think through what might really happen in a similar situation.

Do this: Invite mental health professionals who have been trained in disaster responses and have had field experiences to planning meetings.

Don't: Let someone who has the title but not the credentials or experience dismiss the needs of emotional continuity management during this phase of your planning.

In recent years, businesses have not needed to consider themselves "emergency responders." This impression is no longer valid. With the instability of today's world you may find yourself in a situation in which you must respond immediately and with clarity to save your own life or the lives of your co-workers. The extreme situation that managers of corporate offices in the World Trade Center towers experienced early in the morning of September 11, 2001 has served as a wake-up-call to many businesses, causing them to come up with emotional continuity management plans to handle the emotional impact of a large-scale event.

If you think your little company might be immune to such drama because you are in Padiddle, South Nowhere, and all you do is make little widgets and have five employees, think again. Consider natural disasters, disgruntled employees, a random psychopath with a weapon, rumor, layoff, national economic events that shut down your communications system, a community transportation tragedy, a disrupted shipping process, or the completely unthinkable event that makes the national headlines because no one in their "right mind" would have guessed that such a horror could have happened at little-ol' Padiddle, South Nowhere, in the lobby of the What's-Up Widget Company! But CNN is on its way! The weirdest and most random things can happen – because life is unpredictable.

> Scores of emergency planning texts are available to help your company formulate a drill. For example, you can take an IT contingency book and retranslate the technological risks into emotional risks.

Drills and Rehearsals for Emotions

Scores of emergency planning texts are available to help your company formulate a drill. For example, you can take an IT contingency book and retranslate the technological risks into emotional risks. What are your company's emotional mainframe, software, hardware, database, applications, platforms or communications systems? In other words, who are your strong leaders, your soft followers, your knowers, your doers, your standard-bearers, and your communicators? Or, you could call emergency management providers in your community and ask them to help you create a drill. This book also offers some guidelines. What is important to know is that a drill doesn't need to be fancy, but it does need to be formalized.

Best practices say that drills should be mandatory, well planned, and regularly scheduled. Until participants have had some practice in drilling, a surprise exercise would cause too much emotional stress, and that outcome is the opposite goal from what you would want to have. Emergency preparedness drills which include emotions are intended to prepare participants for a traumatic event and to give participants confidence that they can survive. If the real deal happens, it has been rehearsed and will have a less shattering effect than something that is considered unthinkable. Unthinkable incidents happen, and people are emotionally overwhelmed by the difficulties of incorporating totally new ideas during extreme duress.

Paper drills: A paper drill is just that, a drill on paper. It is a combination of scenarios and written guidelines provided to leadership to pre-think their concerns. The data is collected and shared with all departments.

Table-talks: A table talk or tabletop drill is one that is held around a table. In other words, it is all talk and no physical action. It is an opportunity for participants to share and talk through their concerns, ideas, and expectations to become familiar with each other, as well as with emergency policies, procedures, and exercise compliances.

Dress rehearsal or walk-through: A physical practice of the elements of the drill. One step away from the table-talk and two steps away from paper. More real, but very controlled.

Job function: This drill tests specific jobs, people, or departments.

Evacuation Drill: Participants act out an evacuation with simulated hazards, like stairways with participants acting like dead bodies, moulage, smoke, debris, and loss of communications. Surprises are built into the drill and the plan will need to adapt to the situation.

Full simulation: A full simulation is a real-time action replication or mockup of what a disaster might look like and feel like. Although it is artificial, it is the closest proximity to real-time incidents. The most labor-intensive type of drill, simulations may prepare employees more for a real disaster than any other form of drilling. An emergency situation is simulated as closely as possible. This exercise should include all company participants, emergency personnel, local emergency agencies and others.

6.10 How to Set Up a Drill for Continuity Management

The week of September 11, 2001, I was scheduled to participate in a multi-agency aviation disaster simulation emergency drill. Hundreds of people were involved. The leadership thought it might be appropriate to cancel the drill under the circumstances. Everyone involved stated something to the effect that, more than ever, we needed to drill. The emotional contexts of the participants were profound during the drill. Although we had all drilled many times before, there was a new meaning to the practice. It was the first time that my teams really saw the need for post-drill debriefing, using my drill buddy systems plan, providing personal emotional support for one another, and really using the emotional continuity management tools they had learned from me in countless, tedious trainings. It was the first time team members thanked me for pounding into their heads that, during a real event, they would have unexpected emotions. It was the first time that a significant and powerful leader who had been a major obstacle to the addition of emotional continuity management during disaster drills made a special effort to thank me for pre-training his employees. They knew what to do and called in the proper resources from within their own company.

- Establish full buy-in administratively.
- Determine leadership.
- Prepare with paper drills and table-talks prior to simulation drills.
- Define the goals of the drill.
- Develop appropriate and safe logistical settings.
- Develop appropriate scenarios.
- Create scenario assignments.
- Consider management of a real emergency or unexpected event during the simulation.
- Review plans and gather feedback.
- Conduct the drill.
- Collect results.
- Celebrate the closure of the drill formally.
- Debrief participants and planners without critique.
- Planners then can evaluate the success or failure of goal achievements.
- Add or subtract necessary components and schedule next drill cycle.
- Send thank-you notes to all participants.

Consider:

- What questions will you need answered to make good decisions?
- What resources will you need in each case?
- What resources will you activate immediately?
- What resources will you put on stand-by?
- How will you approach administration, employees, vendors, and ancillary participants?
- What plan will you write?
- What policies for emotions will you want in place?
- What people with what qualifications will serve you best?
- What level of emotional impact will this possibly have?
- What risks will there be for solo or group emotional spinning?
- What tools will you use to manage the emotions of employees?
- How will you take care of yourself as you participate?
- What would be the estimated costs of this for your company?

▷ What would be the estimated costs for your company if it was unprepared for a real emergency?

6.10.1 Creating a Space for Emergency Emotions

Drilling and exercising for emotions in events allows the brain to make a space for the experience. Post-traumatic stress disorder (PSTD) is an extreme consequence of seeing or experiencing something extreme that is unexpected and potentially life-threatening or being in the presence of a real death. The mind says, "Some perception in my inner worldview has been shattered forever." The difference between trauma and difficulty lies in the perceptual distortion presented by the incident. For example, a firefighter will generally not become traumatized by fire. On the other hand, someone who has never seen a large fire can become traumatized when they see flames roll across a floor like an ocean wave. That same firefighter, who is seasoned to fire, may develop PTSD the first time he sees an eyeball rolling across the floor. That is not something the mind is prepared to see the first time. Some firefighters would say, "Oh, gee, there goes another darn eyeball. That's the third one this week." Another firefighter might find this was his emotional last straw.

To manage severe emotions well includes creating a place in the brain for the possibility of new and challenging information. It is as though you see an unidentified flying object (UFO) land in your patio. Even if you are a believer, your brain will now have to accommodate the image in real-time. If you believe in UFOs, your worldview includes UFOs. If you do not believe in UFOs, your world may be temporarily or permanently shattered. If your company has UFO drills, even if you don't believe in them, and a UFO lands in your lunchroom at work, your brain will have already begun the initial process of accommodating to the concept of how your team will help each other respond in unexpected events, and it will be less likely to shatter into emotional pieces. Of course, it is not really necessary to drill specifically for unexpected UFO invasions in the lunchroom, or for the possibility of horrors like rolling eyeballs. What is helpful is to create an emotional climate in which your employees can begin to develop a repertoire of thoughts, ideas, words, and images to manage emotions that may surface during an incident. Unfortunately, many people with PTSD report that no one would talk to them about their feelings, especially at work.

> When I went to New York City in September of 2001, I knew what my job was, even though my mind and heart were shattered by recent events. I had participated in many disaster drills... The unexpected is somehow less daunting when you rehearse for the unexpected.

When I took piano lessons, I was constantly annoyed by the requirement of playing scales over and over and over. When I gave my first large concert performance, my fingers went in the right places even though my heart was pounding with stage fright.

When I went to New York City in September of 2001, I knew what my job was, even though my mind and heart were shattered by recent events. I had participated in many disaster drills, and in fact had been involved in a large multi-agency aviation disaster exercise before I was called on to go to NYC. When I arrived at my post, my practice apparently paid off because I left the scene knowing that my humble contribution of services helped.

Rehearsing, practicing, and drilling in advance, preparing my own support team to be ready to take care of me when I returned, calling people at home daily, laughing when laughter was available, crying when crying was appropriate, carrying my self-care tools with me, remembering the policies and procedures of the work and the situation, and managing emotions from small to huge all helped me to do my job, and these things continue to make an ongoing contribution to my recovery. The unexpected is somehow less daunting when you rehearse for the unexpected. Sometimes it seems silly and pointless. Other times it is precious.

I am reminded of a story I heard about British soldiers in POW camps during World War II. Apparently, they had a higher rate of survival than others because they continued to rehearse and drill even when incarcerated. They would arise at the proper time, make a formation, do calisthenics, and mime regular activities like eating, shaving, and drinking tea in elegant imaginary teacups in an effort to maintain a sense of order within the chaos. These soldiers were prepared and ready for whatever came up. When rescue came up, they were in better shape than their counterparts who had not drilled on a daily basis.

I am a strong advocate of improvisational music, therapy and life in general. My personal affirmations include gratitude for spontaneity and astonishment at the mysteries of life. I am also keenly aware that there is order in the universe and that disasters, catastrophes, terrorist events, traumas, and even minor inconveniences disturb our order, and thus cause us to be in an altered state in our efforts to regain order. I tell my clients that it is not the fear or difficult emotions that are the problems in life; rather, it is the desire to hire a moving truck and relocate your emotional furniture into the drama and stay there. I encourage people to feel their feelings fully and then move forward with their feelings as an active, energetic part of their full texture. Feelings are okay. And, we still have to get things done.

There used to be a toy produced called Weebles (Hasbro, 1969). They were small people-shapes that had a rounded base so that when a child pushed the toy it would wiggle but not tip over. The advertisement for the toy went something like, "Weebles – they wobble but they don't fall down!" I call real survivors "Weebles," as they are the ones who can maintain some integrity with their own human emotional experience and get the job done.

6.10.2 Emotional Continuity Management Drill Scenarios

Scenario A
Your community is located within 50 miles of a mad cow disease outbreak. You manage a food industry company that has contracts with health care services and other local contracts. You manage 34 full and part-time staff that works in two shifts. Your boss had informed you that your team must remove all beef from the venue.

Scenario B
You just found out that you are pregnant and you have not told anyone yet. A co-worker discloses that she is leaving early today to have an abortion and wants you to finish her assignment without telling anyone.

Scenario C
There is a running joke in the office about mentally handicapped people. Your brother has schizophrenia. Someone tells you a new joke.

Scenario D
You have been struggling with weight loss for two years, a daily struggle. Co-workers make fun of "fat" people. There is a potluck lunch today, and your boss asks if you are coming.

Scenario E
Your new boss takes you and a colleague out to lunch, and insists on driving after a few martinis. Last year a drunk driver killed a dear friend.

Scenario F
You have diabetes. Do you tell your colleagues how to help you if you become ill?

Scenario G
You cheated on your time cards. A co-worker finds out.

Scenario H
Your spouse is an alcoholic. There is trouble at home. The boss wants you to work overtime. This means your alcoholic spouse will be driving the children home from school.

Scenario I

You are a member of Alcoholics Anonymous, and you have been sober for two years. Associates who party on the weekend are scorning you for being a party-pooper. They think you don't like them. They invite you out again.

Scenario J

You are gay. You have not told anyone. Someone asks you what you think about gay marriages and if you know any gay people.

Scenario K

You are taking anti-depressants to tolerate your difficult working situation. At a meeting you are asked what improvements might help the organization.

Scenario L

Your religion doesn't allow you to work on Saturday. Saturday is the championship game for the company bowling league. Bowling is at the center of all social events and social discussions throughout the year. Bowlers are more likely to get the promotions and often are given opportunities to travel to out of town conferences.

Scenario M

You are having an affair with a co-worker. Your lover tells you about another co-worker who is committing fraud.

Scenario N

You accidentally intercept a love letter on company letterhead to a co-worker on your team.

Scenario O

Your boss asks you to do something that frightens you.

Scenario P

Your co-worker asks you to help cover up an error she made.

Scenario Q

Your co-worker tells you an unsavory secret about your boss.

Scenario R

The National Weather Service has upgraded the hurricane to a Category 4 and recommended evacuation. You are hosting a group of visiting industry professionals from a foreign nation. Their translator just walked out of the meeting.

Scenario S

An employee that left the company a year ago, before you were hired, comes into your office with a weapon claiming he was mistreated by the last manager.

Scenario T
Your company is forced to shelter in place for two days because of a toxic chemical spill. (A truck overturns, a railroad car goes off the track, a local chemical plant has a fire, etc.)

Scenario U
Your boss has a sudden heart attack and dies in the employee lounge during bring-your-children-to-work day.

Scenario V
A toilet overflows during the weekend causing major foul flooding in your office. You have a deadline for a project that is set in stone!

Scenario W
There is one confirmed case of smallpox reported in the United States. Contact your local health department, the Center for Disease Control (CDC), or World Health Organization (WHO) to find out the profound ramifications of this terrifyingly real possibility.

Scenario X
You suspect one of your employees is a sex offender.

Scenario Y
Your company has an emotional terrorist in a key position. This employee begins to focus attention on your management skills.

Scenario Z
You have a snake in your office.

Other Possible Scenarios Could Include These

- Your cubicle mate comes to work covered in bed-bug bites.
- A rumor of outsourcing has erupted. Mass layoffs are threatened.
- Someone in the company has committed cyber crime.
- Money is missing from the cash drawer.
- The office manager is not following through on tasks and is calling in sick frequently.
- The boss changes his/her mind every time something is almost finished.
- You work in tornado alley in the Midwest, and new employees are hired who have never been near a tornado.

- Your office is on an earthquake fault.
- 15% of your employees are related to active duty military units deployed to the Middle East. The news this week is not good.
- Four of your employees are pregnant, and the office is scheduled for repainting.
- Two of your employees have been married to the same man.
- Two of your employees have been married to the same woman.
- Someone in your company has a child die.
- An employee starts showing signs of mental illness.
- Someone in your company is devastated by the loss of a beloved pet.
- One of your employees insists on rearranging key equipment and the staff is upset.
- 37% of your workforces are military reservists called to active duty.
- A key employee disappears.
- Your competitor raises the stakes and you lose a valuable client.
- An employee has a chronic cough.
- Office communications have been disrupted.
- Your company files for bankruptcy.
- There have been news stories about toxic leaks. There is an odd smell at your office. Someone starts vomiting.
- Your boss comes to work saying his child has an extremely contagious disease.
- Someone forgot to "save" an important 83-page document and it was lost.
- Your office shares a common wall with another company that has had a fire.
- You hate your HR manager. Your HR manager hates you.
- A scandal implicates your company.
- A severe winter storm collapses trees onto important job performance equipment.
- An employee who is a combat veteran is upset with the war in Iraq.
- Transportation to your office has been disrupted.

A Successful Workplace Intervention

It is not unusual for a company – even one with good policies and procedures for employee conflict resolution – to call in a mental health professional for an intervention to avoid further conflict, controversy, and potential damage to reputation. In cases like the one that follows, the intervention led management to see the need for an ongoing policy and program that would prevent – or allow speedy response to – emotional conflicts.

The Crisis

A hospital with 600 employees found itself in crisis when growing antagonism between groups of employees escalated into a public fist fight between two medical professionals. The hospital used standard methods of employee conflict resolution: HR had worked with the individuals and then had referred them to an employee assistance program (EAP), but the conflict continued. Finally, the problem came to the attention of the CEO, who – after six weeks without a resolution – initiated the action of calling in Dr. Vali to advise the company and work with management for a solution.

The Triggering Mechanism

Dr. Vali identified quickly that the original trigger for the violence was staff response to an administrative decision to remove a vending machine from the break room. Since the hospital cafeteria was not open at night and no other food service was offered for that shift, the removal of the vending machine was interpreted as a symbol of management's lack of support for the night shift. The night shift took the vending machine issue personally, another "indicator that they were out of the loop" administratively. When they complained, they were given no alternative solutions but, essentially, were told it was a "done deal, now deal with it." Competition and bad feelings between the day shift and night shift became a system-wide "spin" and staff members picked sides, culminating in public dissension and, finally, the fist fight. Hurt feelings and a sense of administrative abandonment led to anger, petulance, and verbal abuse. The two employees from the fist fight – who represented the tension – had been leaders from both shifts on the same team for a special project. However, their different strengths and talents that had been a benefit to that project had, suddenly and unexpectedly, become the source of their division and antagonism. Other staff members took the emotional tension to heart, escalated the symbolic and literal differences, and exaggerated the issues into personal grievances.

The Object of the Intervention

After initial interview with CEO and the ringleaders of the dispute, Dr. Vali recommended a system-wide emotional continuity assessment, since her research and interviews had revealed additional internal conflicts that had not yet reached the ear of the CEO.

Dr. Vali recommended and management concurred that the system needed to

▶ Calm down.

▶ Establish boundaries.

▶ Get back to the work at hand.

▶ Stop spinning toward out-of-control levels.

▶ Receive alternative education about emotions and business.

▶ Learn new communication strategies.

▶ Develop a policy to manage future conflicts.

Management agreed that success would be gauged via observed increased productivity and an improved level of emotional calm in the general population. The fiscal success of the program would be determined by the CFO and CEO. Finally, improvements in the emotional climate would be tracked regularly via internal systems of HR, Dr. Vali's evaluation, and feedback from employees.

The Agreed-Upon Solution

Dr. Vali introduced a system-wide intervention to train all employees, from top down and bottom up, regarding the nature of how emotions can escalate into conflict and violence and the methods to manage and prevent the escalation of emotions in the workplace. She presented management with an overview to show how the nature of business and the bottom line can be protected while also providing compassionate support for human feelings.

After over a year of debate and delay (as described in the "obstacles" below), the administrators and the HR professionals recognized the need for a standardized plan and policy. Once the CEO was completely convinced, he was involved directly in the planning stage. Dr. Vali was available, but not involved in the direct designing of the plan. While Dr. Vali made recommendations, part of the program of emotional continuity management (ECM) is to not micro-manage it, but to empower the company to do its own homework – and make its own initial mistakes – with backup support.

The Action Steps

▶ Mandatory classes were set for all employees consisting of a 2 hour block in rotating shifts. This was followed by non-mandatory individual meetings, support groups, and other educational opportunities, literature, and workshops.

▶ Each department received a custom-designed, peer-based approach to the special needs of their worksite and job descriptions, understanding the unique nature of each position and responsibility, stressors, and expectations for success.

▶ Every employee received education. If an employee failed to attend the assigned classes or workshops, he or she was mandated to an individual session with Dr. Vali, who evaluated the employee for resistance, emotional terrorism, or legitimate absence.

▶ CEO and top management were given additional training to manage potential adjustments to new emotional boundaries and expectations, and provided with skills training. Employees who did not wish to receive the new protocols were counseled to success or counseled toward new career/employment opportunities and ideas.

▶ During a six-month period, Dr. Vali saw 600 employees in groups of 6-10, followed up by meetings, individual consultations, and trainings. In addition, she remained on call to the company for over two years to manage other micro adjustments to the protocols.

Difference between EAP and ECM

Part of the development of ECM is the idea that there are many possible "go-to" people and resources to manage emotional content. Often, companies do not think beyond EAP or HR for assistance in emotionally charged issues. EAP is traditionally a system that allows 3-5 sessions of counseling for one specific issue. If the issue is not resolved, a gap in services and ongoing support often follows. Also, because EAP is designed to help individuals rather than entire groups, this support does not include the rest of the system. On the other hand, ECM defines problems and issues spanning the entire range of human emotions, helping companies to design resources to match real problems with real solutions. Thus, either EAP or a critical incident stress management (CISM) debriefing might offer the right support. In the process of creating policy, the hospital began to develop a broader range of partnerships for supporting employees.

Obstacles to Success

▶ To begin, the administration was reluctant to change its position about the vending machine decision, refusing to replace it or offer other food solutions to night shift. This position was not flexible and, therefore, became an entrenchment.

▶ The company began with a compromise policy, one that was an "informal understanding" rather than an official company policy and plan. The CEO assumed everyone would comply automatically with his wishes; thus, he resisted the idea of any kind of formal company policy.

▶ An emotional terrorist on the staff regarded the "informal understanding" as an excuse to refuse openly to follow the steps set up for the intervention, working hard to sabotage all policies and workshops.

▶ The CEO had an agenda to keep this emotional terrorist on staff, which allowed the employee to continue to act out for a full year before the CEO saw that the costs outweighed the benefits and fired the employee. Only then did he support HR and the CFO to start sculpting a formal policy.

▶ Other delays included another violent event that was secondarily associated with the tensions in the company.

The Aftermath

After some initial resistance, employees cooperated. Once they saw how the intervention was helping the situation, they were fully on board, and playful and a peer-based agreement ensued. Most people just wanted to get back to work and not participate in the drama. Management concluded that the intervention was worth the investment of money, time, and effort. Violence and antagonism disappeared rapidly as a result of the support and skills training. When Dr. Vali completed the intervention, the company was drafting a policy. The CEO concluded that the company was calmer and people were doing much better; so he didn't feel the need to "rush a new policy," but to take the time to develop it. When Dr. Vali spoke with the CEO about two years after the consulting contract had ended, he reported that the ECM planning continued, and there just were not "the problems we used to have."

Lessons Learned

▶ Be prepared for the costs in money and time for a system-wide intervention.

▶ Start at the top and work down; then start at the bottom and work up.

▶ Get the CEO on board. This one struggled for over a year but eventually saw the financial reasons for the work and did a full buy-in.

▶ Have a policy and protocol in place first.

▶ Call for professional support before the conflict escalates to violence.

Questions for Further Thought and Discussion

1. What does it mean to the bottom line to have buy-in from the top-down and the bottom-up? What would 100% buy-in look like in your company?

2. Does your organization have an anti-bullying policy? Does it recognize emotional terrorism? How would you convince a reluctant executive to see the need for a wide-ranging anti-bullying policy?

3. What kind of "emotion" or "feeling" words are included in your company mission or vision statements? Count how many items reflect objects and how many items reflect human feelings. What does that say about your corporate culture?

4. How would emotional continuity drills, policies, procedures, and 100% buy-in be a value-added strategy for your company? Would that answer change if your company were facing a disaster?

Emotional Continuity
Management for Disasters

Nowhere is a system-wide, in-place, pre-drilled, and ready-to-go ECM plan more necessary than during and after a disaster. And if companies don't plan ahead, there can be more of a disaster after the "real" disaster has passed. The long-term emotional consequences of a natural or man-made disaster can be more heinous than the actual event. Many people recover well and quickly after a disaster. Some Don't: recover quickly. Some never do.

7.1 Phases of Disaster Planning to Consider

7.1.1 Planning Phase

Prior to a disaster incident:

▶ Define qualifications necessary for membership and leadership in the emotional continuity management team.

▶ Select and interview applicants.

▶ Provide training and continuing education.

▶ Provide regular training and practice drills.

▶ Plan task assignments, authority lines, and delegations of responsibility.

▶ Create a disaster buddy system.

▶ Provide chain of command structure to all employees.

▶ Negotiate contracts with external disaster services providers.

7.1.2 Implementation Phase

▶ Provide a central location for communications for your team and outside teams.

▶ Do a disaster buddy check-in.

▶ Initiate pre-planned task assignments, authority lines, and delegations of responsibility.

▶ Coordinate responses.

▶ Coordinate lines of supply, equipment, and information.

▶ Assess needs with an ongoing process of open communications.

▶ Provide a clerical manager for support.

▶ Provide other support services such as communications, logistics, supply.

▶ Orient team to the specific event.

▶ Define event status and review plan.

▶ Profile the participants of the event.

▶ Collect resources, make network connections, implement memos of understanding (MOUs).

- Create a blueprint of actions for immediate response and build in plan for long-term.
- Make task assignments.
- Continue training as needed with regular updates and support.
- Review short-term response.
- Begin discussions of intermediate and long-term responses.
- Continue status updates, consultations, liaisons, MOUs, and provider partnerships.
- Provide expert consultations and trainings.
- Support staff and manage self-care.
- Defuse as needed.
- Document activities.

7.1.3 Recovery Phase

After an incident:

- Debrief participants and team members.
- Continue self-care.
- Maintain liaisons and links with other network connections.
- Ongoing training should continue.
- Discussions on lessons learned.
- Wrap up details.
- Paper work completion, filings, recordings.
- Support process over the long term, no matter how long it takes.
- Send thank you letters.
- Support and encourage buddy sets, and support and reorganize around any buddy losses.
- Provide memorials and commemoration programs.
- Acknowledge and give appropriate recognitions.
- Return to phase one and begin new phase of recruitment for planning for next disaster.

7.2 Increasing Competency of Emotional Continuity Management

7.2.1 Questions to Ask With Every Incident

With every incident ask:

- What can I learn from this?
- Why would I need to continue to hang on to hurt feelings?
- What fear does this expose for me? Why am I vulnerable?
- What sacred issues of mine are at risk or being threatened?
- Can I think of ways to let this go?
- Did I take this issue personally?
- Was it really about me?
- Can I use my spiritual practice and move on?
- Could I let this incident simply pass?
- Would I let this incident simply pass?
- When will I allow this incident to simply pass?
- Can I give myself permission for the feelings I had?
- Is this temporary or permanent?
- Did I make a positive or negative contribution?

> My colleagues who specialize in information technology (IT) disaster planning and business continuity management (BCM) have taught me well. My physical well-being is my hardware; my emotions are my software; and I participate willingly in drills to protect them both.

7.2.2 Preparation is Just Good Thinking

The interruption of business to practice physical evacuations or emotional debriefing appears to be an annoyance until you actually need these skills in reality. Drills with first responders, the American Red Cross, and with critical incident stress management teams have taken my valuable time. I have whined about volunteering my time to "practice." Then an incident happens, and I can't say enough about the value of drills. I practiced. Now it makes sense. Now it is rational and not a waste of my time. I get it.

Whenever I return from a disaster, I am humbled by how grateful I am that someone went ahead of me and tipped me about what it would look like. The faces and names, the debris and the details may be slightly different, but the general texture is the same. And what is always the same is that people are having emotions. I have drilled and rehearsed my emotional continuity management practices and am not surprised when a human emotion is presented to me. I know what to do. And if it is beyond me, I know whom to call. I am not bullet-proof so I anticipate that I might have some emotions. Sometimes I do. Sometimes I do not. But no matter what, my mission is to be helpful and not add to the disaster. I have my feelings. They matter mostly to me. Ignoring my emotions is neither healthy nor useful. Extensive research on PTSD backs me up on this.

My colleagues who specialize in information technology (IT) disaster planning and business continuity management (BCM) have taught me well. My physical well-being is my hardware; my emotions are my software; and I participate willingly in drills to protect them both.

7.3 The Real Deal

I hear stories. When I tell people I'm an emotional continuity management consultant they say something like, "Our business survived the tornadoes, but a year later we were still shaken up." To think disasters are out of the norm is denial at best and insanity at worst.

7.3.1 Understanding the Need for Planning

Thinking, planning, preparing and drilling for disasters is not paranoia. Thinking, planning, preparing, and drilling for disasters is intelligent. People who feel prepared are happier. They can relax and put aside thoughts about disaster because they know what to do if one pops up. They can get on with life. Employees who feel prepared are happier. They can relax and forget about disaster because they know what to do if one pops up. They can get on with work.

It is a fact that people who have within their minds the concepts of what might happen during a disaster are statistically less likely to suffer the long-term effects of a disaster. People who avoid the topic are at greater risk for long-term emotional consequences as a result of a disaster.

When my area was hit with a 6.9 earthquake early one morning, I had no time to think about what to do. And I was in no mood to sort out my choices at that moment. I did what I had been practicing and drilling. I followed up with emotional self-care. I had been drilling that also. When in my first (hopefully last) tornado, I was deeply grateful for the people who had drilled for tornadoes because I didn't have a clue what to do – I was in denial and laughed, thinking it was a joke. They were moving quietly and quickly to the basement as I stood like a deer in headlights.

I have rehearsed being neutral during a conflict. If an angry and raging employee verbally attacks me, I don't have time to think about what to do. Their feelings are immediate and I need to have an emotional continuity management skill ready to go.

I have rehearsed really listening to people. If a grieving and weary employee verbally risks sharing with me their tender story, I don't have time to think about what to do. Their need is immediate, and I need to have an emotional continuity management skill ready to go.

> The regular ways of relating do not work during or immediately following a disaster. Normal cues are missing, images are distorted, and normal emotions and thoughts are temporarily incongruent.

I have rehearsed and drilled debriefing employees. If something needs ventilation, I am ready. I use the tools I teach. They serve me and they serve others well. And I want you to have them all, the ones I offer and anything else you can get to make your life easier!

A disaster is a complicated event affecting numerous connections, intersections, links, and systems of people, places, things, and ideas. Disasters produce changes in human emotions that are both predictable and unpredictable. The regular ways of relating do not work during or immediately following a disaster. Normal cues are missing, images are distorted, and normal emotions and thoughts are temporarily incongruent. Mental health professionals who have been specially trained in disaster management know the unique needs of people in these distorted experiences.

7.3.2 What Managers Need to Provide in a Disaster

Managers need to have at least a basic understanding of disaster exercises, tools, practices, procedures, and resources because they may be the only people available whom the staff trusts. If your staff does not trust you before a disaster, a disaster will not increase their sense of safety. If the manager is clueless and unprepared for a disaster, or has no concept about the effects of disaster on human emotions, chaos can increase and escalate the emotional consequences.

After a catastrophic event, it is often the quiet, centered, and calm voice during the event that a victim remembers. A calm voice of compassion that is resonating with reason and security is the loudest guiding force when madness is swirling noisily about, chaos is ripping apart the fabric of the known, and cacophony is jumbling up signals and signs that have before this moment made sense. Imagine for a moment the stairwells in the World Trade Center building during the earliest morning evacuations. People unsure of the situation quietly and quickly followed well-practiced procedures guided by managers reminding them of the drills they have done before. Now, imagine a firefighter calling a child out from under his hiding place in a burning home. As the firefighter manages strong inner emotional content, the child hears a voice of authority, calm, and direction.

Managing during a disaster is not about controlling the disaster; it is about managing the emotions of the moment. Disasters have a beginning, middle, and an end. Each stage is managed a bit differently. Importantly, there is a pre-disaster phase where the real planning is formulated and rehearsed.

7.4 Changes Occurring with Disaster

During a disaster, changes in divisions of work, power, authority, and perceptions are appropriate expectations.

7.4.1 Power

Power creates change in people during regular interactions and dramatically during disasters. In terms of control, influence, capacities, or strengths during a disaster, it is the disaster that holds the power. Normally powerful people can be brought to their knees, and usually powerless people can rise to superhuman abilities. The power structure hierarchy of any organization may be made impotent by the sheer force and power of a disaster.

7.4.2 Work

Work stops during a disaster unless you work in the disaster industry. Expecting anyone to continue normal activities is at the least unreasonable and at the worst unethical, inhuman, and perhaps even insane. Expect and support a reasonable period of time between the end of the incident and the return of any level of normalcy. The specific details of the disaster should define those expectations.

7.4.3 Authority

Professionals who work in the disaster industry recognize the need for clearly understood lines of command during a disaster. Incident command is set up to provide incident management or authority procedures in charge of the on-scene process of a disaster. They initiate response, assess the situations, and manage resources. This command operation becomes the icon, flag, or base of operations that keeps workers on track in the chaos. In your company, you may need to either be the incident manager during a disaster or delegate one. You also need to create a procedure in the event that you are not available. One of the most difficult discussions after any disaster can be dealing with a manager who was injured, absent, on vacation, or not present for any reason during a disaster for which that manager had authority.

7.4.4 Perceptions

There is an understanding among mental health disaster workers that any victim, emergency responder or mental health disaster worker (including themselves) that they meet during or after a disaster will be in an "altered state of consciousness." The degree of that alteration of thinking is the variable. The relevant issue is never a question of "if" there is an altered state, only "how altered is it?" This alteration means that brains are processing information in a distorted manner because brains under the influence of the incident do not operate like brains not under duress.

Victims and responders are "under the influence" of the disaster and need to be managed like anyone under the influence of a powerful drug. The brain releases significant amounts of brain chemicals directly into the brain-blood barrier, the body releases fight-or-flight hormones, blood moves away from the extremities (hands and feet and brain) toward the center of the body (belly), and digestion stops. People under this influence can do some very odd, silly, heroic, bizarre, unexpected, and dangerous things. The word "shock" is a term that most people understand, but it is inadequate to define the long-term effects of disaster influence. Post-traumatic stress disorder (PTSD) is a good example of the long-term effects. A mother running into a fire to save her child and coming out cradling a sofa pillow in her arms and singing to it as if it were her child because she truly "sees" it as her child is, while tragic, not an unusual example of an altered state of consciousness designed by disaster.

Do this: Honor the enduring power and ongoing dynamic of disasters.

Don't: Hurry the process.

7.4.5 If and When

It is never a question of "if" there will be an incident, only "when."

Now that you know there is a disaster brewing somewhere all the time, every-where, you will know that every day you are either pre-disaster, current-disaster, or after-disaster. That will make your job easier. Many companies gamble that they will have a long, long time before (if) they have a disaster. It is a much more rational policy to assume that you will have a disaster tomorrow, and anything you do today will help you survive it.

Emotional continuity management is not about being paranoid, but it is about being alert emotionally to the reality that disasters happen. The figure for the statistical majority of people who wear seatbelts is higher than the number for those who actually need them during an accident. Risk-takers gamble. Unfor-tunately, that gamble influences others if, for example, you do not manage the seat belts of your charges, your children. Managers need to make certain their employees have on their disaster seatbelts as they move forward. Good parents protect themselves and their children. Good managers protect themselves and their colleagues before something happens.

7.5 Managing Before, During, and After a Disaster

7.5.1 Before the Disaster

- **Acknowledge:** Acknowledge that there is a probability that at some time there will be a disaster that has an effect and conse-quences for your company.

- **Brainstorm:** Make a list of all possible disasters that could ever, even in wildest imaginings, touch your company directly or indirectly.

- **Buy-in:** Establish hierarchical buy-in for your company. If your company refuses to acknowledge the probability that there will be a disaster that will have an effect and consequences, dust off your resume and look elsewhere. Denial is not good business.

- **Plan:** Create a list of partnerships, interventions, resources, policies, procedures, ideas, concepts, supplies, and contingencies for even the wildest imagined disaster.

- **Narrow:** Narrow down your full list to the top ten possibilities.

- **Training:** Get training for anyone who might be involved in any disaster, from the line staff to the authority players in key positions. Training can consist of a small pamphlet to significant, formal education opportunities.

▶ **Partners:** Pre-plan partnerships with local, state, and federal responder agencies and private disaster industry professionals. Write memos of understandings, pay for retainer fees, and publish a list for everyone on your staff. You never know if you will be there to make the calls.

▶ **Normalize:** Make disasters a normal discussion in meetings and planning sessions as you would any other part of company business. Disasters are a "normal" part of life and need addressing in a coherent and open manner in the same spirit you would discuss the furniture in the office.

▶ **Learn:** Although everyone is doing well, this is an excellent time to seek more management training.

7.5.2 During the Disaster

▶ **Self Care:** It is always appropriate to take care of yourself first.

▶ **Survive:** Do what is appropriate to survive a disaster.

▶ **Expect:** Expect emotions of all forms, from immobilized screaming to hysterically funny giggling fits.

▶ **Remember:** Recall the stages of grieving – denial, bargaining, anger, depression, and acceptance. Add to this blaming, resistance, minimizing, aggrandizing, and emotional response and reaction to surprises that you haven't anticipated.

▶ **Remind:** Remind yourself and others that all disasters have a beginning, middle and an end. Beginnings are easy, and ends are a relief. Middles are crazy-makers and seem to last forever, but they do not!

▶ **Learn:** Although this is a difficult time for everyone, it can be an excellent time to seek more management training.

▶ **Review:** Review the before guidelines and repeat what is necessary to stay on track.

> Banal and mundane tasks may keep people from sliding into an emotional abyss of helplessness. An employee who has "power and control" over the wastebaskets may feel less overwhelmed by the power of the disaster and may return to competent functioning more quickly.

7.5.3 After the Disaster

▶ **Manage:** Remember that the disaster cannot be controlled, but you can manage through it. Face the changes and work through the transitions between the activity of the disaster and the end of the disaster when changes have been completed.

▶ **Expect:** Don't be surprised. Encourage yourself and others to not be surprised. There is no "going back" before the disaster; there is only moving forward "after" the disaster. Help people move forward.

▶ **Involve:** Involve people in managing themselves and others. In disasters there is a tendency for people to either help others or become looters. Involve people in helping, even if it is a fabricated task like "we need someone to empty the wastebaskets." Busy people become more focused and feel more security. The rubric is that in an abnormal situation, it is helpful to do something that seems normal. Washing dishes, sweeping, dusting, organizing a phone tree, serving water, and other such banal and mundane tasks may keep people from sliding into an emotional abyss of helplessness. An employee who has "power and control" over the wastebaskets may feel less overwhelmed by the power of the disaster and may return to competent functioning more quickly.

▶ **Listen:** Don't argue, discredit, disagree, or deny people their own perception of reality. People will adjust and recover in their own way at their own speed.

▶ **Okay:** Human emotions are okay. Don't avoid or discourage emotions from your employees. If you feel uncomfortable with emotions, find someone who isn't, and gently direct people that direction. Do not block the healthy process of emotional recovery or it may come back on you.

▶ **Pay Attention:** After a disaster, the rhythm of work has fits and starts as it readjusts to its new flow. Try to move with it without resistance. See or feel it as choreography with new dance steps. Two steps forward, one step back. One step forward, two steps to the side, and two steps forward. Take your time. You will "feel" your new footing soon. Don't be afraid to ask questions or check your footwork from time to time. You don't want to step on toes, but you also don't want to miss a beat. Everything will be uncertain, a period which will then be followed by what seems like rigid certainty, which will then again decay into chaos as it moves back into a more resolved new form. Take your time. Take your time. The disaster is over. Now you have time to figure it all out.

- **Insist:** Insist on being in the loop for information sharing. If you are out of the loop your anxiety will increase and so will your employees' anxiety. It is better to say, "I don't know, but I'll find out as soon as I can," than to say, "I have no clue" and leave people in the dark with no sense of leadership.

- **Communicate:** Share information, listen, wait, exchange ideas, avoid rumors, seek facts, present facts, and offer patience, peace, procedures, and protocol.

- **Support:** Support your people. Know they can handle information better than innuendo. People can handle ambiguity if they are in the loop. Waiting is very hard for most people under duress; so create a formal "what should we do while we are waiting" process. Put things in writing when you can. A quick-fix bulletin board for memos or messages is very supportive for groups of people. Expect people to be distracted. It might help to have a television in the office for a few days. Let people watch it while they are working. Put it in the center of the worksite and not the employee lounge. Don't make employees pretend nothing happened. That will make you look crazy. Expect random outbreaks of group talking when incidents change. Check up on people to find out if they are in the loop or feel like they are.

- **Open up:** Acknowledge stress – yours and theirs. It's okay to say you are stressed even when you are in a management position. It gives you more credibility and makes you more accessible. This doesn't necessarily mean a crying jag with your staff, although tears do not destroy leadership potential. Don't hesitate to ask for help. Quick check-ins with employees – without getting deeply involved in their emotions – are very helpful. It is called defusing and takes the edge off the emotions as a brief respite and release. Find a place where you can defuse also. It should not be with another employee that you are managing.

- **Debriefings:** Create opportunities to debrief your employees. You can train your people to do it, find volunteers, or hire professionals or consultants who have been specially trained in mental health disaster practices.

- **Avoid:** Do everything you can to stay away from group blame-frenzy behavior.

- **Continue:** Continue to communicate and move forward. Check in with people to see if they are moving forward, or if they are beginning to lose ground and need a different kind of intervention.

▶ **Persist:** Persist in assisting people who may need ongoing management support. During normal situations, people need leadership. Before, during, and well after a disaster, people need to keep their focus through the well-balanced position of leaders. Workers who may have lost capacity to work due to loss of technology or services that existed before the incident will need specific leadership to stay connected to the job.

▶ **Learn:** Although this is a difficult time for everyone, it can be an excellent time to gain more training.

▶ **Review:** Review the **before** and **during** guidelines and repeat what might be useful or necessary to stay on track. Another disaster may be in your future.

▶ **Lessons Learned**: In the absolutely most intensely positive manner you can muster after all of this, review every step, before, during and after, with an eye on successes and areas that need improvement.

▶ **Celebrate:** Celebrate your survival!

▶ **Memorialize:** Plan ahead for the one-year anniversary or remembrance moment of the event. Create an annual commemoration for your office. Delegate the task if necessary to someone who would benefit emotionally from the process of creating tribute.

7.6 Managing Disaster Anniversaries

Most adults remember vividly where we were on 9/11/2001. Children may have seen adults weep for the first time, or felt sickened by the television coverage, or became confused as they sorted out how this would affect everyone and everything. A person did not need to be in New York to feel the ripples of that day.

For many adults and children, the tragedies of September 11, 2001 were their first connection to an historical event. People everywhere saw the television footage over and over. They saw the reactions of others. Emotions ran high and to the extreme. People wondered and waited to see what horror would be next. Psychological and emotional terrorism – one planned goal of the terrorists – spread as everyone wondered where the next target would be.

People closest to the terrorist actions suffered the most directly. A study the following year found 11% of New York City children suffering PTSD, and 15% suffering agoraphobia, a fear of public places, because of the attack. Even if you were not in New York City, Washington, D.C., or Pennsylvania on September 11, 2001, you were exposed to a trauma. In the months afterwards, children and adults everywhere continued to have difficulties dealing with their emotional experiences.

> Managers need to be involved actively in open acknowledgment of anniversary events and emotions... provide support, validation, space, and memorial events for everyone.

7.6.1 Grief May Take Months to Resolve

When someone approaches the one-year anniversary of a disaster, noted trauma experts know that this is a difficult day for many adults and children. Tremendous media coverage can be expected in some cases. In other cases, the individual suffers in solitude over an extreme personal incident. Memory images replay again and again, and thoughts and feelings resurface. Some children regress behaviorally and academically around the anniversary of a trauma. Some adults do, also. Fears, worries, or nightmares may come back. Some adults and children will do well; others may have surprisingly strong reactions. David Mitchell, who created a series of writing journals for disaster anniversary management, writes, "As a Disaster Manager and counselor I have seen how ignoring or mishandling anniversaries can create more emotions than the original event. The National Institute of Mental Health and the University of Illinois Extension Disaster Resources agree when they say that children and adolescents, if given support, will recover almost completely from the fear and anxiety caused by a traumatic experience within a few weeks. However, some children and adolescents will need more help perhaps over a longer period of time in order to heal. Grief may take months to resolve, and may be reawakened by reminders such as media reports or the anniversary of the death. And some of the effects of long-term disruptions may not surface immediately; problems may not surface until weeks, months, or even a year following the disaster" (Mitchell, D., 2012).

7.6.2 Managers Need to do the Compassionate Thing

Managers need to be involved actively in open acknowledgment of anniversary events and emotions. They can lead the team or create a team that will provide support, validation, space, and memorial events for everyone. If someone has had a personal loss or trauma on your team, ask how he or she wants to spend that day. If the team has had an incident, help them organize an appropriate tribute. It can be formal and elaborate, or it can be one minute of silence. That is up to you and your company needs. However, ignoring the moment can create an emotional backlash of anger and pain that combines with old memories and feelings of the original event that can become distorted into a full-blown emotional spin. Certainly, the compassionate thing is to take the time to honor the moment. The fiscally responsible thing is to invest some downtime for people's emotions that will allow employees to emotionally regroup and return to productivity.

Disasters are:

▶ Scary.

▶ Unimaginable.

▶ Unpredictable.

▶ Uncontrollable.

▶ Manageable.

▶ Temporary.

Bullies are:

▶ Scary.

▶ Unimaginable.

▶ Unpredictable.

▶ Uncontrollable.

▶ Manageable.

▶ Temporary.

▶ Cockroaches, snakes, tornadoes.

▶ Not too bright and stuck with very limited options.

You are:

▶ Brave.

▶ Blessed with an imagination.

▶ Able to predict certain things in life to be real.

▶ Able to control your ongoing education and excellence by reaching for more daily.

▶ Manager of your own emotions: You can feel them, deal with them, heal them. They are real, and they count, but mostly to you.

▶ Eternal and light.

▶ Smarter than bullies and blessed with unlimited options.

Questions for Further Thought and Discussion

1. Do you think Emotional Continuity drills would change how your employees might manage their emotions during a real emergency? How?

2. List as many possible natural and man-made disasters that could happen during a work day. What kind of disasters have happened in your region of the country where you are located?

3. Have any of your employees experienced a significant natural or manmade disaster? What insight could they offer you in terms of emotional continuity?

4. Compare the amount of money your company spends on Business Continuity, IT Continuity, and Emotional Continuity? What does this mean to your people?

5. If there were a large, unexpected, sudden disaster to happen 15 minutes from now, what would you have available to assist employees to deal with their emotional reactions and responses?

8

Where Are We Going?

Our society is struggling right now with one of its prime focuses on what I call the soul of business. Political competitors are lining up their platforms based on principles that challenge corporate humanity. Are companies the people who run them? Do the voices that are heard speak for a few or the many? What does it all mean? Who are the good guys or bad guys? Are we going to be "okay"? This is a transformative time on our planet in terms of mass consumerism, ecological fragility, the management of transparency versus truth or lies, greed and abundance; people and companies are weighing in right now. Where are we going? It's up to you. And me.

Although it is far from a popular view, I maintain the belief that good stuff will win over the bad stuff. Fear will eventually succumb to faith. The arc of that change may be long in coming, but throughout history progress has been built on that faith, the belief that good things will come. When I speak to organizations about the real fears of pandemics, violence, terrorism, and the ugliest of the ugliest potentials, it is always from a context that is meant to project a sense of empowerment.

> **There will always be more than one story told.**
> **The only part we get to manage is deciding which**
> **story we want to be a part of as we tell the tale.**

8.1 To Be or Not To Be... A Victim

There are two kinds of victims: Real and Not-Real. If you get hit by a bus, are molested as a child, are in a building when it gets hit by an airplane, you are initially a victim. Not-Real victims take such an event and use it to attach Velcro to the back of their hand and on their forehead and walk about with "poor me" all the time. There was no one else who shared their tragedy because it is always all about them.

Thinking you can control the universe isn't rational. The idea of management is rational. You may not be able to control X, Y or Z but perhaps you can manage it well and survive with some semblance of grace. Human beings love to have control. And when control is gone, even temporarily, the situation is ripe for developing character or karma, and as I have said before, the behavior of people in disasters and emergencies ranges between that of being looter or helpers, real victims who recover and Not-Real victims who exploit the story.

In business the same holds true. There isn't a corner on the market of being a chronic victim or a fear addict. But if you understand that chronic victims, those who choose to remain in self-pity, have limited choices, you will also understand how non-victims have a number of choices and make use of them. The future will be created by both. There will always be more than one story told. The only part we get to manage is deciding which story we want to be a part of as we tell the tale.

8.2 The Future Holds Choices for Solutions

The future will present problems. It will also present solutions. You are building your future now. Whatever you put into it will be what comes out of it. This isn't a new thought. In a marketplace that demands fresh ideas based on old thinking and principles, it is smart to use your head and your heart to balance the business and emotions of work.

You can do the same thing as you develop your Emotional Continuity Management plans. Use your imagination. Use what has worked in the past. Find something new. Ask your most creative people to brainstorm the best solutions to old problems. Ask your old wise ones what they think. Mix it up. Make everyone a stakeholder. Inventions are often the direct result of an unmet need.

Since the World Trade Center attacks, future-thinking entrepreneurs and inventors have been trying even harder to come up with even more brilliant methods to evacuate people from extremely high buildings. Great ideas often are discovered after the fact. Polio vaccine didn't happen overnight and not before there were great losses. But passionate and devoted humans worked on the problem to solve it. The future holds solutions. Find them.

Solutions for the Future

Use your imagination
> Think outside and inside out.

Convert energy
> The old energies are becoming scarcer. Transmute one natural resource into another.

Be a master of wise innocence
> Be smart and open. They aren't mutually exclusive.

Lead with leadership
> Take the leap of faith to become the voice of sanity and safety. Stand up out of your chair right now and lean forward into tomorrow. Show others how.

Upgrade into real changes
> Find out what works and custom design a program that is realistic and valued, flexible and filled with energy to change and grow over time.

Prepare to avoid fear
> Protect your company and self by preparing for possible emergencies and not being afraid of things. You can only do what you can do. But do it. Now.

Set your intentionality
> Set an intention. Intent is one of the most powerful tools for success.

Dislodge blockages
> Gently clear the sticky debris of limited thinking.

See again with wise innocent eyes
> People are good. Life is wonderful. Sweetness and beauty are truth. Be smart and look for danger, and then open up to full-tilt playfulness from your wise and innocent self. Look at the problem again. Then ask a third grader for a better answer.

Take inventory
> Don't make assumptions. Review everything gently. Stay awake and alert. Find your way by knowing your way.

New books on workplace emotions are coming out all the time. Authors are writing about mean bosses, jerks, death, violence, bullies and more. As the light is dawning on the day, people are beginning to open their eyes. When I started out shouting from the rooftops most people were doing the best they could and just didn't see it. Some put their fingers in their ears and sang "la la la la la" to avoid it, others listened politely, others ran in the other direction. This was before September 11, 2001. There is absolutely nothing wrong with that avoidance and denial. It is what healthy people do; they press forward, adjust, compensate, and are resilient.

Unfortunately what is going on now is that the "secret" has come out via the media and just the sheer volume of incidents that are occurring. Did they always occur? Possibly, but I don't believe they were this frequent or heinous. That is the bad news. The good news is that writers, trainers, facilitators, and planners are now beginning to present useful tools to address various components of this wave of discomfort. What Emotional Continuity Management© has been about has been the hope that this would happen. My advocacy has voiced a larger concern trying to bring all of these wise components to the table of your planning procedure to explore, create and evolve a system-wide policy of emotional management for employees that encompassed everyone. Everyone. CEOs have bad days also. And so do CFOs. And so do line staff, and managers, and supervisors, and vendors, and stakeholders! No longer is it sane to separate out the units of companies into pockets of prepared and unprepared employees. No longer is it sane to consider human emotions as "soft." Read a newspaper and do the math.

> **For the first time in the history of the organization, which had spanned decades, there was a voice at the big table about how emergency incidents might affect the emotions of human beings.**

8.3 Changing Attitudes, One Meeting at a Time

I was part of a volunteer committee around 1999. I had started by sitting as far from the head table as a newbie should and gradually made it nearer the action of decision makers. The team went around the circle sharing their advocacy in turn, and the community worked at emergency planning taking info from all participants. The "leader" was a hardened professional veteran who earned his stripes in the fire management profession. He was the man, the head man at the *head table*. He made it clear for a long time that my "soft-airy-rose-colored-glasses-psychobabble" didn't fit into the real planning discussion. I hung in there quietly and respectfully. These were powerful "knowers" and I was just that "counselor person" who showed up. But life happened. Disasters happened. Hell happened. And the people who were in leadership were leaders because they could learn. So one day, after a series of particularly horrid wild fires and other subsequent incidents, we had our monthly meeting. I entered the conference room and sought out my "out-of-the-way" chair. But something had changed. The leader stood up in front of everyone and offered me the chair beside him. Nothing was said. There was no verbal acknowledgement. But for the first time in the history of the organization, which had spanned decades, there was a voice at the big table about how emergency incidents might affect the emotions of human beings. It was a big moment for me, for the team, and for the community.

The moral of the story is simple. This is how you develop this comprehensive system-wide program and policy: *One meeting at a time*. As they say, you can only eat an elephant one bite at a time. I have published articles on preparing "go-bags" for emergencies that suggest you start with the absolute smallest unit and then grow your plan over time. You start small and then move forward to evolve your own, custom-designed package of security. There are countless resources available. Shop for what you want. Keep the receipt in case you change your mind. Partnerships need to be flexible. Rigidity is not safety.

It is necessary to develop plans and policies and procedures that move out of the 1950s and into what is going on in the here and now, and tomorrow.

8.4 Keep the Old Foundations While Building the New

I just got a call from a former client who kindly shared the successes my mentoring program brought to his team. He moved to another state and wondered if I would bring my workshop to his new team. He asked if the work had changed. My answer was that "No, the basics still work; and yes, there are changes and adjustments that I have learned work and don't work." That is the demand of the work, moving between the business and the emotions. I think an old veteran carpenter would tell you that a hammer and a nail never change, but what you build over the decades will be different as the creative designs change. Disasters are disasters, emergencies are emergencies, and some of the tools to manage them will be basic, stable, unchangeable "hammers and nails" work. However, if you look at the composition of disasters today as compared to 10 years ago, they have changed. The victims have changed. The perpetrators have changed. Tornadoes no longer just hate mobile homes! Hurricanes and floods no longer avoid huge tourist cities. Violent murderers no longer just slink around in shadows – they hijack airplanes. Sex offenders run human services companies and batterers run churches. It isn't necessary to freak out and run to the hills. It is necessary to develop plans and policies and procedures that move out of the 1950s and into what is going on in the here and now, and tomorrow.

8.5 Signs of Hope

I am so happy to see the signs of hope for people at work. A few years ago, I felt like I was yelling in a canyon, because I could hear my own echo. It was as if people would pat me on the head and tell me I was a nice kid, but take my puppy elsewhere. But things are rapidly changing. Business and emotions are no longer separate topics in the workplace and the management or mismanagement of human feelings is starting to take a toll. Therefore wise people and cutting-edge leaders are stepping up and creating amazing products and venues to mix the oil and water of these apparently divergent issues. I celebrate all those who are doing the work of bringing it to the front.

I was recently tapped for a job bid in India to be a consultant for what they term "occupational hygiene." This is the current state of emotional continuity management – humans and business bottom line working forward collectively.

Occupational health psychology is an emerging field of study that is rapidly taking a lead in the speaking of the "human" side of the equation. New buzzwords like "workplace incivility" are popping up in the media and websites. It's happening. Where do you want to be in 5 years? 10 years? Dinosaurs are resisting. And we know how that worked out, right?

> **Take care of yourself so you can survive to be a true help to others. Drowning people do not make good lifeguards.**

8.6 Not the Last Word

This is not even close to the final word on this topic. I hope it contributes. You need to stay current to manage your own emotions. Find your way. If you live on top of a mountain in total isolation, then perhaps you won't need to learn more. But if you have any interactions with other human beings – in person, via social media, via Internet, or from outsourced random locations – you need to understand that humans are human: good, bad, ugly, and really, really ugly. You can bless them all spiritually, but if someone has an agenda to create chaos or harm, you may want to be prepared to deal with the real deal of that intentionality.

My personal belief is that humans are part of the Great Light of the universe. Unfortunately, some human beings are committed to staying in the shade and others are committed to darkness and devoted to dragging others into a bleak death spiral as they traverse their own abyss. As Bob Dylan, the songwriter-poet suggested, some people are always "trying to get you down into the hole that they are in."

Don't let it happen. Be the light. Recognize what lurks in the shadows and then *turn on the light and give help or get help*! We are social beings and not meant to do some things alone. It is true; some people are just downright scary and are not going to change. Take care of yourself so you can survive to be a true help to others. Drowning people do not make good lifeguards. Get tools. Get training. Go to countless websites and read books from brilliant and passionate authors who also know this is true.

And Finally…

So. I want to wish you light and luck. Why don't you call me. Let's have coffee. I want you to stay safe. Be smart. Write poetry. Crunch the numbers. Dance. Watch a sunrise. Create brilliant policies. Splash in puddles. Bring your best you to important meetings. Cry. Upgrade your computers. Laugh. Drill for the physical and emotional parts of emergency evacuations. Buy flowers. Get over yourself. Show up. *Be a quantum planner, managing both a hard-nose-bottom-line-business and a compassionate-human-being in the exact same location.* Be ruthlessly compassionate and fiscally awake. Take care of the business of the bottom-line capital issues and the compassionate needs of your human capital. Be the quantum! It's what's happening.

Epilogue

If I could ride only a few floors in the elevator with your CEO and take that opportunity to talk about why your company needs an Emotional Continuity Plan, this is what I might say – and depending on how many floors we were riding up or down, I'd expand my information:

- **Emotions at work impact your bottom line.** Whether a small outburst or a full-fledged catastrophic event, just add up the time you spend on the average day handling the emotional turmoil du jour and multiply it by the salaries of everyone involved.

- **Emotional Continuity Management stops spinning from the top down and the bottom up.** It recognizes four kinds of employee: healthy, dysfunctional, pathological, and what I call "emotional terrorists." While most employees just want to come to work and go home, some employees would rather make the worksite a chaotic tornado zone – and most workplaces have at least one of those people on board.

- **Early detection of emotional storm warnings is not rocket science or some secret skill of psychologists or mystics.** Simple and complex human emotions are part of the culture of any company and deserve – or will ultimately demand – attention.

▶ **I own a company that works with CEOs and employees to create Emotional Continuity Plans that help protect the bottom line and create a safer place to work.** Emotional Continuity Management offers a straightforward, compassionate process that will help employees remain productive and encourage disruptive people to go find their emotional squeaky toys somewhere other than your company. They generally leave voluntarily when no one else wants to play with them anymore.

▶ **Emotional Continuity Management training doesn't take long.** Couple of hours. Less for CEOs, once they get on board. And, it is managed internally by peers, not by expensive external consultants.

I would end my "elevator speech" by telling the CEO that this work cannot be left solely to internal Human Resources personnel and internal or external Employee Assistance Providers. It has to be a corporate commitment from the top down. Everyone needs to be in on the process. In the same way as a dress code, it becomes clear almost instantly who is on board with your mission and who is not.

Then at the last stop of the elevator, I'd give your CEO my business card with the invitation to call me so that we could get started to manage emotional risk in your company. At the same time, I'd be wondering to myself if I'd get that call. Some companies want to avoid risks, while others think they are immune and keep rolling the dice. I hope for your sake that your CEO does call. Because you and your co-workers deserve a great work environment so you can just do your job and go home at the end of the day feeling it's safe to come back tomorrow.

Dr. Vali

References and Links

Child molester statistics (2005). Retrieved from http://www.yellodyno.com/html/child_molester_stats.html

CNN U.S. Guiliani describes 9/11 rescue (2004, May 20). Retrieved from http://articles.cnn.com/2004-05-19/us/911.hearing_1_giuliani-terror-attacks-von-essen?_s=PM:US

Duffy, M. (2009, Sept.). Preventing workplace mobbing and bullying with effective organizational consultation, policies, and legislation. *Psychology Journal: Practice and Research,* 61 (3), 242-262.

Enhanced Fujita scale (n.d.). Retrieved from http://www.tornadochaser.net/fujita.html

Fujita, T.T. (1981). Tornadoes and downbursts in the context of generalized planetary scales. *Sci.,* (38), 1511-1534.

Geerts, B. (1999. The Fujita tornado intensity scale. Retrieved from http://www-das.uwyo.edu/~geerts/cwx/notes/chap07/tornado_class.html

Haugk, K. (1988). *Antagonists in the church.* Minneapolis, MN: Augsberg Books.

Hawkins-Mitchell, V. (2007). Taking your own pulse: self care protocols. *Disaster Recovery Journal,* 48-55.

Hothschild, A.R. (2003, May 3). *The managed heart: the commercialization of human feeling, twentieth century edition, with a new afterward.* Berkeley, CA: University of California Press.

Karpman, S. (1968). Fairy tales and script drama analysis. *Transactional Analysis Bulletin,* 7(26), 39-43.http://www.karpmandramatriangle.com/

Kübler-Ross, E. (1997) *On death and dying.* New York, NY: Scribner.

Mental Health America (2012). *Bullying and what to do about it.* Retrieved from http://www.nmha.org/go/bullying

Mitchell, D., Director of EAP, First Choice Health, Seattle, WA (personal communication, 2012).

Romano, S., Levi-Minz, M., Rugala, E., and Van Hasselt, V. (2011, January). Workplace violence prevention. *FBI Law Enforcement Bulletin.* Retrieved from http://www.fbi.gov/stats-services/publications/law-enforcement-bulletin/january2011/workplace_violence_prevention/

Rosenberg, M. (2003). *Nonviolent communication: a language of life.* Encinitas, CA: Puddledancer Press.

Simmons, G. (2001) *The I of the storm.* Unity Village, MO: Unity Books.

Those annoying little things: twists of fate that saved people's lives (2003). Retrieved from http://www.beliefnet.com/Inspiration/2003/07/Those-Annoying-Little-Things.aspx

Webisodes (n.d.). Retrieved from http://www.stopbullying.gov/kids/webisodes/index.html

Whitney, M. (2009, Oct. 25). W*orkplace bullying policies: a template for organizations.* Retrieved from http://suite101.com/article/workplace-bullying-policies-a162445

Bullying Policy Links:

Canadian Centre for Occupational Health and Safety, (2005, Mar 3). *Bullying in the workplace.* Retrieved from http://www.ccohs.ca/oshanswers/psychosocial/bullying.html

CBS Monewatch, (2008, Oct. 20). *How to handle a workplace bully.* Retrieved from http://www.bnet.com/article/how-to-handle-a-workplace-bully/242687

Develop a policy to deal with bullying at work (2005, Nov. 3). Retrieved from http://www.bullyonline.org/action/policy.htm

Sheid, J. (2011, May 22). *Implementing a workplace bullying policy.* Retrieved from http://www.brighthub.com/office/humanresources/articles/88410.aspx

Glossary

acute A severe reaction that is short in duration.

aggressive Determined, forceful, strong energy with a focus, fast, intent, first, taking lead.

aggressiveness Speaking up for your rights (or those of others) in a way that violates the rights of others.

angry An elevated level of annoyance, inflammation, pain, frustration, loss of control, irritation.

annoyance Mild anger, impatience, irritation.

antagonistic An unwillingness to work toward problem solving; if you find one solution, there will be a next level of "problem," energy focused on chaos and upheaval, not resolution.

anxiety Generalized or specific apprehension that is more focused and involved than regular fear, or worry.

assertiveness Speaking up for your rights (or those of others) and expressing your thoughts and feelings in direct, honest, and appropriate ways which do not violate the rights of others.

avoidance Staying away from, not going near, not doing, dodging, circumventing something, someone, or some issue. May be conscious or unconscious.

behavior How someone or something acts, visible, noticeable, use of body, reaction under a specific set of conditions or circumstances.

boundary A real or perceived edge, limit or border between yourself and somebody else, defined territory.

bulletproof Employees who consider themselves somehow mysteriously special, unique, and above all, unquestionably correct. They truly believe they are untouchable, impervious, unrivaled, unchallengable and above criticism. They might blatantly steal and brag about it. Such employees are so convinced of their unique status that they will try to eliminate anything that does not fit into their picture.

bully A person who is habitually overbearing, especially to weaker people. Bullying is a form of abuse that attempts to create power over another group or person to create an imbalance of power through social, physical, emotional, or verbal coercion/manipulation; see emotional terrorist.

burnout Extreme exhaustion.

business continuity management "An holistic management process that identifies potential impacts that threaten an organization and provides a framework for building resilience with the capability for an effective response that safeguards the interests of its key stakeholders, reputation and value creating activities." (Business Continuity Institute, www.theBCI.org).

catastrophic Widespread damage, death, very bad, totally unsuccessful, extensive loss, life-threatening, terrible beyond understanding, total.

charisma Exploitive appeal, charm, with a sense of magnetism and unique allure.

CISM Critical incident stress management.

conflict Energy that engages with other energy to create a dynamic tension that in nature is neutral, but may have consequences. Example: The surf is in conflict with the shoreline. This can create erosion or a fun vacation. The outcome of conflict can be creative growth, war, or both. Conflict is a normal part of life forces in relationship with each other. The consequences are what need to be considered.

consequence The results that follow something else, the effect that follows the cause, this equals that, a conclusion reached after thinking, the results.

contagious Likely to affect others, transmittable, able to be passed by contact.

control Maintenance of power over something or someone, authority, capacity, regulate, restriction of other things, ownership, direction, gate keeping, standard.

critical incident stress management (CISM) An intervention protocol developed specifically for dealing with traumatic events. It is a formal, highly structured and professionally recognized process for helping those involved in a critical incident to share their experiences, vent emotions, learn about stress reactions and symptoms, and be given referral for further help if required. It is not psychotherapy. It is a confidential, voluntary, and educative process, sometimes called "psychological first aid."

deflection Change in course, direction of attention elsewhere, a bounce away.

denial Unconscious process by which unpleasant realities are kept out of the conscious mind.

depression Emotional state with low energy, a slump, sadness, loss of hope, melancholy, dejection or other such feelings of downheartedness. Can be acute, chronic, minor or severe, simple, complex, temporary or part of a disease process that requires professional intervention.

distortion Misinformed information, twisted, malformed, changed from reality into something else, changed shapes, unnatural, altered, different than original, altered form.

duty to warn A legal requirement that some professionals must report violence, or threats of violence. These professionals are called "mandated reporters" and must, by law, call professional agencies to report even a suspicion of threat risks.

dysfunctional Not performing as expected.

EAP Employee Assistance Program.

emotional All human feelings, those defined as positive and negative.

emotional continuity management Business risk management that provides an infrastructure of clear policies and procedures to manage the full range of human emotions in order to protect people and the bottom line.

emotional terrorism The use of emotional mechanisms and behaviors to force or coerce an emotional agenda on someone else with the intention or action of controlling a situation, or accumulating territory; either real, perceived, or symbolic.

empathy Compassionate understanding, responsiveness, identification, and sense of feeling another's feelings.

energetics In the sciences, the study of energy in motion and under transformation.

entitlement Rigid self-aggrandized thinking, which affords permission to "take from" someone else in order to get the deserved or entitled goal, object, or outcome, special privilege, a sense of title, award, or honor that is deserved, whether real or perceived.

entrenched Taking a position that is fixed and unalterable, beyond an opinion or position; it is a "my way or the highway" style of thinking.

explosive Capable of eruption, taking up space violently, blowing up, boom, expanding collapse.

fear Level of apprehension, anticipation of scary stuff or danger, concern.

fiscal Financial.

Fujita Scale Ted Fujita and Allen Pearson were scientists who wanted to predict and evaluate the activities of tornadoes. Prior to 1971, weather experts used a variety of means to try to measure and describe tornadoes. Experts have used the Fujita Scale (also known as the Fujita-Pearson Scale) as a way of linking damage risks to wind speed.

goodwill Non-tangible value of a business.

grief An active process of mourning, emotional pain sorrow, suffering, sadness or severe anguish associated with change and loss.

grounded Steady, firm, balanced, whole, present and accounted for, in the moment.

historical Existing in the past.

hostage takers In the context of emotional continuity management, emotional terrorists who take advantage of the close quarters and long hours of the worksite to take other employees emotionally captive, creating emotional chaos, while using the people and location for their own agenda of control.

HR In business, Human Resources, the department within an organization that recruits and manages employees. Older term for this department was "Personnel." Also seen as an acronym for human relations.

hysterical Wildly excited and emotional viable.

intention Something done on purpose, not by accident, thoughtful choices.

intentional spinning The intentional use and action of displaying and using emotions of self or others to control a situation or to accumulate territory – either literally or figuratively – using force through physical, mental, emotional, or psychological mechanisms of fear, intimidation, implied threats, or outright control.

irritation A level of annoyance, inflammation, exasperation, frustration, low-level anger.

Karpman drama triangle The approach, by Stephen Karpman, is a model of communication within a psychological model called transactional analysis that efficiently removes the power plays from any interaction. Participants in this model take turns acting out the roles of "victim," "rescuer," and "persecutor."

mad A strong level of anger, intense emotion, personal exasperation, annoyance; a traditional term that once meant mental illness.

management Organizing, controlling the affairs of something or someone.

non-verbal Not using words.

passive Submitting without resistance, influenced by other forces, not taking charge of personal decisions, inactive, not actively participating, no authority, accepting.

passive-aggressive A personality that manipulates others indirectly, resists requests and demands with non-action rather than action.

pathological Disease based and outside the scope of what is considered in the range of "normal" or health based.

pathology The study of disease; indication of the presence of a disease.

peace No conflict, no war, calm, serene, no violence, no disturbance, freedom from disagreement, no anxiety.

perceive Notice something; take in mentally, be aware of something.

posttraumatic stress disorder (PTSD) A term that has become controversial. PTSD is a mental health condition that can develop after a person has experienced a frightening or life-threatening occurrence, such as military combat, disaster or accidents, physical or sexual assault, or witnessing a traumatic event, crime, or other significant incident. PTSD is not always a result of such events, and PTSD can occur as a result of what would be deemed a much less significant incident. PTSD has a range of challenging symptoms resulting in long-lasting problems in many areas of emotional and social functioning. At various points in history, PTSD was called "shell shock," "combat stress reaction," or "battle fatigue." It is now a term that is being questioned, although there is no question that the result of extreme incidents causes significant levels of short- and long-term problems. It is only the term that is in question, as professionals learn more about the effects of disaster, war, trauma, combat, assault, abuse, secondary trauma, and catastrophe on human beings.

power Measure of strength, force, control over, authority, ability, influence, energy, status, effectiveness.

projection Image of something, ascribing a personal thought or feeling to someone else that isn't theirs, a representation.

psychosis A psychiatric diagnosis traditionally marked by delusions, hallucinations, incoherence, and distorted and incorrect perceptions of reality.

PTSD Posttraumatic stress disorder.

reaction An emotional response to something or someone, a force exerted as a process in response to another force.

real Actually existing, verifiable, genuine, factual, true, accurate.

reflection Pondering or musing about something.

remediation Positive actions to restore or establish the ability of a person to cope with situations, learn a skill or tool, or become more stable in a performance required for employment stability.

risk management "A process effected by an entity's board of directors, management and other personnel, applied in strategy setting and across the enterprise, designed to identify potential events that may affect the entity, and manage risks to be within its risk appetite, to provide reasonable assurance regarding achievement of entity objectives" (The Committee of Sponsoring Organisations of the Treadway Commission).

righteous Considered correct or justified, a moral code, unwavering truth.

sociopath A psychiatric diagnosis of someone who acts without conscience.

specific Detailed and non-vague, something particularly unique and describable.

spinning Normal emotions that, for some reason, escalate and continue to develop an additional energy beyond the emotions of the original event. Emotional spinning occurs when one or more person joins forces with someone else to form a mutual or collective energy spin. The increasing collective emotional dynamic created by rampant, unmanaged, or poorly managed feelings.

stress In human emotions vernacular a condition that occurs when perceived pressures exceed the ability of mind or body to cope with them in a positive way. A normal and necessary part of life.

sustain Withstand, continue, nourish, hold something, give support, validate, confirm, maintain.

target Something or someone aimed at, goal, focus, point and direction of attention.

tension A level of tightness or looseness between two or more objects. In emotions, it is a state of relationship between hierarchy and proximity.

terror A level of intense and overwhelming fear.

thought One activity of thinking, an idea, intention, plan.

trauma A profound injury or experience with severe emotional consequences with potentially long-lasting influence.

traumatology The study of the effects of trauma.

unintentional spinning Being unconsciously caught in someone else's strong emotional process, and temporary emotional repercussions or consequences associated with the effects of an emotionally charged event.

upset Disruption, distress, disorder, defeat, disturbance.

vague Unclear, incoherent, non-perceptible, foggy.

validation Offering a sense of value to something; a sense of being recognized, listened to, heard accurately.

verbal Using words.

Index

Boxes and figures are indicated by b and f following the page number.

I

Identification tags for emotional
  incident drills, 211
Image armor, 81
Improvisational behaviors, 220
Inflexibility, 104–5
Insider information, 86
Intentional spinning, 15, 43, 148, 263
Interviews with emotional terrorists,
  126, 134–35
Introverts, 194
Irritation, 209, 263. *See also*
  Annoyances as cause of spinning
"It-Seemed-Like-a-Good-Idea-at-the-
  Time" plan, 143–44

J

Journal writing, 143, 145
Justice Department, 212

K

Karpman, Stephen, 116, 123
Karpman drama triangle, 57, 122–25,
  263
Kübler-Ross, Elisabeth, 46, 101

L

Levels of emotional spins, 40
Levels of functioning, 69–72
  in bullies and emotional terrorists,
    70
  in healthy employees, 70–72
  recognizing, 72
  "What's Up?" checklist for, 72–73
Liability costs of emotional spins, 7
Lies and lying, 90–91
Litigation threats, 7, 36
Location of emotional spins, 39
Loss and grief
  change as cause of spinning, 46–49
  defined, 262
  disasters and, 244
  emotions of, 101–3
  stages of, 46–49, 160
  stories of, 104
  trauma survivors and, 58

M

Mad, 76, 263. *See also* Anger stage of
  grief; Angry
Management insomnia, 136–37
Managing emotions at work, 107–21
  conflict management and, 140–42
  in disasters, 236–37, 239–43
  empathy and, 116
  exit strategies, 143–44
  expression of hope and gratitude,
    117–18
  expression of needs and wants in,
    117
  guidelines for, 107–15
  HR department and, 17
  learning process for, 115–21
  problem-solving strategies, 118–19
  problems vs. issues, 139
  self-care techniques for, 111–13,
    142–43
  toolkit for, 113–15, 150–51
  validation and, 117, 119
Mandated reporters, 120
Meetings with emotional terrorists,
  126, 134–35
Memory loss, 53, 58
Mental health, 143
Mental Health America, 96
Military personnel
  collective emotional terrorism and,
    162
  emotional continuity for transition
    to civilian life, 159–67
  resources for, 164
  understanding background of,
    160-61
Misinformation behaviors, 90–91
Mitchell, David, 244
Mood changes, 55
Multi-talented nature of emotional
  terrorists, 189

Q
Quantifying emotional tornadoes,
28–33

R
Range of emotional spins, 39–40
Reactions, defined, 264. *See also* Acute
    stress reactions
Real, defined, 264. *See also* Perceptions
Real vs. Not-Real victims, 248
Recovery phase for disasters, 233
Reflection in emotions management
    process, 118, 264
Rehearsals for ECM, 190–91
Remediation process, 187, 264
Rescuer role in Karpman drama
    triangle, 122–24
Resistance
    to ECM training, 188–91
    by emotional terrorists, 70, 93
    as sign of spin starting, 41
Righteous, defined, 62, 265
Risk management, 43, 77, 265. *See also*
    Emotional continuity management
    (ECM)
Rosenberg, Marshall, 116, 122
Rumors, 85, 184

S
Salvation Army, 212
Security professional standards, 196
Self-care
    in disasters, 240
    emotional health and, 143
    for managing emotions at work, 95,
    111–13, 142–43
    mental health and, 143
    neutrality and, 106
    physical health and, 142–43
    post-disaster, 233
    spiritual health and, 143
    time bullies and, 93
    trauma survivors and, 58
September 11, 2001 terrorist attacks,
    38, 243–45
Severance pay, 5

Sex offenders, 77, 90
Silence as emotional management tool,
    110, 146
Simmons, Gary, 140
Size of emotional spins, 39
Snakes in the schoolyard metaphor,
    127–29
    business application of, 129–32
Social withdrawal as sign of burnout,
    53
Sociopath, defined, 265
Soft technical data assessments,
    197-201
Space for emergency emotions, 219–21
Specific, defined, 202, 265
Speed of emotional spins, 38
Spinning. *See also* Emotional tornadoes
    annoyances as cause of, 54–55
    bullies' exploitation of, 20, 50, 52,
    53–55, 57, 59
    burnout as cause of, 53–54
    causes of, 45–74
    change as cause of, 45–50
    contagious nature of, 19, 19f,
    189-90
    costs of, 2–8, 255
    defined, 15, 265
    dysfunctional car analogy and, 68
    early warning signs, 41–43
    emotions as start of, 16–17
    escalation of, 18–23
    examples of, 59–66
    healthy car analogy and, 67–68
    intentional, 15, 43, 148, 263
    levels of functioning in people,
    69-72
    normal day-to-day feelings vs., 13,
    21, 66–67
    pathological car analogy and, 68–69
    as reaction to something else, 45–46
    stress as cause of, 50–52
    trauma as cause of, 57–59
    unintentional, 15, 266
    violence as cause of, 55–57
    violence resulting from, 22–23,
    23–24b
    witnesses to, 146–50

CREDITS

Kristen Noakes-Fry, ABCI is Editorial Director at Rothstein Associates Inc. Previously, she was a Research Director, Information Security and Risk Group, for Gartner, Inc.; Associate Editor at Datapro (McGraw-Hill); and Associate Professor of English at Atlantic Cape College in New Jersey. She holds an M.A. from New York University and a B.A. from Russell Sage College.

Cover Design and Graphics:	Sheila Kwiatek, Flower Grafix
Page Design and Typography:	Jean King
Index:	Enid Zafran, Indexing Partners, LLC

Title Font:	Nueva STD
Body Fonts:	Sabon and Frutiger

About the Author

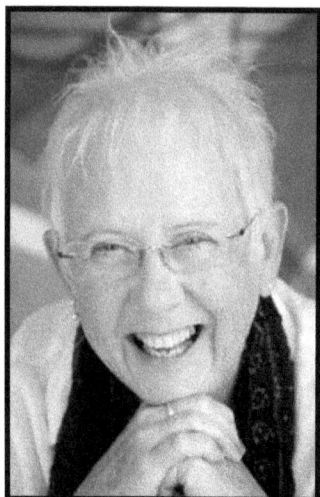

Vali J. Hawkins Mitchell, Ph.D., LMHC, REAT, holds a Doctorate in Health Education and Masters degrees in Applied Psychology and Expressive Arts Therapy and is a highly regarded public speaker, trainer, author, consultant, and educator.

A valued mentor and keynote speaker, she offers critical insights on the real human factors of disaster and emergency planning based on her experiences with major events such as the World Trade Center, Hurricane Katrina, Samoan earthquakes, Indonesian tsunami, and Pacific Northwest Wildfires. She is considered by many as the leading authority in the growing field of Emotional Continuity Management.

Academically, Dr. Hawkins Mitchell has been adjunct faculty member and guest lecturer at a number of universities and colleges, including Washington State University, the World Medicine Institute, and Lane Community College. Dr. Vali, as she is well known, has contributed original research in the area of Psychosocial Dynamics of Families with Pediatric Illness, Tools of Trauma Management for Emergency Care and Health Care Delivery Professionals, and the Use of Quantum Poetry for Trauma Management. She has been trained by the American Red Cross as a Disaster Mental Health provider and National Diversity Instructor, and has been consulting directly with military families and service members in all branches since 2009.

Dr. Vali travels extensively providing custom-designed trainings for individuals and teams, private and government agencies, mom-and-pop companies, and large corporations.

Dr. Vali is the author of *Emotional Terrors in the Workplace: Protecting Your Bottom Line; Dr. Vali's Survival Guide: Tips for the Journey; Preparing a Go-Bag*; and a number of plays, musicals, and children's titles. She is a performance musician and award-winning artist. She is a Registered Expressive Arts Therapist (REAT) and currently has her art studio and professional office in Seattle, Washington.

www.improvizion.com

www.ingramcontent.com/pod-product-compliance
Lightning Source LLC
Chambersburg PA
CBHW071346280326
41927CB00039B/2045